CIRCLING THE SQUARE

صورة الشيء

ALSO BY WENDELL STEAVENSON

NONFICTION

Stories I Stole

The Weight of a Mustard Seed

CIRCLING THE SQUARE

STORIES FROM THE EGYPTIAN REVOLUTION

WENDELL STEAVENSON

GRANTA

Granta Publications, 12 Addison Avenue, London W11 4QR

First published in Great Britain by Granta Books, 2015
First published in the United States by Ecco, an imprint of
HarperCollins Publishers, 2015

A CIP catalogue record for this book
is available from the British Library.

1 3 5 7 9 10 8 6 4 2

ISBN 978 1 78378 234 5
ISBN 978 1 78378 244 4

Designed by Suet Yee Chong

Offset by M Rules

Printed and bound by CPI Group (UK) Ltd, Croydon, CR0 4YY

www.grantabooks.com

FOR ADO
THANKYOU, SORRY, THANKYOU

CONTENTS

CIRCLING THE SQUARE

BEFOREWORD

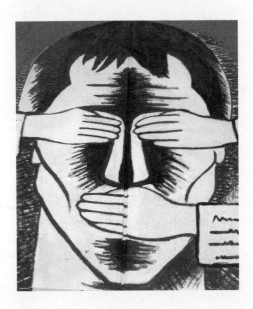

I N CAIRO IN THOSE EIGHTEEN DAYS (*THOSE DAYS!* ALREADY GONE AND replaced by the nostalgia of the misremembered), every day was a new day to be written. I would wake up in the morning and the protesters on Tahrir were waking too, rising from their flower beds, shaking themselves anew, and wondering too: what would this new day bring? Every day we had no idea what would happen, every day seesawed between joy and death. Between the grand metaphysics of a great hope and its realization was the physical reality that opposed it: a stick, a rock, a bullet.

With hindsight it's easy enough to offer reasons for the Egyptian revolution. Analyzed narrative, neat and ordered. Like history in a textbook, each event a chapter I learned when I was twelve: the causes of the French Revolution, the causes of the Russian Revolution, the causes of the First World War reduced to a list, (a) (b) (c) (d) and (e). In this way we can catalog Mubarak's Egypt quite academically:

- aging dictator
- no succession plan (fear that the dictator's widely perceived corrupt businessman son, Gamal, was being groomed to take over)
- obviously fraudulent parliamentary election the previous December
- increase in number of opposition groups over the past five years
- brutality of state security
- outrage at the graphically horrifying photographs of Khalid Said, a nice middle-class young man, after he was beaten to death by the police
- a bulging youth demographic
- widespread use of social networking
- the example of Tunisia

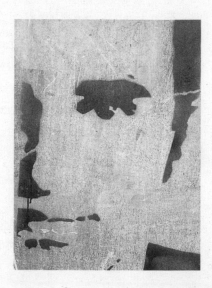

Is this clear? Do we understand better? We can read words on a page that have been organized for us. But notice the volume of white space around the words. What is hiding in this white space? Half-considered tangents and impulses, groping comprehensions and mis-apprehensions . . . so much of history is hiding in the white spaces, dismissed as marginalia.

When the crowds massed in Tunis and then in Cairo I felt a great tug in my gut. I had spent more than a decade in the Middle East. Many conversations with Iraqi Syrian Lebanese Egyptian friends, many evenings, *shawarma* arguments, beers on the table, debating to and fro and cracking black jokes, throwing our hands in the air, caught between two barbed-wire fences: foreign nefariousness (colonial carve-up; American petro-interest and military foot stamping) and homegrown brutal dictatorship.

Yes, I would agree, we British Americans are murderous and hypocrites. You couldn't come in from a bloody Baghdad street and conclude any different. But when I wrote about prisons and jackboot mustaches and suicide bombs and the violence against women or Christians or Shia or indeed anyone-who-was-different, I would whisper to myself: murderous and hypocrites, yes, but we are also self-determination and the Magna Carta and Tom Paine, we are the Bill of Rights and the Enlightenment and a certain sense of decent cricket behavior. And I would be angry with the Arabs—all of them together, because no one can help generalizing in the privacy of one's own thoughts—and silently vent my frustrations: Why must you always be subjective, instead of objective? Can you dare to imagine the rule of law in these sandy lands? If you want something, do it yourself instead of demanding that someone else do it for you and then complaining about foreign interference. Plenty of times I heard my thoughts echoed when Arabs themselves complained to me about Arab shibboleths: pride and patriarchy; clan and religion and that particular pathology of an inferiority complex armored with a sense of superiority.

But I never believed that there was something inherently Arab about Arabs that meant they were condemned to strongmen or to fanaticism. Everyone I ever met in Arabland, every story I ever wrote, seemed to suggest a greater universality of hope and dream. It is very obvious to people who are not free that they are not free; it was very obvious to me that they would have liked to be.

I watched the crowds gather on the streets on TV. They carried smiles and determination. They were shouting, "*The people want the fall of the regime.*" Shouting! My heart thumped with them. I e-mailed editors to send me, please send me! One o'clock in the morning, dishes in the sink, I opened my e-mail to read that Oz had pulled his curtain back an inch and typed two words: "Yes Go."

Hindsight eats stories. It might seem inevitable now that Mubarak would fall; inevitable, too, that two and a half years later the army would take back control. But at the time there was nothing sure about it at all. There were street battles, there were giddy skittish youths, there were tanks, there was an ever-present undertow of reactionaryness. One person would say, "We are not leaving until he leaves!" and thrust their hand in the air defiantly. And the person standing next to them would say, "Yes, but we must be careful. We should wait until things calm down before there are elections." And the man next to him would say, "We should all go back to work because this disruption is destroying the country." And his friend would nod and agree and add, "I trust the army, the army will take care of everything." And then one of the young activist kids hearing this would shake his head furiously and say, "No, they are all the same, all the old guard!" And then another angrier voice would interrupt: "Let's burn down the Interior Ministry!" "No," would come the reply of an old schoolteacher, "no, peaceful, peaceful!"

The crowd was a single thing, but it was made up of individuals and in each Egyptian head resided several competing opinions. Calm down vs. burn down; Islam as sanctuary as mantra as terrorism; army good, bad, the only solution; strongman Pharaoh regime parliament—what does a prime minister do?—voting voting with your feet running away, from, toward, around the corner to catch your breath. This was as true for an army officer stationed at a Cairo crossroads or a pro-Mubarak thug or an official of the ruling party as it was for a revolutionary youth. Every day Egypt would wake up and have no idea what it would do that day, or what would happen. Events hung between one possibility that was active agency, and another that would be delivered as fate (which is to say by Allah or the powers-that-remained) but which was to be accepted as beyond your control. For some Egyptians this was the freedom of their own blank page to write, for others it was terrifying and mystifying and exhausting.

The precariousness of not knowing what would happen next persisted after Mubarak fell. Sparks were tossed into the air and the hot wind blew them hither and thither, alighting in the midst of the demos: protests, sit-ins, strikes, football matches, factories, courthouses, police stations, car parks, train stations. Everything became mixed up together: the old regime with all the new yelling, protesters and provocateurs and secret policemen and military trials and journalists hauled before judges on libel charges. It was very confusing, and the events overlapped each other and the crowds swept over the events like waves.

When editors called I would, of course, say yes. Yes to demands for characters and beginnings and middles and conclusions. But the Egyptian revolution defied historical precedent and it defied, too, the templates of storytelling. There was no protagonist, no leader, no bad guy, no hero. There was a beginning and there was an end, but everything in the middle was a giant sprawling messy epic, unplanned and subject to many plot twists.

The mood swung wildly week to week between optimism and pessimism. As much as Tahrir became repetitive—tear gas, rocks, running, riot police—it was different every time. Moods like joy and boredom and fear and anger swept across its face like clouds in summer storms. How can I begin to describe this? As large and chaotic as it was, it was also an intimate welter. The crowd was a single thing and yet it was full of people. A thousand faces, ten thousand opinions.

I have heard it said that we tell stories to make sense of life, but the more experience I have of it, I don't have a sense of life as a single narrative. I have a sense of it as a mosaic, many pieces fitting into a whole. And now that I am trying to write it, write the revolution, it feels more like a jigsaw puzzle and I am trying to figure out how the pieces fit together. Blur and seams, the juxtaposed and proximate-but-unrelated. I cannot impose order. I would need to be a novelist to write a better truth than these glimpses offer.

But to return to the beginning, which begins, as most stories do, with an arrival. In any case (to plagiarize myself) four days after the crowds first took to the streets of Cairo, on the twenty-fifth of January 2011, I got on a plane.

TANKS

CAIRO AIRPORT REOPENED WHILE I WAS IN THE AIR EN ROUTE TO Amman. The Egyptian mobile phone network was switched back on while I was in the air between Amman and Cairo. The national Internet servers would remain shut down for several days longer.

The Royal Jordanian plane landed at seven P.M., after curfew. There were only three people on the flight, a middle-aged lady with a large bag of oranges, an Italian with wavy ice-cream hair who introduced himself as a correspondent from *Corriere della Sera*, and me. Gelato correspondent and I were heading for the same hotel, and so we shared a taxi. I was scared and glad of the company.

The driver drove slowly down a dark and ominously empty highway. Down side streets I glimpsed dim jumbles of makeshift obstacles, a garbage bin pulled across, a tangle of metal chairs, a length of palm trunk. Figures stretched into shadows thrown by the orange glow of oil drum braziers. The driver turned into one of these streets and the figures emerged, glowing cigarette tips gesticulating circles in the gloom, as a group of men carrying sticks. One stuck his head into the driver's window and the driver spoke

a few words while two others opened the boot to check. We hung
for a moment between friend and foe. Then a cracked grin and a
cheerfully delivered, "Welcome in Egypt." We continued through
residential neighborhoods, at first prosperous—bougainvillea
growing over the walls, wrought-iron gates—then broken, down-
at-heel, narrower streets, narrower apartment blocks, metal shutters pulled down. At every intersection we were stopped by groups
of men carrying sticks or rolled-up newspapers or antique scimitars. Faces peered out of the dark like moons. I saw gunmetal flash
against the dark obscurity of a gutter. Twenty times or more we
were stopped, but these citizen committees, all of them armed,
were, all of them, friendly. At last we reached the hotel without
incident.

Inside Adrien Jaulmes came briskly toward me across the
marble foyer. He was tall and thin and blond, sharp like a yellow
pencil, with a Labrador bounce in his step. I had said good-bye
to him only two days before in Jerusalem. "If I make it to Cairo,"
I said to him then, watching the news from Egypt, "can I sleep
on your hotel room floor?" Adrien and I had been friends since
Lebanon in 2006. He was a correspondent for *Le Figaro,* spoke
English beautifully—"please forgive my atrocyous accent"—and
had the calm ease in dodgy situations of a subaltern under fire.
(In fact he *had* been a subaltern under fire; he had been a lieutenant in the parachute division of the French Foreign Legion,
a fact that he held modestly in reserve.) I thought of him not as
French at all but as an Englishman from another era, sandy colored, pink around his sunburned edges, and decent. He stood up
when women approached his table; he liked to wear hats appro-
priate to the occasion, Panama in the summer, straw boater on a
yacht, astrakhan if it snowed. He was always reading an enormous
book, he mumbled, he was easily startled and charmingly knocked
things over. Once he spilled a cup of coffee and I am sure I heard

him say oops-a-daisy. When he said good-bye he said bye-sie bye. I think he got it from a J. P. Donleavy novel.

A tourist family were sitting in the lobby bar, worried, marooned among their baggage. The mother held a small quiet son in her lap. The father held a wad of tickets like a bunch of wilted flowers. Adrien was smiling at me. "You made it after all! Do you want to get your own room? You are very welcome to stay with me," he offered, solicitous, polite. "It's up to you."

We went up in the lift to the eleventh floor. The room was very comfortable five-star luxury. Adrien had requested a balcony overlooking Tahrir and the concierge had laughed, "Twenty years I have worked here and this is the first time no one wants a Nile view!" From the balcony I could see the square, shaped like a giant teardrop with a traffic circle in the center. We could hear intermittent gunfire. A small crowd huddled at a far curve. In the dark it looked indistinct, drawn in smudged charcoal. On the Corniche, running along the riverbank, the National Democratic Party building was still smoldering. Yesterday had been the Day of Rage. Adrien lit a cigar and described it. "It was really extraordinary. I never saw so much tear gas. You couldn't see through the tear gas. The protesters were so determined. They were on the bridges, trying to get over the bridges onto Tahrir, and the police were lined up against them. They kept running for hours at the police and the police were really ferocious, batons hitting and driving trucks into the crowd, and then suddenly—it was weird—the police lines broke or disappeared—I couldn't see which—"

As Adrien spoke tanks labored up the Corniche with a heavy mechanical lumbering growl, backing up and around, biting their treads into the soft asphalt. The people now occupied the square, but the army had deployed around it.

"What are they doing?" I asked Adrien. He stood, cigar between his thumb and forefinger, leaning on the balcony railing. He made a wavering motion with his other hand, as if to say, who knew, anything was possible. A tank snorted, grinding over a traffic island.

"Tanks don't like to be in cities," he said. "They prefer the countryside."

I n the morning we went down to Tahrir.

The crowd was small. People were tired and unslept. They sat on curbs, hunched over their knees, eating a breakfast of foil triangles of Laughing Cow cheese squashed into *baladi* bread to make a rough sandwich. The alley cats sauntered abroad with their tails in the air.

"Cats like revolutions," said Adrien, bending down to say good morning to a tiger with an eye patch who looked at him coldly and went back to his chicken bone. "No cars on the street and lots of garbage piling up."

We laughed at a homemade placard one of the protesters carried of a Laughing Cow drawn to look like Mubarak's face.

"They have the same jowls!" I said.

"Dictators fall when people laugh at their ridiculousnesses," said Adrien.

"I always thought that dictators fall when the powers-that-be lose the will to shoot people," I said. This was my theory left over from the collapse of the Soviet Union. "Shooting into crowds is pretty effective," I told him. "Whiff of grapeshot. Napoléon ended the French Revolution like that. Iran two years ago. Same thing."

"Journalists are always reporting the last uprising," Adrien pointed out.

"History doesn't repeat itself," I agreed. This was another theory that appealed to me.

We wandered among the crowd on Tahrir as if we were walking through a strange garden. A garden in a clearing with big buildings all around. The square without cars took on an alternative topography. Curbs carved paths, heavy green metal railings made cul-de-sac enclosures out of pavements, brick traffic islands were patios, grassy paisley verges were made into picnic spots, flower beds were soft earth and apparently good—for the exhausted protesters I saw there, wrapped in blankets—as people beds. I did not have my bearings yet. Adrien and I climbed over the heavy green metal railings in front of the Kentucky Fried Chicken restaurant and walked across the tarmac to the central roundabout. It was a little hill in the middle of everything, a raised circle of grass, rimmed in brick that made for a prime sitting stoop. Through the day more people came. The circle was the eye and marches revolved around it.

"We're looking for Mubarak! If you see him throw him into the Nile, where the geese can eat him!"

We explored from pillar to post, from an old landmark to its new incarnation, describing by this journey the evolving geography of the square. The turbaned statue of Omar Makram, who had led the uprising against Napoléon's occupation, was now plastered with handwritten posters as an information point. The Hardee's restaurant had become, by its corner location and its bright signage, a meeting place. An alley between two buildings with a concrete sentry box for the doorman was a toilet. The toilet alley led to another alley where there was a little mosque underneath a lean-to roof between two buildings that had been turned into a field station. Blister packs of pills and rolls of bandages heaped up on the *minbar*, rows of men in their stocking feet lined up for prayer. An old man was leaning against a pillar, heaving with an angina attack, sobbing for his son who had been killed the night before, shot, he said, by snipers on the roof of the Interior Ministry.

Through the afternoon Adrien and I circumambulated the square. From the Hardee's corner past the American University in Cairo with its private lawns locked behind a laurel hedge; past the giant-toad Mogamma building, repository of all Egyptian bureaucracy; past the grand Omar Makram Mosque (which screened the view of the big-block American embassy, just behind it); past an abandoned Italianate villa above which towered the bland fortress of the InterContinental Hotel, where Adrien and I were staying; past the elegant Arab League building, built in the sixties when Nasser still dreamed of pan-Arabism; past a stretch of blue metal fencing that hid a giant sprawling building site that had been a building site for so long that no one could remember if they had ever known what was being built there; past the staunch and classical red-painted Egyptian Museum; U-turn at the wide neck of the square that gave into a snaky mass of highways and bridges and access roads and underpasses; and then we walked back into the heart of the square, along a facade of old downtown elegance, balconies stuccoed with swags and flowers and cherubs with broken noses, that housed, on the ground floor, travel agencies and tourist touts. All of Egypt and all her history were thus arranged around the perimeter of Tahrir. Stellae, monuments, state, statements, statues. And here in the center stood the people wanting to change it all.

The atmosphere was tentative, milling. There was a kind of stillness and expectation to the scene. Two tanks were stationed next to the American University gate guarding the entrance to Qasr al-Aini Street, where the parliament and several ministries were located. One soldier was sitting on top of his tank eating a plastic bowl of *koshari*. Next to him, standing two rungs inside with his head and shoulders poking out of the hatch, was a lieutenant colonel. A group of protesters was standing in front of him pestering him with questions.

"How long will you be here?"

"Until you all calm down," said the lieutenant colonel, irritated. He did not seem comfortable with this awkward mix of military with civilians. "You are all taking it too far. You've been silent for thirty years and for them that means that you were happy. Now you have demonstrated. You have delivered the message, but if you keep going you are going to rip the country apart!" Someone from the crowd threw up a water bottle and the lieutenant colonel caught it. This was the basic tradition of Arab obligation, desert rite, water from one man to another, a gesture beyond enmity. The lieutenant colonel accepted the water with a nod, but he was still upset. "I want to know where is all this stuff coming from, where is the money coming from?" He seemed to assume that the crowd was paid for. Fifty-dollar bills in their pockets and eating Kentucky Fried Chicken! according to the slur broadcast on state TV. He swept his arm over the jostling protesters. "In whose interest is all this? All these demonstrators actually don't care!" he declared, his thoughts contradicting each other. "They don't care about their own children!" He was angry now. "To me my children are more important than who is the president. If you really care, go home, see your children! See your wife!" He pointed at the crowd, demanding, accusing: "Do any of you here have children?!"

"My children are home," came back a voice, "but I am here for their sake."

The tanks were stationed at several entrances to the square and all afternoon Adrien and I wondered what they were going to do. (There was no infantry deployed at all.) Some of the tanks had been spray-painted with flowers and hearts and slogans. *Down with Mubarak!* The crowd continued to grow. The sky darkened, the air grew thicker. As if in answer to the limbo, at about four o'clock, a loud, aggressive revving began. A column of twenty-five tanks began to advance into the neck of the square by the Egyptian Museum. The crowd came forward to confront them before they could get into the wider expanse of the square. People held hands to make a cordon. The column halted with a grinding jolt, but the tank engines continued to growl powerfully. The crowd inched forward gingerly. There was a wariness in front of these big beasts. One man touched the armored nose of the lead tank. Another did the same, and then another, until the crowd was flowing all around and in between the tanks. They patted their hot metal flanks and called to them in soft voices as if to tame them.

The faithful lined up for the sunset prayer; amid the quiet murmur an imam called for deliverance and freedom. And suddenly there was a great deafening searing screeching. It came from the sky, terrifyingly loud. We put our hands over our ears, all heads turned upward. The crowd shrank back against the green metal railings. Little gray triangles, hard to see against the cloud cover, two fighter planes swooping, buzzing us. Tearing, ear-splitting roar. On the second pass we regained our composure. The crowd swelled back, stood hands on hips and raised their fists at the angry birds. Another screaming pass right over our heads and the crowd yelled and jeered defiantly, *"We won't leave! We won't leave!"*

The jets flew away and the crowd, tested now and finding themselves a little braver, began to sing to the tanks. *"The army and the people are one hand! The army and the people are one hand!"* The chant grew with confidence, and it occurred to me—but only much later, because at the time standing there in front of the tanks, everything was held in suspense and unknown—that the crowd at first did not believe what they were chanting. They did not know whether the army would shoot, what orders had been given to the tank commanders, what the shrieking jets were meant to signal. They sang to the tanks a wish, growing stronger in voice, hoping, by fortitude, to make it true. They were co-opting them.

The chanting rose until it drowned out the background drilling of the tanks' engines. The drill was subsumed to a hum and then stopped altogether as the tank commanders turned their engines off. The crowd gathered around them, handing up water and packets of sugary pink wafer cookies, chatting to the soldiers who came out of their turrets and sat cross-legged on the aprons of the revolving gun platforms. "We are your brothers!" they told them. Women tossed plastic roses for the soldiers to catch. A man hung a placard from the nozzle of a cannon that read, *The people want freedom.* People posed for photographs against the row of wheels inside the tank treads, V sign for victory, *I was here.* Some handed their children up to the soldiers, who let them sit for portraits on the long gun turrets, turned, for the moment, into climbing frames.

"Will you shoot at us?" the people asked the lead tank commander, because it was still unclear: were the tanks Egyptians or the army or Mubarak?

"You will shoot at us if you are given the order!" one man insisted.

"Will you shoot at us?" the crowd asked.

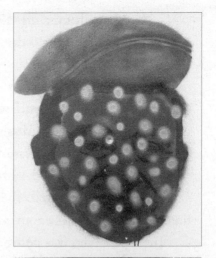

"No, I will never do that," the commander told them. "Not even if I am given the order."

Later in the afternoon I went to see Hisham Kassem. Hisham was known as an urbane and measured commentator, and I had first met him in the summer of 2008, when I went to Cairo to report on the bread riots that spring and the protest movement that had resulted. It had been July, hot, and Hisham had come straight from a courtroom, supporting an opposition newspaper editor who was being prosecuted in a spurious libel trial. "I thought these days of prosecutions were over," he had sighed back then, discouraged and tired. The heat and the repression of the courtroom had infected him with weariness and summer lassitude. "No, I don't worry for myself." He shook himself out of self-pity, shuggling another cigarette out of the pack. Hisham had

worked in human rights for twenty years; he had started Egypt's first independent newspaper and had it wrested from his hands by the powers-that-be. From time to time state security agents rang his doorbell for "a chat"; he assumed his phone was bugged. "Twenty-seven years Mubarak has kept this country on pause," Hisham told me, drawing on his cigarette, pulling himself back into analysis mode. "Egypt is like an old building covered with scaffolding." We talked about the bread queues in the spring and the demonstrations on April 6, and he became a little more optimistic. "Something is changing," he had told me then. "This apartment is right opposite the prime minister's office; I moved in six months ago and the amount of sit-ins and protests—if I had known I wouldn't have moved here! Even fishermen, doctors, and these are not political people. There is a feeling of quicksand, anything can happen."

Hisham lived just off Tahrir Square, opposite the parlia-

ment, and Adrien and I left the tanks halted by a line of protesters and walked around a barricade to get to his street. We found
him in a state of exalted shock. Outwardly he looked the same
as he had three years before, a handsome man in his fifties, gray
hair in a square frame around his face, luxuriant mustache, but
he was shaking and he put out his hand to show me. He had
never been to a demonstration in his life before; his opposition
had always been in conferences, in opposition parties and written editorials. But he had gone out on the streets on the Day of
Rage. He had been with the demonstrators on the Sixth October Bridge. The police had beat him, and he said he had felt the
blows almost as a personal affront. He had felt angry, and the
force of his anger had surprised him too. The government was
beating him! All around him people were shot and bleeding. He
fell and was pulled upright by strange and friendly arms. "There
were people from the upper classes, people with plenty of money
and no problems, there were people wearing rags, different generations. They want dignity, they are sick and tired of Mubarak
and his brutal police apparatus. It's about the little guy carrying
bottles of vinegar against the tear gas. People helped me when
I fell down, and I found that I did the same." On the bridge he
saw the police vans revving into the crowd and protesters attacking these evil things. He picked up a rock and threw it. "I threw
rocks with the people," he said, still disbelieving—the violence,
the street, his own action, all of it. "Thirty years of my life under
that buffalo!"

Hisham realized at some point during the rushing and fighting that the police shotgun trucks were attacking more sporadi-
cally. Protesters began waving cars down and siphoning petrol
from gas tanks into empty bottles. Hisham watched them tear
strips of T-shirts to make wicks. "Then I thought: *I don't want to
be a part of any arson. The police are still here and you cannot defeat
the police. In the next few days when this calms down they will prob-*

ably arrest me. Or they will just shoot me and someone will be thanked for it. In any case we'll wake up tomorrow and nothing will have changed. But. We will have shown him we are determined, and that must mean something."

Hisham left the demonstrators and walked home. The streets around his building, around the parliament, were hell upside down. Police vans on fire, police trying to drag barricades across roads, kids everywhere, *kids*! On the roofs he saw the black silhouettes of snipers. He could hear gunfire coming from the direction of the Interior Ministry. Safe inside his apartment, he made himself a sandwich and turned on CNN. The camera panned across the black smoke and bright orange flame. "I nearly cried when I saw the NDP burn!" he told me. "Can you imagine? For the last thirty years—for thirty years! Just when you have given up!" He took a draft of coffee. The TV was still tuned to CNN. Crowds filled the whole screen. Ticker-tape news scrolled continuously. Hundreds of thousands of protesters were demonstrating in every city across Egypt, the police had vanished from the streets, tanks ringed Tahrir, a curfew had been imposed from four P.M. to eight A.M. Cut to footage of Mubarak standing in front of a blue curtain, hands set squarely on the podium, addressing the nation. Ahmed Shafik, former head of the air force and minister of civil aviation, was appointed the new prime minister. Omar Suleiman, chief of intelligence for twenty years, was appointed to the long-kept-vacant post of vice president. The cabinet had been sacked.

"The cabinet is zilch, nothing!" Hisham laughed. Everything was happening so fast and was so suddenly upside down and hilarious. "The ministers themselves will tell you in private: 'I don't make policy, I get orders from the president and I carry them out.' Mubarak ran things like a war room." Then he laughed again. "This I think is the first time I have used the past tense and Mubarak in the same sentence!"

The Day of Rage was a fulcrum moment. It tipped history from demonstration to revolution. Something very important happened on January 28, but in all my conversations with its participants no one could say what. Over the year and a half I lived in Cairo after the revolution, during the many occasions I was present during fighting, riots, rock throwing, I began to realize that witnessing something did not give you any good sense of what had really happened. In fact it was the opposite. In the midst of the fray (or rather on its edges, where I usually stationed myself) you were blinded by tear gas or running away. The scene was jumbled. You could only see a very small part of it; it was hard to distinguish attackers from attacked and certainly impossible to see who had "started it." "Witnesses" were frightened and spouting all sorts of rumors. The more I went to protests the less I could see. A person bearing witness was the most unreliable narrator of all.

I arrived in Cairo the day after the battles on the bridges and so I had to reconstruct events secondhand. I don't know if checking sources against each other is a better way to figure out what happened than checking them against your own view. History, reportage, memoir; survey, facts, story; and which is the truest? (Fiction of course!) On the Day of Rage, at some point in the late afternoon, the police stopped attacking and ceded the streets to the protesters. The disappearance of the police on the Day of Rage was the first conundrum of the Egyptian revolution. In the months after the revolution, I kept asking, why?

One of the people I asked was a reporter who had witnessed the battles from a balcony. We met in a bar. Ahmad was nice and young and helpful. He had seen the famous photograph moment, ranks of kneeling, praying demonstrators strafed with water cannons. He had seen knots of protesters running forward and beaten back again. All afternoon he watched the to and fro; all afternoon the police line held. At around five P.M., Ahmad

told me, he went down to the street to see better. Then it happened suddenly. The police stopped shooting and retreated.

Why? Why did the police just stop? At that moment? Because
the police hadn't only stopped attacking the protesters on the
bridges, they had vanished like the retracting arms of a startled
sea anemone, en masse, all at the same time, in every city across
Egypt, even from police stations, even from their sentry posts
in front of foreign embassies. That night the protesters burned
Mubarak's National Democratic Party (NDP) headquarters, the
face of the regime, and they burned dozens of police stations all
over Egypt. The protesters occupied Tahrir. Tens of thousands of
policemen took off their uniforms and went home and sat there
for weeks, inactive, some of them angry, some frightened, some
even ashamed.

In all the excitement and melee that followed, this specific action, or *inaction*, had been lost. Ahmad and I scratched our heads
and ordered another beer and discussed the how-why. Maybe the
protesters had been too many and the police were overwhelmed.
Maybe the police had run out of ammunition, maybe their lines
were breached. Ahmad shook his head from side to side, the better to rattle his memory.

"There was an officer there, maybe he told them to—" He
stopped. "I don't know." He wasn't sure what he had seen. "But it
was definitely not an orderly retreat. They were running, just running in every direction."

What orders had been issued, and by whom? President
Mubarak? The interior minister, Habib al-Adly? There were rumors of Adly making frantic phone calls to the presidential palace screaming for help because the Interior Ministry was under
attack. But the chain of command, who said what to whom, was
never made clear even during the investigation and trial when
Adly and Mubarak were prosecuted for being responsible for the
deaths of protesters. Perhaps whatever orders had been issued

had existed only by word of mouth, perhaps they existed on an audio file at Military Intelligence headquarters. Perhaps there had been orders to shoot and these had been countermanded or ignored. But the fact remained—do facts remain? Is a fact like a rock? Perhaps I should not use the word *fact*. Perhaps *consequence* is better, but a *consequence* must have a *cause*—and the cause in this case is unknown.

How-why unknown, but that night the apparatus of the dictatorship, the police, the great wall of enforcement that had protected the regime, was out of the equation.

On the twenty-ninth of January—or was it the day after that?—it was announced—who announced it?—that Habib al-Adly and the police chiefs of Cairo and Giza and several other senior police officials had been placed under a travel ban. This seemed to signal some sort of arrest, but at the time I had just arrived in Cairo and the news was subsumed by the roaring maw on Tahrir and I registered it only fleetingly. Only months later, sitting with Ahmad, mulling over timelines, trying to force events into a narrative, I realized that there was a large piece of the puzzle missing. Who was in charge that evening? Who had ordered and orchestrated what amounted to the decapitation of the entire senior hierarchy of the Interior Ministry?

I continued to ask around: newspaper editors with a line to the Ministry of Information, TV news producers with certain military connections, a shadowy former intelligence general who was starting his own political party, and a friend of a friend who was a Military Intelligence officer: what the hell ever happened to Habib al-Adly?

"He's in prison." Grunt, raise a glass in ironic adieu, who could pity this reversal of fortune?

"But who arrested him? Why?"

"Ah—yes." And my interlocutor would pause and curl their fingers a little tighter around a glass of whiskey, perhaps to ward off any premonition of his own reversal of fortune . . . Well, there were different versions: Adly had been extracted from the Interior Ministry by the army because it was under siege by protesters, he had been shut up in his house under guard, he had been taken away somewhere for his own safety.

Something larger was at work. This was the moment that defined the revolution. The police left the stage. The crowds surged onto Tahrir and remained there. But it was never clear to me whether the fulcrum was tipped by the weight of the people or whether someone had pulled a lever.

TAHRIR

BUT QUESTIONS WERE FOR THE AFTERMATH, FOR LATER PONDER-ing. It is not that we didn't ask them at the time—Adrien and I spent one morning touring smashed-up police stations, some semifunctioning, some abandoned—but the sheer force and drama and spectacle of Tahrir was so magnetic that we couldn't bear to be away from it for long. A hundred thousand faces crammed into close-up foreground . . .

Every morning we went down onto the square. It was like being at the center of the world. Days and faces serried, gloried, blurred, repeating, recurring, new friends from this morning, old friends from yesterday afternoon. We were accompanied by Dahshan, our translator. Dahshan was one of the new generation of Egyptians that all the foreign correspondents fell in love with on Tahrir, young, hip, American pop culture referenced, techno savvy, English speaking. He was absurdly overeducated: He had grown up in France, the child of university professors, and was fluent in several languages. He studied political science at the American University in Cairo and economics at Sciences Po in Paris and had done a second MA in international development at the Harvard Kennedy School. He had interned and consulted at the Arab League and the World Bank, with the Dubai government and the UN; he had lived in Ramallah, researched in South Lebanon, overseen reconstruction in Indonesia after the tsunami, and been an election observer (twice) in South Sudan. He flew back to Cairo on January 24, 2011. "This was a protest I wanted to go to," he told me.

Dahshan was obviously entirely overqualified as a translator. We happily followed him about, round and unbounded, as he tweeted the revolution, grinning with glee, worriedly texting for news of the brother of a friend of his who had disappeared two days ago; restless, curious, running on adrenaline as we all were, darting away to take a picture of a tank or bumping into his friends who lived in a tent under a sign that read *The Freedom Motel* or being interviewed as one of the "revolutionary youth" by CNN.

Every day the crowd was larger. Tents were planted on the grassy traffic circle, field hospitals grew over corner stoops, stages were erected and piled with loud speakers. Placards, slogans, and manifestos were handwritten in ballpoint. Everywhere were megaphones, microphones, choirs, chanting, cheering.

News was word-of-mouth: Strikes in Mahalla . . . More dead in Alexandria . . . Tanks deployed to the presidential palace in Heliopolis this morning . . . Mubarak is going to address the nation tonight . . . Did you hear they found three police informers in the crowd and beat them up? . . . The Al Jazeera crew are out of Mukhabarat custody, thank God . . . The Muslim Brotherhood leaders have been arrested . . . The Muslim Brotherhood leaders have escaped in a prison break . . . No, it was the police who let all the prisoners out to destabilize the country . . . Yeah, I heard this from my cousin who is married to an officer in Asyût . . .

What I remember most was the happiness and camaraderie. Everyone shared water and Laughing Cow cheese sandwiches, everyone was together: Zamalek girls with Gucci sunglasses and poor boys from the slums with broken sandals, old toothless men, women in *niqab*, mothers carrying babies, fathers hoisting their sons onto their shoulders to see democracy for the first time. I found NDP members and off-duty army officers in jeans and polo shirts; there were hip tweeps in Che Guevara T-shirts and Ultras, football fans, who had long experience in fighting the police. There were pious men with scratchy beards and prayer calluses, civil rights lawyers and opposition politicians and preachers and rock singers and famous actresses who toured the square with little mobs of admirers.

Afterward I would wonder at those glorious days. The excitement and the amazement of it all was overwhelming. Everyone helped each other. Everything was shared. It was a utopian Egypt, without class or parties, where whether you were religious or secular didn't seem to matter. It amazed the Egyptians too: they were emboldened and proud, and it surprised them that they could feel these things after so long. And very soon Adrien and I found ourselves caught up in this infectious spirit; we cast our doubtful impartiality to one side and from time to time I caught myself chanting along: "*Hold your head up, you are an Egyptian!*"

Now we have a voice!" an oil rig worker told me. A young female surgeon wearing a red head scarf told me she had been on duty at the October 6 University Hospital and seen the live bullet wounds. I diligently wrote down names and quotes. A man called Hassam Fedawy was overexcited. He sat on the curb beside a man with a bandaged head and told his story of the Day of Rage. "At first facing the police we were shaking. I told everyone to embrace the police and they put their arms around them; actually they are very skinny!" An old wrinkled woman with eleven children and a tumble of Ottoman coins dangling from her ears said, "State TV is not showing the reality. And they are letting prisoners out of the prison to frighten us. We are not frightened!" A gray-haired, soft-spoken English teacher who did not want to give his surname because he was still afraid said, "I am not working according to any party. I am without a party, I have just my sandwiches." Abdul Rahman, with an MA in business: "The situation is changing dramatically. It's impossible to know what will happen in two seconds." A well-dressed man speaking accentless English: "Don't quote me as a diplomat! There would be an investigation and even though they wouldn't know it was me, they would probably use it against someone they suspected for something else . . . The president must go . . ." Assr Hassan, an engineer at Vodafone dressed in camouflage trousers and a red and white checked *kaffiyeh,* told me the marches were the most beautiful thing he had ever seen. "There is a collective consciousness. Even after the phones went off there was a kind of national telepathy of where to go."

It seemed that the whole of Egypt was on Tahrir, all barriers and visions and class and prejudice pushed aside. A seventy-five-year-old former French professor with a single tooth; a Coptic couple, arms entwined, recently engaged; a man in a dirty *galabia* and a short bristle mustache who waved furiously and said, "All of us in Egypt, Muslim, Christian, don't want *him!*" A teenager who pulled up his baseball cap to show a bandage where he had been "whacked by a rubber bullet on Friday." A professor of material science who had been trying to register a new political party for fifteen years. A lawyer from the lawyers' syndicate: "It is just the people, there is no leader." A doctor, a dentist. A pharmacist who spoke in measured academic tones: "I am interested in the social aspect: all my life of thirty-five years we knew ourselves to be a bit aggressive—the traffic, the sexual harassment. These were negatives and we somehow believed that we were not really good people. Since Thursday we have noticed changes in ourselves."

I remember, in particular, a human rights lawyer whose offices had been raided the night before, a dozen arrested, who told me, wry, determined: "There is no plan, but we must proceed."

H ello, I am the media coordina-tor," Ahmed Naguib said, in-troducing himself.

"Of what?"

"Of the revolution!"

We were caught in a dense pack of people between the back of a stage and a travel agency that the Muslim Brotherhood had taken over as a kind of unofficial Tahrir branch office. Naguib was big with curly hair and bouncy enthusiasm, and he opened his arms wide like a friendly bear to shepherd us through. He told us he was not Brotherhood himself, but he was impressed with their coordination of food, medical supplies and people. The travel agency was only a small cramped shop front and it smelled of sleeping men and feet. The Brotherhood was deliber-ately keeping a low profile because it was an article of faith on the square that no parties should display their own banners.

Most days we would stop by the Brotherhood travel agency and ask Naguib, "What is happening?" and Naguib would laugh. "What's happening? This is anyone's guess!" But then he would tell us rumors and news—the youth had been furious with the Nasserists who put up a Nasserist flag; had we seen the couple who got married on the square? Had we seen the priest and the

imam holding hands with crucifix and Koran aloft? A general had
shown up yesterday and tried to tell everyone to go home but the
crowd had booed him and he had angrily retreated; there were
people coming from Upper Egypt, even from Aswan . . .

WAR AND PEACE

Last night Adrien and I watched the battle scene of Borodino in Bondarchuk's version of *War and Peace*, made in the Soviet sixties heyday of grand epic cinema when budgets were unlimited. Here is a battle unfolded, probably the best battle scene ever filmed— but it is not a single scene but many.

At the beginning the light is bright morning tinged with gold and expectation. The infantry marches in rows of platoons, companies, columns; whole regiments maneuver across the plain. The scene is stretched as far as the camera can pan, over undulating ground, with its dips and gullies and strategic hills, artillery on the high ground, cavalry prancing across the sward and puffs of white smoke like cotton-wool cannon fire. For a moment we see Captain Tushin diligently and enthusiastically firing his cannon, and then the action swings, smoke blackening over the seam, to the battle for a farmhouse. The French infantry, transformed from anonymous marching formations into individual soldiers (look at their great mustaches!), dart forward with their bayonets fixed into the orange billowing fire. Bondarchuk's direction travels a long tracking shot, left to right, from a splintered interior, furniture overturned, pots and possessions scattered, to a balcony where the Russian defenders are retreating through a jet of flame sent up like a conjuror's crescendo. Now cut to Napoléon himself, standing on a grassy promontory receiving reports from his staff officers, who gallop up from the flanks, dismount and salute. Behind him stand a line of marshals in fine blue broadcloth uniforms encrusted with gold braid; in front of him, a little ways off, lonely, is a campaign chair set up in case his gout begins to trouble him. But for the moment he is pacing and the battlefield is lost further than he can see beyond the screen of smoke, pockets and actions unknown to him, hidden behind ridges, cut off and surrounded by the enemy or unreported because the messenger was killed. Sweep the camera as the cavalry gallops thundering past, French cuirassiers with plumed shiny helmets, their horses' hooves kicking up swaths of dust. The foreground in this shot is a ditch piled with wounded and you can watch a cameo of a soldier dragging his wounded comrade. Prince Andrei is commanding a regiment kept in reserve. He is frustrated; the battle is being fought by others (or is he somehow relieved? He was wounded at Austerlitz and he understands the horror of it all— but we are not sure whether he is willing yet to surrender to reality or his conscience and denounce the futility of the horror . . .). He tells his soldiers that they may sit and wait, rather than keeping them standing in ranks, and the camera lingers across the front line, each muzhik occupied in an individual and separate task, one oiling his rifle, one darning a sock, two playing cards, one rolling up a ball of string, one repairing a leather strap. Elsewhere on that grand plain and canvas the battle rages. Infantry form into squares and cavalry maraud their bristled edges but cannot break through. We can see this from above as if we were sitting on a nearby hill. Pierre, in his white rabbit top hat and white rabbit gloves, cannot see anything for the moment because a splotch of mud has hit him in the face and smeared his spectacles. He finds himself with Tushin's artillery, who seem to have adopted him as a kind of mascot . . . the cavalry are advancing again, across a shallow river . . . here's a gully filled with splayed corpses . . . the infantry are marching, *gauche, gauche, gauche,* shouts the sergeant major, tamping out the rhythm . . . a curtain of horsemen divide and fall away to reveal a line of infantry, load, ready, fire, and they shoot into the rushing enemy cavalry and riderless horses run together in terrified herds.

What I mean to describe is someone else's description of a complicated event. Bondarchuk copies Tolstoy's technique of swinging from bird's eye to mud. From the sweeping panorama helicopter shot, cut to the ground, to the intimacy of a single moment, a soldier lugging his friend to safety, Prince Andrei, irritated, whisking the long grass with his riding crop. From a blurry cavalry charge to the detail of the loops and swag of the gold braid covering the blue broadcloth uniforms of French marshals. Alternate fog and clarity. Perspective hovers wide, then draws tight. It moves from history's great leaders to the dilemmas of officers, to the humble muzhik soldier cleaning his boots, the berserker stripped to his waist, ramming powder and charge down a cannon's throat or carrying his friend, life and death arguing over his soul, up a mud slope, out of the fray. Because on a field of battle everyone is subject to the same mighty maw.

But who determines its outcome? Is it the generals who have ordered the positions, as Pierre thinks when on the eve of the battle he tells his friend Prince Andrei his concerns about the shape of the Russian deployment, or is it, as Prince Andrei furiously corrects him in riposte, the spirit of the men that matters, their morale, their response to history's destiny thrust upon them?

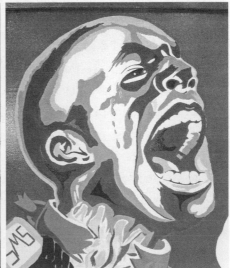

Eighteen days. But they are only eighteen days in retrospect. At the time nobody knew there would be eighteen days. At the time nobody knew what the next day would bring. It could bring death or glory or no change at all. In retelling I can turn events into sequential chapters—"The Twenty-Fifth," "The Day of Rage," "Mubarak's First Speech," "The Battle of the Camels," "Wael Ghonim Sobbing Patriotically on National TV," "Mubarak Speech's Refusing to Resign," "The Last Day." But history does not progress toward an inevitable goal. It does not know what it is doing.

At the time I scribbled incidents in my notebooks, dialogue, anecdotes, things I noticed and overheard—but now these are kaleidoscopic in my memory; they fall into different patterns every time I turn the lens against the angle of recollection.

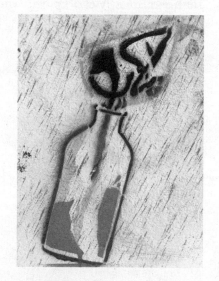

The crowd fought to get onto Tahrir on the Day of Rage. In the Battle of the Camels, they fought to stay on it. Shorn of the police, unsure of the army, the regime, such as it was now—Hosni, his wife and two sons—rallied a last-ditch effort. Networks of cash-in-hand thugs were mobilized.

Thousands of these pro-Mubaraks marched to take back Tahrir. Midday, Adrien and I watched a large mass of them pushing up the throat of the square. We retreated to the far perimeter but got separated from Dahshan on the way. Mobile phone frequencies were jammed; I couldn't get through to him and I dared not look down at the phone for too long in case of being trampled in a stampede. The rival crowds swilled against each other, a strangely calm sea—but I couldn't see where their front lines met, only that there was a great milling of people, no breeze, currents unknown. I turned and said to Adrien, "There's only one way this will go." He said, "Shall we leave while we can?" I nodded.

We got back to the hotel and immediately went outside to our balcony. I lit a cigarette. From here we could see the wide expanse of Tahrir. I watched as the great crowd parted like a bolt of cloth tearing. People were running. And then I saw two lumpy shapes bouncing among them. I squinted carefully and looked at Adrien, cigar resting in his hand on the railing.

"I think those are camels!"

Dahshan reappeared an hour later, cherubic, panting, frightened, furiously tweeting pictures of bleeding foreheads on his mobile phone. We watched from the balcony and ducked inside to watch, in stereo, the CNN coverage. The muezzin called for the sunset prayer and on the safe side of the square the ranks of faithful lined up while the women chipped at the curbstones, quarrying for ammunition. From time to time we could hear shouts go up.

"Hold your positions! Don't be afraid! If they take the square, we'll never get it back!"

"Stay here tonight," I told Dahshan, "we'll make up a bed on the floor." He nodded. Stones were flying over as if it were a medieval siege; flames shone under a large laurel tree, but we couldn't see what was burning because the knot of defending protesters was too dense. The pro-Mubaraks shouted, "Mubarak! Mubarak!" and the protesters hailed them in stones, clanging the alarm for reinforcements on the green metal balustrades. There were skirmishes now at every junction onto the square. I counted them.

"There are nine roads that lead onto Tahrir," I said out loud, "not including alleys and cut-throughs. There's no way they can defend it."

The stones plinked metallically against the armored flanks of the tanks; the Arab League stood illuminated, white and impassive. I watched a doctor in a white coat and surgical gloves help the wounded back from the front line to a corner beyond a red VW Beetle, inexplicably parked in the midst of the fray. I could see red blood seeping across the T-shirts of the protesters. The pro-Mubaraks came in force, carrying a long banner of the striped Egyptian flag unfurled above them like the turtle shell of a Roman legion: red, white, black. We watched them line up Molotov cocktails on the tarmac and hand the bottles to the best throwers in the front ranks, and then watched the throwers lob them into the mass defending the square. Some dropped their burning bottles, and patches of flame erupted all over the road. One landed by the tires of the red VW Beetle, which began to burn. One landed at the feet of a demonstrator, who stamped on it, bright sparks in the purple dusk, as the hem of his trousers caught fire and others rushed forward to drag him back and beat the flames out with their jackets.

The protesters made rushing attacks on the pro-Mubaraks, pushing them back across the bridge. Several times we watched a vanguard run out to chase them away and then return, hauling with them what they could scavenge to make a barricade: blue fencing from the adjacent building, police barriers, road signs, a bench wrenched out of a bus stop. Over and over again the protesters ran forward scattering the pro-Mubaraks. Each time the pro-Mubaraks crept back, their number was diminished. We watched their shadows leaking away into the night.

The morning after the Battle of the Camels Adrien and Dahshan and I went down to the square early. We walked through a gap in the barricade, past garbage heaps that could be set alight in defense. It was already a beautiful day. Protesters lined up to greet those come to join them. "Welcome to Tahrir!" they sang, bang-ing drums. "Welcome to freedom!" I walked between them with tears in my eyes.

All around us was the scene of quieted aftermath: Kids and young men exhausted, splayed on the ground or curled under blan-kets. Boys shoveling stones into flour sacks for ammunition in case the thugs came back. The defenders of Tahrir walked about slowly, dazed, ragged, red-eyed, heads bandaged, arms in slings or limp-ing. They had fashioned helmets from anything they could find, scavenged armor: upturned buckets and saucepans, three empty plastic Pepsi bottles wrapped with gaffer tape, a slab of paving tied under the chin with a length of bandage.

Ahmed Naguib was in his usual place outside the Muslim Brotherhood travel agency headquarters. He held his arms out wide to embrace the morning.

"Oh, you can say what you like about the Brothers! But last night they were on the front lines, saving our revolutionary arses!" Dr. Mohammed Beltegi, a member of the Brotherhood Guidance Council, came out from the interior, harried, smiling, holding his phone to one ear with one hand, holding off supplicants with an-other, offering, as he hurried away, late for a meeting, a quote or two for an outstretched microphone. "Egypt today is a different Egypt!" I had seen Beltegi on the square every day, emerging from the fetid interior of the travel agency always neat and natty, with his special blend of cryptic optimism. That day his thin hair was mussed on his high dome forehead, and his tie was awry. "I see you are in the same clothes as yesterday," I observed, teasing him a little. "Yes, I slept here last night," he admitted, "my two sons were on the square, I couldn't leave them."

The fighting had been heaviest at the entrance to the square beside the Egyptian Museum that was overlooked by a stretch of elevated highway. Here the protesters had built a giant bar-ricade of burned buses fortified with concrete blocks. Rocks were still going over in occasional fusillades. When I climbed up on the windowsills of the burned buses I could see clumps of pro-Mubaraks lurking behind the concrete pillars under the flyover. Adrien and I stood there trying to take in the scene. A scuffling, jostling clot of protesters came past, dragging a plainclothes pro-Mubarak they had found, half of them trying to beat him, half of them trying to protect him. "Don't hand him over! We should keep him!" "No! We'll tie him to the fence!"

To the side of the frontline barricade was a field hospital, little more than a collection of blankets laid out on the pavement. Here we met Sherif Omar, a mild and handsome pharmacist, a volunteer medic. His white coat was covered with blood. "I look like a butcher!" he said apologetically. Bullet wounds, yes, five or six dead at least; one had died bleeding in his arms. He looked away for a moment toward the roof of an abandoned grand villa where protesters were flinging rocks and jeering at the remnants of the pro-Mubaraks cowering on the other side of the barricade. He continued his litany: head injuries from rocks, hundreds, too many to count. As we stood talking, there was a commotion, kids jumping over the burned-out cars and climbing on their roofs for a better view. Coming through: a general with gold stars on his shoulders escorted by a company of red-bereted military police. The general tried to stride purposefully forward but had to pick his way through the rubble. He advanced toward the blue string cordon around the field hospital and came straight up to Sherif.

"Take all this away and pack it up!" he told him. The general was angry.

"Why didn't you protect us from the thugs last night?" Sherif was angry too.

"You would like me to fire on people? With these tanks? One shell and you would all be running!" The general said this in a belligerent tone that implied a deep and career-long satisfaction with the efficacy of superior firepower. "What is *all this*?" He spread his arms over the mess. "*All this* is the work of foreign forces who want to destabilize Egypt!" Sherif began to remonstrate. The general was not interested in backchat. "Go home, all of you!" He pointed at the circle of faces around him. "Go home and put an end to this silly business!"

"You would call the blood of Egyptians silly business?" Sherif the pharmacist stood up tall.

The general ignored him and continued to call for order. "We are resolved to clear the square as soon as possible so that traffic and normality can resume."

"What are you going to do? Shoot us off the square?"

"No, we can't use violence, *but* . . . we can be very tough with people," the general warned.

"What do you mean by 'tough'?"

"Like from a father to a child," replied the general, wagging his finger.

"Thirty years, the same patriarchal crap," said Sherif under his breath. Under the visor of his military cap, the general's eyes were shaded, but I could see his mustache flex in fury. He took the head of a nearby wounded protester in his hands and unwound the man's bandage. "Look, it's just a bruise!" he cried, as if exposing a charade. Then he moved on to another man with a wad of cotton taped to his scalp, trying to rip it away. The bandage would not come off because it was stuck with dried blood. The general caught the man in a strangle hug and violently kissed him on the forehead, as if he was a recalcitrant son whom he simultaneously loved and despaired of. The crowd had grown to several hundred, attracted by this strange scene, and was pressing closer, wary of the red-beret military police but angered by the general's assaulting, insulting embraces. The general stepped back, tripping over a pile of bricks, and addressed the pressing faces. "You all have the right to express yourselves but please save what is left of Egypt!"

"We're not leaving until *he* leaves!" the crowd chanted back.

"I will not speak amid such singing!" The general humphed and turned his back and retreated toward the military encampment by the entrance to the Egyptian Museum.

Every day more tents went up on the central traffic island. The grass was trampled to dust and in places it was so crowded with tents and pegs and guy ropes that it was impossible to walk between them. The Freedom Motel guys broke into a streetlight and jury-rigged electricity to charge their mobile phones and computers. The Internet had been switched back on; there were plenty of pictures and video to upload. Nearby poor families curled up together in nests of plastic bags and blankets. A veiled woman told of her dream of the prophet Muhammad circling the square, a psychiatrist held a small crowd spellbound with his theory that Mubarak was a psychopath, people passed out pamphlets rebutting Prime Minister Ahmed Shafik's apology for the violence at the Battle of the Camels. Girls made heart shapes with the dug-up paving stones now not needed as ammunition against the thugs. Eggplant-shaped village women made sandwiches on a bench next to the boarded-up Hardee's. The pissoir alley that led to the makeshift mosque-hospital reeked for days until someone sluiced it with disinfectant.

Egypt is our mother and we are its child!
Tomorrow a million!
Be a man and step out!
The people and the army are united!
We're not leaving; he is leaving!
Leave!
Leave!
Leave!

The crowd was a tremendous thing. Every morning we woke up to its noise, every night we went to sleep to its roar.

"It is extraordinary," said Adrien, standing on the balcony with a cigar. From this purview Tahrir was a single organism, but when we went down and walked among it, it became a million selves, and it was overwhelming.

One side of the square was shadowed by the gray toady hulk of Mogamma. The Mogamma building was the repository of all state functions, bureaucracy, forms and registrations: births, deaths, marriage licenses, visa extensions, exit visa exemptions, resident permits, restaurant permits, national IDs, Interior Ministry police, the Mukhabarat. Corridors, officials, files, folders, indigo ink stamp pads, seals and documents of attestation, window number forty-two for payment, take the receipt to window number thirteen, leave your passport, come back tomorrow at two P.M. Throughout the eighteen days the army had cordoned the plaza in front of Mogamma with a few soldiers. Interestingly the protesters never tried to storm it. It remained implacable, even forgotten, throughout the events.

"You cannot live in this country and not visit that building," Ramy Shaof said to me one afternoon, pointing up at the edifice. Shaof was a well-known activist, half Palestinian, half Egyptian. He was married to Ragia Omran, a flame-haired human rights lawyer; I think Dahshan must have introduced us. "My security file compiled over the last twenty years is in that building," Shaof said, his eyes twinkling. When I got to know him better I saw that his merriment was his defense. Smile at your oppressors! Because after all they are ridiculous! "I even know which room it's in, top floor, second-to-last door on the left." Shaof had studied war strategy at King's College London and spent a lot of time in demonstrations in Palestine during the second intifada. He had plenty of experience with barricades and tear gas. "It's a hobby," he said, shrugging, wily, impish, entirely unapologetic. He was worried about people who were missing and had compiled a list of five hundred names. "We have been checking hospitals; they could be detained in military prisons or dumped somewhere in the desert." Dahshan nodded. His friend's brother, he told Shaof, had been missing since the night of the twenty-seventh. He had stopped answering his phone; everyone was concerned. He worked for Google in Dubai, "one of us," said Dahshan. Wael Ghonim? Had he heard anything? Shaof frowned.

"Yes, I know. A lot of people are looking for him. Probably he's been arrested."

An ordinary-looking man, bald with a zipped-up windbreaker, pointed his mobile phone in our direction. Everyone had mobile phones and cameras on the square, but for a minute, two minutes, the bland bald man didn't move, just stood there filming us.

"What do you want with this?" Ragia Omran asked him, standing on her tiptoes. She was small with a big frizz of red hair and was wearing a T-shirt that read: *THE SOLUTION.* The man ignored her and continued filming. Ragia confronted him, hands on hips. "Why are you filming us?"

"For my memories," mumbled the man as he walked away.

On the stage set up next to the statue of Omar Makram, Ramy Essam, long-haired heartthrob singer of the revolution, his top lip split and swollen from the rock fights during the Battle of the Camels, was singing one of his funny strummy tunes of rebellion: "Bow Down Bow Down You're in a Democracy!" His bassist played with a bandage wrapped around his chin. Ramy Essam sang his song about the old donkey and the young donkey. *"Give me the cart, you're getting old, the passengers won't notice,"* sings the young donkey. And the old donkey sings back to his heir apparent, *"But be careful of the passengers because if they wake up they'll poke you in the arse eighty million times!"* The protesters waved and clapped and whistled. The girls in the crowd blew kisses. Ramy bowed and then tapped the microphone for attention: "And now we would like to ask you lovely people to go to the Egyptian Museum to guard it!"

Ramy Essam was followed on the stage by a group of Al Azhar Islamic scholars wearing their traditional gray robes with the red *tarboosh* wrapped in a white turban on their heads. They sang Islamic psalms and the scholar with the microphone reassured the crowd: "This peaceful demonstration is not a religiously forbidden dissent."

Adrien and I watched the young hip techno kids melt away and be replaced by a more serious and larger audience, head scarves and imminent beards, who sat down on the tarmac and listened respectfully.

At prayer time the faithful lined up in curving rows, laid out improvised prayer mats: *kaffiyehs*, newspapers, an Egyptian flag and slogan placards. They wiped their hands in the dust to clean them because the Koran says that if there is no water and you are in the desert you can use sand to clean your hands before you pray. When they touched the ground with their foreheads they all had a little disc of dusty grit that stuck there with the sweat.

Wael Ghonim was released after ten days detained by the State Security police. He appeared suddenly on Twitter: *Freedom is the Bless that deserves fighting for it*. Wael Ghonim was driven directly from the State Security prison to the cable channel Dream TV's studios. He was exhausted from days of interrogation, overwhelmed and disoriented. Yes, he admitted, he had been the anonymous administrator of the "We Are All Khalid Said" Facebook page, which had done so much to encourage people to take to the streets on the twenty-fifth. Dahshan watched the interview with us, shaking his head, confused: "None of us knew." He remembered Wael only as a quiet kind of geek, as someone in the background of the room.

Wael Ghonim had been held in solitary; he had no idea of the crowds that had engulfed the country. He spoke raggedly, rapidly, sitting forward on the TV studio sofa and leaning toward the camera, earnestly explaining, almost imploring. He had never imagined that so many people would go out on the twenty-fifth; no, they had not been backed by any foreigners, they were only Egyptians who wanted a better Egypt. The presenter showed him footage of the fighting on the Day of Rage and of the camels charging the protesters on Tahrir, and his voice cracked and broke. He appeared raw and open; he declined any leadership or hero status. His face fractured with emotion—pained, scoured, wrenched—and his hope shone like a beacon from this agonized honesty. His sincerity was searing; suddenly all the lies and innuendos and smears of the naysaying state media who called the protesters Kentucky Fried Chicken–eating mercenaries, stooges of foreign interests and beards of Islamic fundamentalism were swept away.

The next day the crowds on the square were double, and every day afterward the numbers increased into a tidal wave. A hundred thousand, two hundred thousand, half a million. The revolution turned carnival and began to smell of popcorn. Tea sellers suddenly proliferated on the square, samovar kettle balanced on a length of plywood, glass mugs lined up, each ready with a tea bag and an inch of sugar. Roast sweet potato sellers, boys hawking buckets of ice water and Pepsi. I bumped into Shaof the activist leaving Tahrir because it was so full he couldn't move. He was laughing. "At first we couldn't get onto the square because of the police; now we can't get onto the square because of the protesters!"

It was almost the end. It had to be the end now. There was a general strike; they said eight million people were on the streets all over Egypt. Mubarak would address the nation tonight. Hundreds of thousands gathered in Tahrir to hear him speak. The old man gripped his presidential podium as if for support and I remembered Hisham Kassem's word, *scaffolding*. But the old man with the dyed black hair kept his vigorous sneer, his mouth drawn down at the corners, with age, gravity, jowl. He droned his patriotism, his fear of disorder, his unshakable belief in the great and proud nation of Egypt. On the square in the crowd we couldn't hear very well through the scratchy blur of the loudspeakers— some people held radios and mobile phones next to their ears— and as he spoke there was bewilderment. We all held our breath, partly straining to catch what he was saying, partly in respect, partly in expectation. Mubarak drew his measured gravel tones, grave and stentorian, into long syllables. The great and proud nation of Egypt listened for a while and then all around me, one by one, I watched men take off their shoes and hold them aloft in contempt. When Mubarak finished speaking there was a great rending groan. We were near the Freedom Motel tent and one guy screamed and collapsed, heaving and bucking against his friends, who tried to hold him. His brother had been killed, apparently, during the Day of Rage. He could not be calmed. We walked away at midnight hushed and disappointed.

The following day was Friday. Bright blue, as if the rancor of the night was bleached out by the promising sunlight. There was a sense, inarticulate, that whatever *he* said was moot now; history had been done and could not be undone. What next, what to do, was a practical question, but the chapter had already been written and we were galloping to the end, greedy to finish it up. Tahrir had become a city, every day a little more organized with added amenities. I watched a team of builders pouring concrete for a plumbed-in shower block in the middle of the traffic circle. Throughout the afternoon marches set off from Tahrir headed directly to the presidential palace in Heliopolis. Shaof was grinning. For the first week of the protests he had slept somewhere different every night and continually swapped mobile phone numbers, but now he had stopped taking these precautions. He spread his hands out in victorious amusement at such a turn of events. "End of story. Game over . . . the fear is over!"

There was a great debate on Tahrir: whether to march on the presidential palace (but peaceful, peaceful!) or to stand firm and unified on the square. Word came through that a crowd was gathering at the presidential palace. Adrien was stuck writing on deadline. Dahshan and I discussed whether to go or not. The presidential palace was twenty kilometers away in Heliopolis, distance, traffic, checkpoints . . . the crowd forming outside the presidential palace might not do anything but stand there all night; on the other hand if they pressed against the army . . . there were tanks stationed there with their cannons pointing at the crowd . . . if something happened . . . something was bound to happen . . . or nothing might happen.

While we were debating:

Omar Suleiman, a thin, dour, ascetic man with a bald head, his expression a permanent and serious frown. Omar Suleiman, who had taken off the uniform of the Military Intelligence general and put on a somber navy blue suit when he had been appointed Mubarak's vice president the week before, appeared before the country in what appeared to be a wood-paneled corridor. His face was long and there were dark pouches under his eyes. His voice was heavy, like stones being pulled back to the shore. Behind him stood a square man with a square haircut and thick eyebrows drawn down sternly. This accidentally in-the-frame man remained as stiff as a guard but his eyes flicked left and then right and then left again.

Omar Suleiman spoke briefly:

"My fellow citizens, in the difficult circumstances our country is experiencing, President Muhammad Hosni Mubarak has decided to give up the office of the president of the republic and instructed the Supreme Council of the Armed Forces to manage the affairs of the country. May God guide our steps."

We heard a great wheeling cheer going up from Tahrir and we began to run toward it.

Dahshan and I ran hand in hand, so as not to lose each other in the rushing glee. The crowd was jumping and leaping and shaking and pressing forward in a great heaving mass. Waving hands and fists and flags, stretching skyward. Many limbs of one body, bare arms reached up with the glowing rectangles of mobile phone screens, like a phosphorescent twinkling in the dusk. Conga lines and hugs and elbows jagged, banging drums, screaming wild reckless elation, exploding flares. The noise was like a solid tidal roar and I was a drop of water surfing, swept along. The grinning faces painted patriotic stripes, red, white and black; glimpse of baby on shoulders; teenager scrambling up the slender streetlight with a flag held in his teeth; pinch-ass squeal; old man in a wheelchair—all this was a blur. I did not take out my notebook. For a moment I stood among the teeming amazed and just tried to look at it.

Dahshan let go of my hand. He needed two hands to clasp his mobile phone and type the little buttons.

"Look up!" I yelled in his ear. "Look at this!"

He continued, head bent, and made no reply.

"Hold your head up! You're an Egyptian!"

Dahshan muttered something to stop my bugging him. His attention was entirely concentrated on his phone; he was furiously tweeting. I was furious at his distraction. Look up! In case we're trampled on—look up! Your country, *you,* are the center of all history, look up at it!

Dahshan tripped, knocked into a careening reveler, righted himself, looked back down again. But his phone screen had gone black. He shook the phone. He pressed on-off. He looked up at me but I only frowned at him. He remained in thrall to muscle memory, his eyes as blank as the screen, thought to fingertip, reflexively tip-tapping at the unresponsive buttons. He shook the thing. Nothing. The screen remained ineffably black. He looked at me with an expression of miserable wonderment. We stumbled forward. The crowd was heaving. Dahshan kept shaking and jamming at his mobile phone, but it was no use. For many minutes in the midst of that roaring joy he was so bereft he could not speak.

Hands reached out and hauled us up and over the row of people sitting on the curb, onto the circle. We were caught in the tent city, tripping over crosshatched guy ropes, blocked this way with boxes, that way by a cul-de-sac of two tents tied to each other and lashed to concrete reinforcing-rod uprights. Dahshan's glare was fixed to the ground. I looked about and saw that everyone around us had their phone held to their ear or was taking pictures with them or tapping messages into keypads. And I thought, *I should not be irritated, he only wants to tell as we all want to tell the amazing*. Many other people were also shaking their phones with great frustration, redial redial. Then of course I took out my own phone. I wanted to call Adrien, who had stayed behind in the hotel to write his story on deadline. "I can't tell you what day it's going to happen," he had said laconically at breakfast a couple of days before, "but I can tell you at what time: precisely at five P.M., twenty minutes before my deadline." Call failed. There was no signal; so many phones were calling that the volume of radiation had jammed the frequencies.

Dahshan and I hopped through the jagged wires and stays, trying to avoid stubbing our feet against the metal tent pegs, and found our way to the Freedom Motel. Everyone was dancing. One of Dahshan's grinning activist friends clapped him hello on the back and Dahshan tried to manage a smile and, in trying, found one, wan but broadening. We shouted at each other, but it turned out after all that there were no words and no one could hear anyone anyway. Drums banged, flares shot high fire in the darken-

ing sky. People climbed to the top of streetlights to wave flags and everywhere was a sea of red and black and white stripes. To one side, I saw a traffic light. It had been turned off for the duration of the eighteen days but now was suddenly illuminated. It shone like a beacon, but all its lights together, like its own private joke, red orange green. Stop, wait, go.

HASSAN

ONE ORANGE-COLORED DUSK HASSAN AND I WERE WALKING ACROSS the Sixth October Bridge—or was it the Fifteenth May Bridge that runs elevated above Twenty-Sixth July Street? I always got the bridges and their revolutions confused. The *khamsin* wind was blowing sand in from the desert. Billowed ocher clouds made hulky silhouettes out of the restaurant boats moored along the riverbank. Grit in our teeth; wiping yellow paste from our eyes.

"Oh look, a snail on the bridge!" Hassan pointed out, curious, amid the loose stones and ravines of cracked asphalt. Little snail making a glistening slime trail that seemed for a moment, under a waking streetlamp, to glitter in the dirty velvet-bagged obscurity.

"How did it get here?" he wondered. "It must have taken years to crawl all this way."

I met Hassan because Dahshan had flown off to Tunisia-Copenhagen-Geneva to participate in conferences as a real-life Egyptian revolutionary youth and I needed a translator. It was April, a couple of months after the revolution. We met at the

corner below my apartment next to the statue of Um Kalthoum. The first thing I noticed was his Egyptian curly hair sticking out in every direction in a giant halo fro. He was young, smooth faced, a kid really. He was wearing a Sex Pistols T-shirt. He put his hand out, a little tremor, polite and nervous, and introduced himself in perfectly accented English. Of course he had never been out of Egypt; I was to later discover he had barely been out of Cairo and never been on an airplane.

"There's a demo going on at the Syrian embassy," I told him. "We need to go right now. It that okay?" He hesitated only for a moment before nodding and we jumped in a taxi.

The crowd at the Syrian embassy was only a few dozen. I recognized some faces from Tahrir. Hassan was quick with sentences and obliging. We had a good half hour of talking to people—we had missed the stone throwing, I think. The sentry had retreated inside, the gate pulled shut and a meter extra of metal sheeting affixed to the top of the surrounding wall. The embassy had turned itself blind to the shouting street. Hassan was easy and engaging; he had the talent of a natural charm stranger-to-stranger in a crowd. I thought he would do very well, underneath the great big hair.

"Tomorrow?" I asked him as we parted, and he smiled with relief. Then something about him clenched—the way his hands thrust back into his pockets as if there was nothing in there to impede them, the looseness of his jeans around his skinny frame, his hung head turning away . . .

"Here," I said. "As an advance." I gave him a hundred-dollar bill and got a bounce and a big grin in return.

Afterward I always said that I rescued Hassan from a call center, but this was not strictly true. He had actually quit a couple of months before the eighteen days. He was down to his last few pounds when I gave him the hundred-dollar bill. Still, he politely refused when I offered it to him and I had to insist. He had worked for the technical support call center for three years; he started as soon as he left school. His grades were not high enough for the English-language or -literature departments of Cairo University. "The system made me stupid," he told me. He had fives for English and German, but his Arabic wasn't good enough for languages; he was good at math but not biology, so he couldn't be a scientist, and his history teacher had taken against him. So he enrolled in the faculty of tourism guidance at Ain Shams University and never went to class. When I met him he had failed two years in a row and his father was yelling, "Graduate graduate graduate!" because he couldn't apply himself to get the degree that every respectable middle-class male born Egyptian needed if they were ever going to get a job—a good government job— because God knows there were only two million other boys in Cairo in the same position as he was.

Instead he went to work at a call center. Four hundred dollars a month, which was, as Hassan was tempted to point out, more than his father earned as a producer of cultural programming on state radio. Every day Hassan commuted two hours across the entire breadth of Cairo, across that maximum city of twenty million souls, from Heliopolis to one of the new satellite towns, built in the desert, named, like many things in Egypt, Sixth October, after the great victory against the Israelis in 1973. He answered calls from Samsung mobile phone customers in the UK and Ireland. "There were a lot of complaints, there were a lot of problems,"

Hassan told me as he tapped at my iPhone to switch from GSM to Wi-Fi and change the settings in some clever way that meant the battery ran down slower and download an app that updated Cairo traffic jams in real time. "Samsungs are shit."

The call center was a large dull rectangular building in a purpose-built business park named, with Gamal-era progressivism, Smart Village. The first time he saw it, Hassan thought it was a spaceship: wireless headsets, digital track pads, large flatscreens arrayed around each desk. Eight hours in a cubicle in a flat wide room that took up a whole floor and had a low ceiling that sat flat on any horizon. He was drilled: twenty seconds to diagnose the problem, "Hello, Samsung technical support. You have reached Steve. How can I help you today?" Two hundred eighty seconds to finish the call. The customer would be jolted from on hold: weary or chatty or pedantic or worrisome or furious or incapable of explaining what their problem was. Steve talked them through checklists, menu scroll down, click on, kept his voice bright and understanding. He learned British geography and postcodes so that he could direct callers to their nearest service center. Sometimes the line crackled and people asked, "So where are you really?" He wasn't supposed to tell them, but he usually did. Cairo. Egypt. "Och, I'm sure it's nice and sunny where you are! It'll be tipping down outside here in Leith." The distance of a whole world of possibilities (even rain!) bungeed down a phone line. Eight hours over night shift strapped to a headset; six A.M. back on the bus jammed in the traffic. Headphones in his ears, Jimi, Jam, Stones; rime of dust inside the bus window. Often he would give his seat up to a woman encumbered with her own female bulk, several shopping bags, a small child, and then he would have to stand the rest of the way, tired, with his knees bent like springs against the lurching of the bus and the elbow of the man next to him poking his ribs every time they hit a pothole. When he got home his father would compress his lips instead of saying hello, or he would look up from his newspaper for a moment to say something about Allah and hard work because he had become more religious lately and had prevailed upon his wife to put on a head scarf. His mother would be shuffling in the kitchen or in bed with her bad back again. She used to work in the Ministry of Industry and Foreign Trade, but that was ten years ago; she had been on full-pay sick leave ever since. There was a girl he liked, but her stepfather was rich and her mother was always taking her away to Paris or Beirut for holidays. Hassan shrugged in the retelling. Meh. I came to know this signature shrug well. It was a give-up shrug, meh, can't do anything about it, better not to think about it. Hassan was a naturally happy, easygoing person and I guessed that his mind shied away from disappointment to protect him. In the same way, when I first met him, he shied at high fences of political concept. Too complicated. When I talked about democracy or political systems or I tried to explain what a monopoly was in the middle of an interview with a trade union activist, he put on a comical hangdog confused expression, knotting his eyebrows, and then immediately let go of his consternation with an easy shrug, *meh*, as if to say, *Well, it doesn't matter anyway.*

Hassan had a quick smart brain and a sweet empathy. Soon he was given the job of defusing "escalation calls." He became the go-to troubleshooter for the floor, what they called a phone flyer. He figured out a way for phone users to transfer the data from their old Samsung phones onto new Samsung handsets with new software. He wrote a users' manual and made a PowerPoint presentation to his quality control manager. She sent it to Korea for approval and he was awarded a certificate: *Teleperformance awards Hassan five out of five for innovation.* The English supervisor promoted him to the human resource department. Hassan was pleased with this progress; he worked in an office, not a cubicle; he had another fifty dollars a month; and he recruited plenty of his friends and filled up his quota. Then the English supervisor left and was replaced by an Egyptian who told Hassan that the rules required a university diploma to work in human resources and sent him back to the headset. The grit of the long commute and the injustice settled in the cavities of his teeth. He had a friend who taught scuba diving in Sharm el-Sheikh who said he might be able to get him a job there. He knew someone who was in the merchant navy who said he could become a sailor and see the world that way. He had an uncle who lived in Milan who said he could always sleep on his floor if he got to Italy. Italy! He had friends who had gone to London and Amsterdam to study, but you needed an Egyptian degree to apply to a foreign university. He had friends with German or Spanish visas or passports, but you needed a certain amount deposited in a bank account for a Schengen visa. Someone told him about an agency that sent Egyptians to work in America on six-month "internship visas," but they couldn't guarantee a salary and there wasn't any housing provided. More than anything Hassan wanted to leave Egypt. "Graduate graduate graduate," said his father. "If you want to leave this country you have to graduate first." Hassan shrugged.

Through the first days of the revolution Hassan went to work as usual. The government had blocked all the country's mo-

bile phone frequencies and shut down the national Internet servers, but the international call centers maintained VPN connections. On the twenty-ninth it took him four hours to get home because the whole of the city was clotted with popular committees setting up homemade checkpoints. He desperately needed to pee. He sat in the front seat of the bus with his legs bent up, pressed against his bladder. Every time the bus stopped his bladder stabbed him with a renewed urgency. After that he decided to give up going to work. His father continued to commute to the state broadcasting building, a giant circular sixties monolith, known by the name of its Italian architect, Maspero. The building was just along the Corniche from Tahrir Square, but it was more than a week before the state TV news cameras began to report on the protests. For Hassan's father, life went on more or less the same with some added inconveniences. "What do these stupid kids think they're doing jamming up the whole city and no one can get to work?" And the apartment was crowded because Amir, Hassan's elder brother, came to stay with his wife. Amir and his wife took Hassan's room and Hassan slept on the sofa. The apartment only had one bathroom and it happened more than one morning that Hassan would stumble in to brush his teeth and encounter his sister-in-law in her long sleeping gown with only a cotton head scarf tied around her head, and wake up to her outraged screaming.

Amir was Hassan's half brother. His mother's first husband was a corporal in the presidential palace; his mother didn't really talk about him. He had an older sister too but she had broken with her mother and married and they never saw her. "It's a fucked-up family, like most of them," Hassan said. "It's all my mother's fault we can't talk to my sister. She didn't like her husband. It's Egyptian nonsense. My mother is tough; she's yelly. When I was a kid she stuffed food down my throat, tyrannical, '*Eaaaat!*' She could kill me with a look, just a look, she didn't even have to raise her eyebrows. And I would wish I wasn't born."

Before he worked at the call center Hassan had done telemarketing for an online directory. His mother was suspicious. "This is a spy company! What are you doing there? I'm going to report you!" (When he worked for me, his mother remained convinced that I was, like most foreigners, a spy. "What do they want from Egypt? Why is she here taking this information?") For the duration of the revolution Hassan's mother was a shrill warning, waving her finger, admonishing those who would destroy the peace and calm and order. She cried when Mubarak spoke to the country and called Egyptians his sons and he their father. Amir was against the protesters from the very beginning. "They are just destroying everything! They want to ruin the country!" Hassan rolled his eyes. Amir was always whining. Hassan thought it was a bit pathetic that he and his wife ran home to Mummy all the time. He was a chef but he left his job at a hotel because they served alcohol there. "I don't know why—he's not even that religious," Hassan said.

In the evenings his father sat with Hassan on the sofa watching the revolution on Al Jazeera English and BBC World and smoked a shisha. Hassan thought what he had thought since the beginning when he saw the invitations on Facebook to come down to the street on the twenty-fifth: "Oh, fuck this, it's just another protest and nothing will happen." When the Internet was restored he went online to the website of every western embassy in Cairo and applied for asylum. (No one replied.) He picked at his guitar but nothing made his mother crankier than idly strummed chords. His father seemed to follow the revolution along with the shifting tack of the state TV pronouncements. From irritation and outrage, grumbling darkly about foreign forces and agendas, to a certain grudging . . . respect? His father had come from a village, graduated from Cairo University, bought a motorcycle, traveled to France, worn his hair long in the seventies with a droopy mustache, done well, gotten a good and respectable government job.

"Those kids are doing what we never could do," he said after the Battle of the Camels. Perhaps it was meant as a barb for Hassan, who shrugged back at him and said, "Nothing will change."

It was the same as it had been for the twenty years he had known it and despised it. The problem with Egypt was Egyptians. Scrape and scheme and scratch your neighbor's living from his plate. Block you, stop you, keep you down in some dead-end cubicle.

For several nights his father went down to the street armed with a metal curtain rod and protected the building with a group of neighbors. Sometimes they heard a gunshot and the whole family would go out onto the balcony. There were rumors of thieves caught and robberies, but they never saw anything disrupt the street below, impassive almost, ficus tree on the corner, cars parked along the curb, and the parallel tracks of the Heliopolis light railway shining like fluorescent tubes. At night Hassan slept on the hard sofa with the slat that dug into his back and was woken up at five A.M. when Amir would shuffle into the kitchen at that godly hour to make tea. The ATMs were all empty and so were Hassan's pockets. In the later days his mother relented in her cry of alarm—"I forbid any of you to go to Tahrir, I say no no no, with all the thugs on that square, and if the thugs don't beat you, you'll get arrested by the army, which you should if you're out at a time like this"—and let him go out, and he walked to a friend's house with his guitar and sat up late playing chords and singing old Guns N' Roses songs.

The management at the call center desperately tried to get everyone to come in to work, offering bonuses for those who would risk the trip. Hassan said he had had enough of them, no way he was going back there. Ever again. Flog yourself across a city full of tanks and armed civilian-police-military checkpoints to answer calls for an extra fifty bucks and then be told you weren't good enough because you didn't have a university degree even though you were doing that job and doing it well for a whole six months? Hassan stayed on his sofa and slept through the revolution.

WELTER

HAD MET DR. HUSSEIN THE VERY FIRST TIME I WENT TO CAIRO, IN another age, in the winter of 2000. I was escaping from a broken heart in Tbilisi; he was just divorced. Dr. Hussein was a prominent gynecologist like his father and grandfather before him and lived in an apartment above the family hospital on the island of Roda. On a clear day, if the smog was not too bad, you could see six pyramids from his balcony, three beyond the gray blocks of the city at Giza, three further outlines south at Sakkara. Dr. Hussein, eyes like gravy, *sympa*, a gentleness that came from dealing with women in distress and in tears, was a balm to my wounded state. He took me to the seaside at Alexandria, to parties, to afternoons in the winter sunshine on the terrace of the Gezira Sporting Club.

In 2011, Dr. Hussein still lived in the penthouse above his grandfather's maternity hospital with the view of the pyramids. In the intervening decade he had arranged his life very comfortably. Most Friday lunchtimes found him at Café Riche, where there was an informal gathering of intellectuals. Weekends were spent by the pool at the Gezira Sporting Club or diving in the Red Sea. He had plenty of girlfriends, whom he treated generously and who came and went without too much drama. He'd taken up photography and would travel once a year to an exotic locale, Cambodia, Vietnam, Uzbekistan. His pictures were colorful and clear—limpid tropical light, emerald-green rice fields—and he made prints and put them up in the hospital corridors. The patients all said they cheered up the place.

Dr. Hussein had interned in Cairo's public hospitals; he knew very well the ugliness of neglect and vested interest and grime. Sometimes we would talk about the system and how it had gotten that way and what could be done about it. In particular the statistics for stunted malnourished children made me shudder. But the system was too large and complicated for us to really comprehend, or to understand how to fix. Our discussions always foundered.

"It's the mentality," Dr. Hussein would say, unwittingly echoing Hassan. I would nod and suggest, "Maybe you should think about doing something grassroots. Like volunteering or a mobile clinic in a slum." And Dr. Hussein would nod and say, "Yes, it is a good idea." But good ideas are easy enough to come up with, especially by Westerners for whom a functioning state system is an assumed birthright. The actual doing of good is much harder to organize. Dr. Hussein delivered all the society babies, but I know he also treated poor women for free. He was kind, he was well-read and well-informed. He was my best friend in Cairo and helped me in a thousand ways, without hesitation, whenever I asked, which was often. He never did start a mobile clinic, but in a funny way, looking back, out of all my Cairo friends—even the dedicated activists—Dr. Hussein's commitment to Egypt's emerging politics would be the most consistent and longest lasting.

One night—many nights—we sat on Dr. Hussein's balcony, a wide view above the fray. Below us, the black Nile flowed spotted with party boats lit up with pink and blue neon like iridescent water bugs. The clanging thump of the Araby disco reached us intermittently on breezes. We were an assorted assembly of friends and acquaintances, bloggers, activists, politicians, feminists—the English-speaking liberal elite who had gone to the American University in Cairo or studied in the U.S., who had second passports and parents with bank accounts in other countries. We were, we knew, a self-selected unrepresentative group. We gathered on Dr. Hussein's balcony and drank whiskey or gin-tonic or Campari-soda and we talked back and forth. For three years there was only one subject, the revolution.

The army and the square, the army and the Brotherhood, the army and this new word: SCAF, which stood for the Supreme Council of the Armed Forces, which no one had ever heard of before and was now ruling the country. And who/what was Field Marshal Tantawi? President? Transitional caretaker? Just another general-ruler like Mubarak and Sadat and Nasser before him? And what about his "road map" for the country and the referendum for the constitutional amendments? Should we vote yes or no? Was it too soon for elections? And did you see Alaa Al Aswany's fight on TV with Mubarak's last-ditch prime minister—that smoothy Shafik? Novelist versus premier! An ordinary citizen questioning the leader! Ah, but Al Aswany was really too rude! No! He was great, he didn't let Shafik glide off with his suave bullshit and his V-neck sweaters. And Shafik, did you see what he did? Wagging his finger, thumping his chest and declaring himself more patriotic! And then Shafik resigned the next day!

A month or so after Mubarak's fall, I met Aly, Dr. Hussein's second cousin, one evening on the balcony. He was tall and had curly hair and one of those eternally beautiful Egyptian faces, cast several millennia ago from reddish Nile mud. Aly was half a generation younger than Dr. Hussein, but they were great friends. Both bachelors about town, both engaged by the revolution with a hope that they, as members of the educated engaged elite, could perhaps offer more than noblesse oblige.

Aly had gone out onto the street on the twenty-fifth. Of course, after the revolution everyone you ever met declared they had been on Tahrir from the very beginning, but Aly was not puffing and I was curious about the very first moments.

"Why did you decide to go?" I asked him.

He thought for a moment, squinting diagonally at the sodium-orange obscurity of the Cairo dusk.

Aly told me he had met up with friends on the evening of January 24. There was a big group of them, a dozen or more, all young professionals, gathered debating, at the Jazz Club. Three bottles of whiskey were on the table, two of them empty. After all, the next day was a holiday.

"I think we should go," Aly had said, definite, palm on the table. Until the day before he had been hovering fifty-fifty. There would be a heavy police presence. (The holiday was Police Day.) There would be violence and arrests. And the likelihood was that it would be just another pointless demonstration, a few hundred people surrounded by an even greater number of State Security.

The friends talked openly with each other, though they didn't usually discuss politics. Not so much out of fear, Aly thought, but simply because they were resigned to stasis. For a couple of weeks now Tunisia had buzzed softly through Cairo conversations. Aly had logged in to the "We Are All Khalid Said" Facebook page and seen all the messages of solidarity and exhortation. The cymbals clashed, high-hat swish, a certain discordance between the jazz and the cocktail-party hum of the bar. It seemed odd to Aly that even a week ago the idea of protest had been something abstract, even unthought of, and if thought about at all, easily dismissed with cynicism.

"It won't make any difference," one of their number, a banker, said. "It's just a risk for no purpose."

"Those of you who have lived outside of Egypt think differently, you think things are possible, but this is just not reality," said another. Aly made a wry face at this, but perhaps they were right: he had a Canadian passport and a degree from McGill, and had worked in London; he had only returned to Cairo a couple of years before to become a partner in his family's law firm.

Aly tried to convince the rest of his group. He was a lawyer; he made his case:

"Look, we all come from a privileged background, right? So taking this into account, what is our risk analysis? I would say the probability of us getting killed is low. We also know that because we come from connected families, if we are arrested, we would get special treatment, get detained for a short time and then released. So I am looking at the optimistic side of the risk spectrum and saying, look: it's not that likely that something really terrible is going to happen to us. And even if the demonstrations don't succeed"—Aly spread his hands wide, to concede this was the most likely probability of all—"we won't have to regret not doing anything and we can say, *At least we tried*. Not like our parents, who have done nothing for thirty years and watched Egypt stagnate into this mess."

At the end of the evening eight of Aly's friends had agreed to join the protest. Three said maybe. The rest demurred. The nays did not make excuses, they just didn't think it would amount to anything.

The next day Aly went out onto the street with a hangover. Five of his friends showed up all; four yeses had dropped out overnight and one maybe had decided yes after all. They marched with several hundred others, chanting, navigating the police lines, blocking intersections. They managed to get onto Tahrir in the midafternoon and arrived amazed to find themselves cheered by the few thousand already gathered there. Aly was standing very close to the police line when the first rocks went over. He described things carefully, weighing remembered moments for accuracy. What had he really seen? Once or twice I interrupted, "Sorry, did you say *see* or *seem?*"

The rocks went over in a barrage and the police picked them up and threw them back. There were also gun cracks. Aly began to run back from the front line, thinking that it was stupid to throw rocks at the police because it only provoked them, but he stumbled and looked down and saw his friend Seif collapsed on the ground. Seif was curled up with his arms around his head, rocking himself, covered in blood. Another friend crouched down too. They couldn't tell what was bleeding—Seif was the doctor among them—everything was very chaotic, some of the kids were running after police vans careening through the crowd. So much blood! They pulled off Seif's T-shirt and saw dozens of red-ringed black pellet dots on one side of his torso and continuing along the underside of his arm. Bird shot. They wiped away the blood with his T-shirt and could see that the wounds were not deep. After a few moments, Seif sat up. He was all right. People around them said, don't worry, he's not critical, it's better to let him rest a bit, not drag him around trying to find an exit and make him bleed more.

After a while, despite the to-and-fro battle at several entrances to Tahrir, they managed to get Seif to hospital. All the time more people kept arriving on the square. It became clear the police were outnumbered and they stopped trying to attack the crowd. The night before, Aly and his friends had debated what would constitute a success. Five thousand? Five thousand people would be something! Now Aly looked around and saw he was part of crowd numbering thirty thousand or fifty thousand or more. Everyone was calling and texting excitedly to tell their friends, *Come! Come! Something is happening here!* At dusk the authorities jammed the mobile signal in the vicinity, but by that time it was too late. By nightfall Aly was grinning because all of his friends who had been at the Jazz Club the night before had come to Tahrir, all the no-shows and maybes and naysayers as well as all their girlfriends and wives and a further, outer circle of friends.

Aly broke off the telling for a moment and leaned over the balcony railing watching a wedding dancer hip-swaying on the deck of the party boat passing below us. I asked him again why he had decided to go, because he had told me a story in lieu of answering.

"You know," he replied, "I can't really remember exactly why." I watched him trying hard to think back to the time *before*, when even the possibility of all that had happened seemed impossible to imagine. He marveled, blinking, a little uncomprehending, that this coin-toss moment had come up heads.

Another drink?" Dr. Hussein came over to rescue us from white space and dangling participles. "So, cousin, what are you going to call your group?"

Aly laughed. He and his Tahrir friends were thinking about the next step.

"It doesn't have a name yet. It's a Facebook thing. It's just about fifty or sixty of us who were on the

square together. We were considering forming a center-left party but now we are thinking we should look around at one of the parties establishing themselves and join them as a bloc."

Now everyone on Dr. Hussein's balcony began to talk at once.

"But there are so many—"

"Anyway Hamzawy—yes, the one with the seventies fro; what is up with that safari jacket?—and Shobaky are talking about a liberal party. On the left there's a new socialist reform movement, that's a group within the wider party."

"What party?"

"I think they are going to call it the People's Coalition Party."

"Hahaha! The PCP!"

"I'm definitely voting for that!"

Dr. Hussein interrupted.

"There's Abu Ghar, who's a gynecologist, who's forming a party. Amr Hamzawy has split off from that group. I asked my dad to call Abu Ghar and he's going to send a representative to talk to our group on Saturday."

"So you will be the gynecologists' party?"

"Yes, the gynecologists' party . . ." Dr. Hussein was laughing too. "Basically our group, which doesn't have a name, is going to form a coalition with that other group that doesn't have a name so that we can join a party that still doesn't have a name."

REDS

I watched Warren Beatty and Diane Keaton in *Reds* again. *Ten Days That Shook the World:* all the sweep and drama of the Russian Revolution observed by John Reed, agitprop reporter, with Beatty's twinkling blue eyes and chiseled cheekbones. But watching this time, what I noticed more than epic and heartthrob was the talkiness. Almost all the scenes were debate. The first half of the movie is set among American socialists-syndicalists-communists trying to organize an American left in a New England cottage, earnest ideologues up against an ornery union and a solid status quo. Their

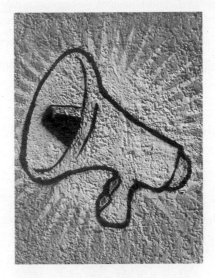

grandstanding arguments fill the air with smoke, cigarette and metaphorical. Jack Nicholson lurks in the corner, playing Eugene O'Neill with a quiet seducer's leer. The second act is Petrograd in the maelstrom of the Bolshevik October takeover. John Reed, Comintern delegate, rallies and rails among a babel of Italian, French, German, English and Tatar on the floor of the International Soviet; committees, meetings, the constituent assembly, the third Congress of Soviets. It is a movie of argument, fists on the table, shouting, storming out, shaking heads with warning, wrong roads, necessary roads, faction, action, reaction.

Cairo February, March, April, after the eighteen days, was like this too. In corner and café and hotel lobby, between *bawwab* and banker, across the *koshari* counter, radio call-in show commented on by the grumpy taxi driver. Every Friday the square filled up again with men holding forth in a circle, cross-purposed, finger-pointing. Someone up on the stage shouting into a microphone. At the end of *Reds* John Reed dies of typhus in a Moscow hospital as the Bolsheviks fight a civil war to consolidate the revolution. His efforts and dreams are unreconciled, and the screen devolves to a black backdrop. Fifty years have passed, and the film concludes in documentary and retrospect. John Reed's friends and comrades, real people, not actors, tell their recollections in interviews, old now, wise and defeated.

The protesters from the square now sat in cafés and talked about forming groups, committees, blocs, NGOs, parties, Facebook groups, YouTube channels, pressure groups, think tanks, unions. Suddenly everyone was making a documentary; new newspapers started up with names like *Tahrir* and *The 25th;* there were photo exhibitions of the revolution set up in the foyer of the opera; graphic designers painted graffiti portraits of the martyrs on city walls around Tahrir. Vendors set up stalls selling revolution T-shirts. Shop windows were full of Egyptian flags stitched and sequined onto evening bags, sparkly earrings, watch straps. Egyptian-flag stripes were painted across walls and gates and around tree trunks. The Mubarak metro station was scratched off the map and in the Tahrir station hall there was a gallery of revolutionary art. Billboards lining the highway for soda and pizza and mobile phones all touted the new Egyptian pride as advertising. In the evenings there were memorial concerts and charity fund-raisers for the families of martyrs. Debates were held in hotel ballrooms and the auditoria of universities; politicians, former judges and generals went on talk shows and kicked off presidential campaigns: How can a civil state include Islamists? What about the Turkish model? . . . Should the senate be appointed or elected? . . . A presidential term should be limited to five years! . . . Do we want a

president or a prime minister? . . . Right now we need to establish
a presidential council committee, because the army is controlling
everything . . . The core of any democratic system is account-
ability. . . . And what about Mexico, which is a democracy but
they had to fire all the police because they were in bed with the
Mafia . . . And Pakistan? Let's not forget the experience of Iraq!

O ne evening I sat in the lobby of
the Four Seasons Hotel with a
couple of journalists and four activists from the Coalition of the
Youth; two of them were liberals,
one a Marxist, and the fourth was
a member of the Muslim Brotherhood. At the adjacent table sat a
party of senior police commanders
in black uniforms with brass stars
and laurels on their shoulders. A
pianist warbled Cole Porter melo-

dies and my porcelain teacup tinkled in the saucer when I put
it down to take a bite of almond tuile. The activists explained
their position, four sides of a revolutionary square. The journalists
leaned forward to catch each sentence. Yes, the army was trying to
talk to all sides, no, the army had its own agenda; yes, there would
be elections, but not yet, but in the meantime the referendum on
constitutional amendments?

"Will you be voting yes or no?"

"No."

"Yes."

"Yes."

"No."

Out of the blue-black street Hillary Clinton swept through the

revolving doors and crossed the foyer at a brisk clip, surrounded
by a small knot of entourage and two agents in dark suits with
earpieces. The four activists made rueful grimaces; they had all
refused to attend the meeting with the American secretary of state
in protest against her close ties to Mubarak.

The question on the table was a grand one. Would this be
democracy as the Americans understood it, one man (or woman),
one vote, and liberty for all, or was this going to be some hybrid
balanced on the twin pillars of Arab political default: strongman
and Koran? This big question was spliced into the concerns of
the immediate, medium and long-term: Hillary's visit, the role
of the Supreme Council of the Armed Forces (SCAF), military
detentions, the constitutional referendum next week: what did
it mean for a transitional road map? Falling currency reserves,
a mooted IMF debt package. The journalists turned, inevitably,
to the question of Israel. What policy would a new Egypt pur-
sue against its neighbor? Would the Islamists uphold the Camp
David Accords? It was here the four activists joined hands for a
moment (metaphorically).

"Well, Israel is an enemy for all of us . . ."

Hillary stepped into the lift, which carried her up and away.

"And what about civil liberties, what about homosexuality?"
asked the other journalist, scratching his temple.

The Muslim Brotherhood activist frowned and leaned back in
the soft gray chenille sofa opening his palms, passing the question
to the liberal with a shaggy Egyptian fro.

"This is your department," he said, discomforted, but amused
too at the shared discomfort.

The liberal demurred. "That's way ahead of where we are now."

The reporters made shorthand loops in spiral notebooks. I ate
all the almond tuiles. Eighty million people were embarking on
an uncharted experiment into Arabic democracy, a great ball of

popular hydrogen pumped to burst and rolling off a cliff—but at least pretty much all Egyptians could agree that they didn't like gays and they didn't like Israelis.

Walking out across the lobby I bumped into Naguib, the spokesman of the revolution.

"Heya!"

I hadn't seen him since Tahrir Square on the morning before Mubarak fell. We gave each other a big delighted hug. He was coming out of the roundtable with Hillary Clinton, grinning and tired and energetic all at the same time. I explained I had been sitting with a group of refuseniks.

"Well you might as well go and listen to what she has to say," he said.

"So now that everyone has a group," I said, "what's the name of your group?"

"My coalition is one of the six founding coalitions of the co-ordinating committee of the masses," Naguib replied without batting an eyelid.

"What's the politics? What's the leaning?"

"I am as liberal as a conservative could be and as conservative as a liberal could be."

"Are you going to run for parliament?" I asked him. Naguib smiled.

"I don't think so." Naguib spoke slowly, running his hands through his brilliantine curls, still thinking about it. "I had the experience of responsibility on Tahrir. I was organizing medicine, food, tents—everything. And if I was elected from my part of the city, where there is a big section of slum, it means a high proportion of the people I would be responsible for would be living below the poverty line. How could I sleep at night? That's

way too much responsibility. Whoa." He put out his hands to
rein in an imaginary horse.

There had been no leaders on
Tahrir. Wael Ghonim spent
much of his ten days in prison con-
vincing his interrogators that he
was not the mastermind head of
this mythical overnight media sen-
sation, "the Revolutionary Youth."
The generals spent a lot of time negotiating with the Muslim Brotherhood to tamp down the protests,
not quite realizing that the Muslim
Brotherhood were not in control of
the crowds. The beguiling beauty of Tahrir had been its collective
nature; no organization save word of mouth. During the eighteen
days, everyone was committed to the same cause: "*Leave!*" Initially
the lack of leadership was the revolution's strength—no figurehead
to arrest, co-opt or defame, according to the usual best practices.
But after Mubarak fell it quickly became its weakness.

The revolution had no leader. The revolution had espoused no
ideology. *Freedom! Bread! Social justice!* Egypt had no political parties except for the Muslim Brotherhood and some discredited old
leftists and Nasserists. None of them had any idea of what to do
next and had been so long in sleepy opposition that political re-
flexes had long atrophied. No one had any template or plan and
in all the crazy months to follow no one ever really came up with
one. There was a new word called *transition*. At first this was vague
and promising.

In the early months, there was a whirl of activity. But now

I look back and it seems we were all just rushing around a hole. For example, there was so much calling up and meeting and talking that Egyptians, overwhelmed by the constant ringing, stopped answering their mobile phones. At first people just ignored the calls from numbers they did not recognize; brrring, click to silent, continue conversation. Later it was impossible to get even close friends to pick up for weeks at a time. Phones vibrated on tables like buzzing flies. Texts tinkled and piled up like tin cans on a string. Facebook instant messages sometimes worked if you could catch someone online. DM via Twitter produced an instant response, but only from activists under the age of thirty.

Sketches, finger drawings in the air, scribblings on restaurant napkins. For the moment it didn't matter that there was no plan because everything was possible and everyone was so pleased and happy to congratulate each other on this lovely extraordinary revolution that had made everything possible—*Look! we are voting next week! Constitutional referendum! Everyone will have a purple finger and we will say yes or no! Then everyone will get a pay raise because the thieves won't steal all the money, and my bumpkin neighbor with the son-in-law in the police who likes to dump his trash right outside my door will be taken down a peg or two and learn to be respectful like a neighbor might be in, say, well, Sweden, where everything is fair and even the street kids have shoes and also gloves!*

Never mind that most people (the majority) had spent the eighteen days watching TV on the couch—they became known as the Couch Party—muttering, "I don't know what these kids are doing." Grumpf. "They'll burn the whole country down just because they want to have a bonfire party!" Mubarak was gone. Now there was this big new shiny word that was called *democracy*—a word that we all reminded ourselves came from the Greek, *demos*, "people," merged with *kratia*, "rule." Fridays on the Tahrir continued protests and intermittent violence. I re-called studying *Coriolanus* at school, Shakespeare, lamenting the fickleness of crowds. I mentally amended the etymology to "rule of the demo-nstration."

I remember going to a debate televised by the BBC at the American University of Cairo. *"This house believes that for the sake of Egyptian democracy elections should be postponed."* No one quite understood the motion. Was it to do with the constitutional refer-endum that had been called for in two weeks' time? Or was it about other elections? Parliamentary? Presidential? In any case, for the

sake of argument, the Muslim Brotherhood had decided to vote yes; accordingly the revolutionary youth had aligned themselves to vote no, but no one really understood the conse-quences of either.

I bumped into George Ishak at this debate. George Ishak had been the leader of the Kefaya (Enough) protest movement, founded in 2005. He was grandfatherly and gracious. "Come and sit down, my dear!" He called everyone "my dear." He was a Copt but he played with his prayer beads between his fingers as he described the frustrations of the fractious liberals. Too many personalities. After a pleasant chat he excused himself; he had an appointment with Naguib Sawiris, the richest man in Egypt, who was forming a party that didn't have a name yet. When I asked him what he was going to do, George Ishak demurred—a respected elder statesman with real revolutionary credentials, he was almost too polite to choose a side—saying, "I don't think I am going to join any party myself."

I went to listen to a question-and-answer session with the political science professor Amr Hamzawy—the housewives' favorite because he had big fuzzy Leo Sayer hair and was smoothly handsome and was always on TV—and the leader of the Wasat Party, a moderate Islamic faction that had split off from the Brotherhood. The audience was made up of professional urban middle-class conservatives. The men sat on one side of the audience, almost all of them bearded and absorbed in their mobile phones; the women, wearing *hijabs* and long buttoned manteaux, sat on the other. Amr Hamzawy, wearing his customary safari jacket, delivered a lecture on liberal democracy. The leader of the Wasat Party then spoke about his project for Islamic civilization. The audience had many questions: Where was the balance of power between mosque and state? Would a liberal secular state outlaw *hijab*? Would a liberal secular state prevent a man from marrying more than one woman? Would a liberal secular state give homosexuals sexual freedom? There was a lot of concern about this foreign *liberal secular state* thing. What about the prostitutes who stood openly in shop windows in Amsterdam?

"Is this the direction of freedom or the collapse of freedom?"

Hisham Kassem, the commentator, watching CNN as usual, remained unconvinced by the sudden enthusiasm for politics. "Democracy is a grind, nine to five. People don't realize this. You don't wake up in the morning and everything is nicely arranged in stable independent institutions. It's hard work over a long, long time." Hisham was going to start his own newspaper, a long-held dream of his. He would have investors, not a proprietor, and he would be the editor in chief.

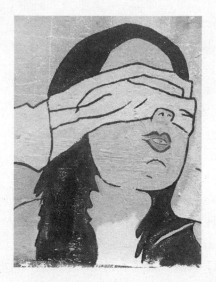

So many things were happening simultaneously that it was impossible to know where to look. The black-clad State Security force was announced disbanded. Six floors of the Interior Ministry were gutted by fire caused by an electrical short while there was, coincidentally, a demonstration going on outside. Alaa Al Aswany's secretary called to tell me he couldn't meet me that week because there had been a plot revealed by a State Security officer (this force apparently not disbanded after all) to assassinate him and several other notable revolutionary figures. There were fights between Salafis and liberals in Alexandria. University students protested against appointed rectors, journalists protested against appointed editors, lawyers went on strike to protest a new privilege awarded to judges, the judges went on strike too. Then the government announced a law banning protests and strikes. Protests and strikes continued. Walk across Tahrir, past the empty parliament building, toward the Ministry of Social Justice, and there were dozens of groups demanding redress and rights. Combine harvester drivers, disabled in wheelchairs, graduates from the postal faculty who could not get jobs in the post office because positions were all tied up with nepotism, called "*wasta.*" Even the State Security force (now renamed "Homeland Security") protested, because it turned out that most of the rank and file were military service conscripts pressed into service against their will and paid a pittance.

BACK TO THE SQUARE

Every Friday through the spring aftermath Hassan and I went back to the square. I was beguiled by Tahrir. It still held for me a utopian promise: *I had seen it.* I had fallen in love, with yelling *no* and the scrappy kids and the *hijabi* mothers and the earnest activists, with all the stories and drama and gossip and news and friends. Tahrir remained a powerful totem, talisman. Every time I walked across it I scuffed my sneakers in the sandy gaps in the sidewalks where the paving stones had been dug up to throw at the police and I was again transported by the dizzy, heady wonder of it. For a while I held a theory that Egyptians were divided into those who had been to Tahrir during the eighteen days and there-fore carried the joy of the possibility they had witnessed there, and the Couch Party, who had stayed at home. Off the square the complaints were grumbled: *Stupid kids that will destroy the country, and who is benefiting I want to know? And how do they have money to go to Tahrir instead of going to work? Who is paying them while the economy is going down down and I haven't had work for three weeks because the foreman won't come to Cairo from Banha with all the bandits on the road and the price of cooking gas is going up and my daughter cannot go to school without wearing her head scarf because some Big Beard will spit at her and Egypt needs a strongman as we all know and anything else is just idiocy and something foreign because IsraelAmerica is behind this to their own ends to make Egypt weak.* I paid them no heed.

Hassan was not convinced either.

"You'll see. It's just stupid Egyptians and they will screw each other and then we will all have to live in a worse mess."

"But something is happening here," I said. "It will get better. This is just the transition."

"Meh. Whatever." Hassan shook his big fluffy fro like a dog

shakes water out of his ruff. "I opened a bank account yesterday. Embassies want proof of deposits to give you a visa. This is my first step to getting out of here."

The Big Pharaoh was a great friend of Hassan's and it was a rare Friday we did not bump into him on Tahrir. Hassan was a skeptic; the Big Pharaoh was a revolution cheerleader. He disproved my theory about people who had and had not been on Tahrir during the eighteen days, because the Big Pharaoh had never gone to the square during the revolution, but afterward, almost as if to compensate for this original sin, he never missed a protest.

Even when the square became muddled with riots and backroom machinations through the summer and into the autumn, the Big Pharaoh was always grinning and excited. He was tall and lanky-gangly and waved his arms when he talked like he was juggling cherries. He had a stutter, but this did not stop him from talking rapidly, intelligently—he was the best analyst I ever found in Egypt—and as quickly as you met him and liked him, which was instantly, you forgot about it altogether. He tended to go to protests alone because he didn't like to be tied down with worrying about other people when the running started. Often we would be talking to him and then there would be a crack and a crowd-scatter and he would bound off, closer into the fray. We would lose him, last seen crouching beside a bollard, head bent to tweet or dodging around a corner while holding up his iPhone to take a picture.

The Big Pharaoh was his Twitter name and he hid it from his family. His family were middle-class and anxious. When the revolution began they didn't want to let him go out onto the streets. They had no love or pity for Mubarak but Mubarak was stability and security. If not Mubarak then what? Chaos? The Muslim Brotherhood? Before the revolution his parents never talked about politics at home. His older brother was an engineer and he was the same. "They are all phobic," the Big Pharaoh told me, "afraid to get into trouble, afraid to be arrested. This is the nature of my parents, to be afraid of confrontation." His father was sympathetic to the protesters, he could see they wanted something better, but who knew what thugs and plainclothes police and Islamist beards were mingled among the crowds. Better to stay out of it. For the entire eighteen days the Big Pharaoh was forced to sit on the sofa and watch until he felt like he was about to explode.

The Big Pharaoh didn't go to Tahrir until it was all over, and then he felt as stupid as a tourist. The first protest he joined was at the State Security archives two weeks after Mubarak fell. The protesters confronted the secret agency of the state, stormed the gates and looted dossiers inside. Apart from the burning of the NDP headquarters on the Day of Rage, this was the only time protesters ever breached a government building. At the time it felt like a wall being pushed over, but when the fires were stamped out it was clear the wall was still standing. The Big Pharaoh went home and found his father holding his head in his hands in front of the television.

"Did you see what they did? They stormed the State Security archives!"

"Really?" the Big Pharaoh replied, mock astonished. "I hadn't heard that."

THE SINGER OF THE REVOLUTION

After the State Security headquarters protest, a small core of revolutionary youth returned to Tahrir. Ramy Essam, handsome singer of the revolution, was among them. The revolution was not finished. The army had taken over. The revolution had not even, they began to realize, begun.

"For two weeks we were all very happy and we weren't scared of anything and we had trust that everything was going to be better. But then we realized we were wrong to leave the square because the revolution didn't finish with Mubarak leaving. Mubarak was just the symbol. So we decided to go back to the square on the twenty-fifth February and this is the first time the army beat us up. We went back on the ninth March and they beat us again."

As he spoke Ramy Essam touched his guitar, scratched and bandaged with tape, hanging from his neck, his left hand on the fret, right hand tapping the soundboard like a drum. He was resting between outdoor sets one Tahrir Friday, still a dreamboat, even with his new short hair. He had a new song, riposte to the Couch Party, bitter-funny: *Laugh, you revolution, hahaha, they told you what, we are spies? Laugh, you revolution, hahaha, they told you what? We are ruining the country? Laugh, you revolution, hahaha, they told you what, we eat KFC? Laugh, you revolution, hahaha, they told you what, we took one hundred euros?*

"We were the people who never left Tahrir and faced death more than once. We are the real revolutionaries." Ramy Essam

and his friends had been on Tahrir on the night of the ninth of March when thugs and plainclothes State Security came through breaking down the tents and beating and taking people. Ramy ran with other protesters toward the army near the Egyptian Museum for protection. But the opposite happened. The soldiers began to beat them even more brutally.

One of them grabbed Ramy and pushed his head down so that his face was in the dust and crunched his boot against his neck to hold him there. *"We will show you who the Egyptian military is!"*

They drag-hauled him along the ground, roughly grabbed at his clothes and pulled off his shoes and his trousers so that he was cowering in his underwear. The soldiers herded others too, pummeling them into the courtyard behind the gates of the museum's entrance. Beaten down, bleeding knees. He heard barking.

"Ramy the singer, get Ramy!" He felt them scraping his scalp, sharp, nicking cuts, shearing his long hair with razors and broken glass. They kicked him in the ribs to make him quiet. He lay on his stomach on the ground and then they beat his back.

"What with?" I asked.

"I didn't see it," said Ramy, "my face was in the dirt."

"I didn't see it either," said his friend Yaris, who had been beaten in the museum courtyard that night too.

"But it felt like a big electric stick."

"Yes," said Yaris, "like a cattle prod. And they were shouting: *'So that you stop speaking against your masters!'*"

"They really said that?" Ramy asked, surprised. "I didn't hear that."

"Yes! And then I asked them: what do you want me to do? And they answered, *'Just shut up.'*"

The soldiers kept them for several hours, kicking and shoving the bloodied bleating group, maybe a hundred of them or more. Some protesters were taken away in police vans. Yaris said he had seen a figure in the dark next to him with blood covering his face and had asked this man his name. His friend had replied, "I am Ramy Essam. Don't you recognize me?"

No one wanted to believe the army had done these things. That night female protesters had been taken off the square, put in a military prison and subjected to forcible virginity tests. When the women's lawyers and activists began to speak about their treatment, people were slow to believe them. I remember Dr. Hussein saying at dinner when the story first began to circulate, "It doesn't sound right to me." It seemed, at the time, too gruesome, too outlandish, unlikely. The army had done this? The army who were one hand with the people? The army who were the protectors of the revolution?

Huge numbers of people were now detained in military prisons. Ragia Omran, indomitable flame-haired human rights lawyer, was representing some of them. "Thousands," she said under her breath, red frizz bobbing, hurrying between the journalists' syndicate, press conferences and the military prison. "No one knows how many, they won't release any lists."

Fridays on the square: yelling and chanting. Tea sellers and face painters and other opportunists. Hassan and I would wander and listen for a bit and then we would repair to Café Riche and meet Dr. Hussein for lunch. He would be sitting at a table with friends and café acquaintances: doctors, lawyers, an Al Jazeera correspondent or two, old poets and retired ministry officials who liked

to vent their cynicism. Mobile phones on the table buzzing intermittently, cigarette smoke curling through the conversation. The TV was tuned to the protests but we had stopped watching them. Magdi, the owner, sat behind the desk by the door in a niche he had burrowed into over the years. On his desk, books and papers and folders were piled up and crowned with an ashtray. He kept one eye, an eye that seemed to swivel independently of the rest of his expression, on the door. Incomers were nodded at or rejected. He didn't like those people who pushed themselves into the middle of a discussion and kept repeating their opinions. Dr. Hussein ate the schnitzel; I always ordered chicken livers in gravy with potato chips and garlic cream salad. I would make little crunchy sandwiches out of the chips and the liver and drag them through the garlic. Filfil would bring a Stella beer for Hassan. Filfil had been a waiter at Café Riche since he was thirteen years old. He was now ninety, a wizened stick set with two gleaming currant eyes. I always greeted him by name but he never acknowledged me and I never saw him smile at anyone. Filfil, always at hand, standing as straight as a soldier, had known the café when Naguib Mahfouz held his weekly salon there and even before that, when the communists

would be let out of prison by the British and would come to bor-
row money from their friends. In those days when there was a
police raid, they used to escape through a secret door in the basement that let out into a side alley. Filfil had known the old days
of cosmopolitan Cairo when the polyglot denizens, Armenians
and Italians and Greeks and Levantines and Jews, took their
tea at Groppi's in the afternoons and dressed up to go to the
cinema. Filfil's face, unmoving and uncommunicative, had been
engraved with years into a lithograph as statuary as the portraits
of Cairo's illustrious dead intelligentsia of the past that hung on
the walls. He never exchanged pleasantries, he never passed the
time or commented, even when there was tear gas in the street
outside and everyone was crying into their lentil soup.

"That's just Filfil," said Dr. Hussein. "You'll never get a word
out of him. The whole world turns upside down; he probably didn't
have anything to say when Nasser took over either."

Dr. Hussein met with Abu Ghar's group. They were going to
form a political party and call it the Egyptian Social Democratic
Party, and Dr. Hussein and his second cousin Aly were going to
join them.

"When we say *social* we don't mean socialism," Dr. Hussein
joked, "we mean social."

We laughed and then we ordered coffee from the quiet and
inured Filfil, perfectly imperturbable, perfectly eternal Egypt.

TEWFIK HOUSE

I MET DAVID AND NORA ON DR. HUSSEIN'S BALCONY TOO. NORA WAS half Egyptian, half American; David was a hydrologist from Washington State. Old friends of his; Dr. Hussein had once been engaged to Nora's sister, and he had delivered Nora's babies. Nora tucked her long legs under her body, ran her fingers through her blond hair and drank deep from the large gin-tonic. All was woe. They were camping in friends' apartments, refugees, turned out of their home with three children. It was maddening. Everything depended on *inshallah*.

The Gezira Palace on the leafy island of Zamalek in the middle of the Nile was built by the *khedive* Ismail Pasha to receive the European dignitaries on the occasion of the opening of the Suez Canal in 1869. The cost of building the palace and downtown, a whole new district of elegantly swagged French and Italian facades ("My country is no longer part of Africa, we are now in Europe," the spendthrift *khedive* announced), was so great that the exchequer was bankrupted. The French and the British took over the purse strings, and much, including the grand, half-oriental-gilt, half-classically colonnaded Gezira Palace, was sold off. The palace became a hotel and was eventually refurbished as a Marriott. The palace gardens, which occupied an enviable slice of real estate between the Gezira Sporting Club, where the British and the Ottoman elites hobnobbed and played tennis, and the Nile, were sold to developers in the 1930s.

Nora's grandfather bought a plot and decided to spare no expense in building an elegant apartment house on the site.

"In those days most of the architects were Italians," Nora's father, Ghaly, remembered. Ghaly was a grand gentle man, a retired doctor; waves of white hair lapped his mahogany face. "My father's architect was an Italian and my father told him build it, no matter what the cost."

The building rose in a line of similarly well-appointed apartment blocks built along the riverfront at the same time. *Tewfik House* was picked out in art nouveau plaster letters painted brown against cream on the lintel; the foyer was lined in blue-veined marble. The facade had ornamental columns. Above, brick and parapet, eight stories and two penthouses. Wrought-iron balconies jutted out like bay windows, with just enough space for two chairs and a circular café table; gin and tonic at sunset. On the Corniche side the apartments had the all-important Nile view; on the back they looked over the green and pleasant spaces of the Gezira Sporting Club.

During the forties, many of the apartments were occupied by British colonial officers. When the British left, generations of Tewfiks moved in. Nora and David and Anna and Zoo and Alexander lived on the fourth floor. Nora's parents lived on the floor below. Various aunts, Ghaly's several sisters, lived above. Some apartments, those categorized, during the Nasser socialist muddle, as free from rent control, were let out to foreigners for large sums. The row of twenty or so apartment houses built on Ibrahim Pasha's garden had become the grandest address in Cairo. Leafy Zamalek, just across the river from downtown, conveniently close to the Gezira Sporting Club and adjacent to the Marriott with its elegant arbored terrace. Nora's balcony looked over the river where ibis stalked a mass of floating reeds.

The ancient German iron cage elevator clanked reassuringly between floors. Two *bawwabs* sat outside on comfortable warped plastic chairs, nodding to guests, helpfully ferrying packages, loading cars for weekends away. "Mrs. Nora? Oh, she's not home yet, but go straight up, Mr. David is there." And I would walk in from the dusty honking street to the coolness of that timeless marble foyer, catch a little colonial breath and take the wonderful old jickety elevator up.

Nora and David had gone down to Tahrir Square on the first night, the night of the twenty-fifth. They took a bag of oranges and sandwiches for the protesters. Nora told me she remembered the square was very dark because the authorities had turned off the streetlamps; the crowd was young and somehow relaxed but at the same time expectant. People were talking to the line of riot police visors, saying things like, "We are doing this for you," "This is about a better way of life," "We are not your enemy and you are not our enemy." Nora was astounded and amazed, as everyone who was there was, by the atmosphere of fellowship and selflessness and determination. Nora was a Tewfik, part of the elite, had gone to college in the U.S. She was well connected; she had plenty of friends in common with Gamal, for example. But there was never any doubt that she was on the side of the revolution. She and David walked through the crowds, bumping into people they knew, handing out oranges, marveling. They left at about one A.M. and just half an hour later, the police came through with truncheons to expel the numbers that remained and chase the protesters through the adjacent mazelike cut-through lanes of downtown.

The violence with which the protesters on the twenty-fifth were met convinced Nora and many others to go down to the street on the Day of Rage. She packed supplies of vinegar-soaked baby wipes and extra bottles of water and a couple of towels in a backpack. All anyone could talk about was whether they were going to go down tomorrow or not. Everyone was agonizing. "I have kids, is it irresponsible? Will it be safe? It won't be safe, they are shooting at people. If we go we can die." Nora told her friends, "You're right. But I have no doubt that I am going."

Nora was in the crowd that tried to fight its way across the Sixth October Bridge. The same crowd as Hisham Kassem. She saw a young handsome well-to-do boy in a striped sweater fall next to her with a brass cartridge case stuck in his neck, which was pumping blood. For a long time this was the only thing she could remember clearly when she tried to recall the events of that day. At nightfall she went home and watched the NDP headquarters burn from her balcony across the river.

Zoo clambered up, squirming, kicking against her restraining arms, reaching his three-year-old hands through the ten-foot-high railings she had installed (wisely; Zoo was a climber) and asking, "What are the blue flashing lights? Is it the police?"

"Those are the ambulances, my love."

"What for?"

"For the people who are hurt."

"Because the police hurt them?"

"Yes, my love."

"Because the police are the bad guys," Zoo pronounced solemnly. Anna, his elder sister, haloed in her customary quiet, retreated from the window and went to her room to read. Alexander was not quite toddling yet and sat fat on the floor, engrossed with a pile of cookie crumbs. David came in from the kitchen, pouring a glass of wine.

"More again tonight?"

"Yes, Dad, more again," replied his eldest son and replica. The two of them had the same compact wiry body, the same dark hair framing twinkly triangle faces. For a moment they watched the lights and sirens across the river in mirrored concentration. On the opposite bank of the river was the circular hunk of the Maspero building. Orange flames danced in the dark. Something was burning.

"Look, Dad," Zoo said, excited, "a fire engine is on fire!"

David and Nora and the children had American passports. A few days later, finally, after they had waited several days with packed bags on standby for the signal, the embassy called to tell them they were being evacuated. Nora hurried to get everything ready. She thought: *I should stay this is my country I can send the kids out with David and I should stay this is my country but these are my children and I must go with them.*

Anna waited patiently by the door with her own bag, David was checking every drawer for the passports, Alexander was crying for something to eat and Zoo scrambled over the bags, racing down the stairs, banging on everyone's doors to say good-bye. Two aunts from upstairs, Jou-Jou and Tati, came to see them off. They were old twins; one admitted to the age of seventy-one, the other would allow no more than sixty-eight. Jou-Jou had red permed hair that made a frizzy cap; Tati preferred a dyed-blond chignon. They were mirror opposites: Jou-Jou was fat and powder-sugary, dressed in pinks and turquoise, heavy costume jewelry weighing her wrists; Jou-Jou was lean from power-walking around the track at the Gezira Sporting Club every day and preferred a demure palette of neutrals and navy blue. Both had made frequent visits to the plastic surgeon over the last twenty years, and their faces were stretched so wide that their lips appeared as alien features, plumped caterpillars scored in brown liner pencil. They bent down and kissed the children and told them to be good little travelers. Nora wrested her bag from inside the doorway, stumbling into this family knot between her and the elevator. She couldn't quite push through to open the doors and then there was a clank and the wooden box glided upward, called to another floor.

"You are going! And all this rushing!" Jou-Jou reached out and smoothed a lock of Nora's hair.

"You will take care!"

"It will be safer in America. You're so lucky with your passport, Nora."

"Oh, Nora, dear niece, you should give us your key, just in case. We can keep an eye on things for you."

"In case thieves come, or squatters come."

"Because the police have all gone now!"

"The police are the bad guys!" said Zoo.

"Who told you that, little boy?"

Nora said: "Oh, thank you, it's fine really, my father has the key in case there's any problem."

"Oh, but in case he decides to take your mother away."

"In case it becomes too dangerous for *all* Americans—"

"And if there's a problem with the pipes—"

"Because water damage is terrible."

"The whole building could be at risk if we couldn't get into your apartment to fix it."

"That's always when you hear the worst stories about flooding and everything ruined and half the building falling into the street."

Nora reached through the wall of flapping aunts and pushed the button to summon the elevator again. David came out onto the landing with the two large bags and seeing the family good-bye commotion, his wife heaving Alexander onto her hip, he called out to her to lock up behind him, he and Anna would carry the bags down the stairs and see them at the bottom.

"It's extra insurance, dear niece."

"But my father . . . ," said Nora. She looked at her watch, at

Jou-Jou's moon face ringed with beige makeup that made a smooth stripe against the mottled tortoise skin of her neck.

"If anything should happen—"

"Oh, not that anything would happen, but just to be on the safe side . . ."

The elevator reappeared. She took her keys on their Snoopy key ring out of her pocket and locked her door. The keys were in her hand. Jou-Jou held out her palm in the space between Nora and the elevator door.

"It's just better knowing that everything will be safe and sound."

Nora gave her the keys, little brass keys against a soft plump palm, and squashed herself and Alexander and two carry-on cases into the elevator. They had only an hour to get to the airport. Depending on the traffic—which could not be depended on—and the checkpoints . . .

The day Nora and David and the kids were evacuated was the day of the Battle of the Camels. All night I watched the rock hurling to and fro from the balcony. Nora called her father from the airport.

"Can you get my jewelry? I left it in a bag on the dresser. I couldn't decide whether to pack it or not."

Ghaly Tewfik went upstairs to retrieve his daughter's jewelry for safekeeping, but his key didn't work in the lock. Perhaps he had the wrong key—ah well—he'd figure it out in the morning. Later that night he heard something moving in Nora's apartment above him and he went upstairs to investigate. He banged on the door, but only silence came back. Perhaps he had not heard anything after all.

In the morning light of the day, he went upstairs again. His twin sisters, Jou-Jou and Tati, were coming out of the apartment. He was surprised to see them there and then, suddenly realizing, not surprised.

According to the Islamic law of inheritance, a son receives twice a daughter's share. Ghaly had four sisters and two brothers; each had their own several children.

Tewfik House was held in common by all of its heirs, its income apportioned accordingly. For the last few years, however, inevitably, as grandchildren grew up and grew their own families, it became clear there were not enough apartments for them all. According to Islamic law, from the grandchildren's generation, only Nora and her sisters were entitled to one whole apartment in the building. Ghaly had many times suggested that the building be divided up into individual titles among his siblings, apartment by apartment. But his siblings could not agree on the calculations of share and ratio and square meterage that did not exactly add up to whole apartments. What about the apartments that were still rent controlled and produced little income? What about the penthouses, which were larger? What about their daughters and sons and their families? The arguments had gone back and forth for several years, inconclusive.

Tati and Jou-Jou crossed their arms across their bosoms and barred his way.

"Nora gave us the key, you see. She's fled Egypt for good, that's what she told us."

"She's not coming back! She said she never wants to see Egypt again."

"Ran back to America!"

"And we are not to let you or your wife into the apartment under any circumstances."

"That's what your daughter Nora said."

"She was very specific on this point."

"Because it's ours."

Ghaly rang Nora in Washington. Nora called her eldest uncle.

"You will never set foot in this apartment again. The best thing for you is to let us find you another apartment. We will move your things and when you return you will find all your belongings safe and sound." Nora called her other aunt, Fussy.

"You are the daughter of sixty dogs!" Aunt Fussy shouted at her across the Atlantic. Aunt Fussy's husband owned homes in London and Paris and one of the biggest yachts in the Red Sea; high-ranking generals were frequent guests at their beach house.

"You'll never get into your flat and we'll throw your belongings onto the street! My daughter married well, remember, to a man hand-in-hand with Gamal. You're an American! Who knows what agendas you have concocted."

A few days after Mubarak stepped down, when the choppy waters had seemed to return to some semblance of level sea, Nora's father employed a lawyer. Akila Mohammed was a busty square-shaped woman, head scarf, sensible shoes and a lumpy suit jacket over a bulky rectangle of trousers, a no-nonsense, practical woman, the Egyptian middle-class stalwart. She was the type of woman I would often come across in Cairo, indomitable and a little fierce, easy to anger but just as quick to smile and to proffer a cup of coffee and a piece of cake.

After twenty years of handling internecine property disputes, Akila Mohammed had ceased to be shocked by the nefarious. The closest families revealed their basest emotions. Avuncular uncles turned into slum landlords, stepmothers into avaricious ravens; previously kindly brothers never spoke to their sisters again. When I asked why there was so much of this miserable familial strife she would reply, with a fatalistic shrug, "Allah has put down the laws of inheritance and if we followed them properly there would not be any problems. But there are arguments between people and people are full of hatred and envy and greed and poverty."

A few days after Mubarak fell, Akila Mohammed filed a complaint of invasion of private property at the police station in Zamalek. The police station was open as if it was operating normally, but the atmosphere was subdued. Usually she had to armor herself against the nugatory interrogatory: *What do you want? Why have you come back today? Wait here! No, you cannot. He is not here.* Followed by, in slanted underwhine whisper, *Perhaps a little tip for my teatime?* But this day the desk officer would not meet her eye; he looked down at his hands, at his shoes, at the floor, somehow cowed or embarrassed. "Hold your head up like an Egyptian!" she told him, teasing him. The officer did not reply. He took her completed forms in silence.

This initial complaint was sent, according to procedure, to the general prosecutor's office in the building of the Abdeen Court downtown. The prosecutor referred the case for investigation and issued an interim ruling that no one could enter the apartment nor could anything be removed from it until judgment had been determined.

Nora and David and the kids returned to Egypt in early March. They imposed on friends, moving every few days. Barred from their home, a vagabond family, everything in limbo. Afterward Nora shuddered to recall this time. "It was like being in a very primeval state of suspended dislocation." She took up smoking again.

"When are we going back to our brown house?" Zoo would ask plaintively.

"As soon as the floors are fixed from the water pipe that burst," Nora told him.

Zoo did not believe this story.

"I promise I'll be good, I promise I'll never be bad again, only please let me go home." Once when they were driving along the Corniche little Alexander waved to Tewfik House receding through the back window, and Nora's heart broke for him.

There had been a revolution. There must have been. After all a dictator had been toppled and pictures of the delirious crowd had been celebrated on the front pages of every newspaper in the world, headlined in giant bold print. I moved to Cairo and rushed about filling notebooks with politicians parties debates activists referendums.

But stop *talking* for a moment to look around; Cairo was curiously unchanged. People went to work and came home again. The trains ran and stuck in the station as usual, the *foul* sellers set up their rickety chariots every morning for breakfast, the buses ground the streets into dust and mixed it with diesel vapor for a tasty smog. When I came home late, even past midnight, the old man in his little laundry shop would still be ironing. Thump swoosh thump swoosh, rhythm of the always. It was a revolution but nothing had revolved. The head had been cut off but the body, state corpus, remained. Its limbs moved in the same slow way they always had, entangled and blind, like a bandaged mummy or a malfunctioning automaton. I muddled metaphors for this strange being. It was a time that felt like a hammock swaying between what had happened on Tahrir and something that would happen next. No one knew quite where authority lay in the gap between—between one ruler and a rubber stamp that had not yet been die-cast.

Everyone was waiting to see what would happen. But everyone was waiting on the sidewalk, as if it would happen independently from people making it happen. This *transition*—from dictator to the unknown—was called "getting back to normal" by the Supreme Council of the Armed Forces, a committee of nineteen generals that no one had known existed and that had now assumed control of the country.

The investigating prosecutor took witness statements from Nora and her father and interviewed the aunts and uncles named as co-conspirators. Akila Mohammed assembled evidence, bank statements, rental contracts, telephone bills, electricity bills, to document Nora and her family's residence. The contents of the apartment were officially inventoried. The prosecutor took statements from several tenants of Tewfik House who testified that Nora and her family had lived on the third floor without incident or prejudice for six years. Ghaly went to see the prosecutor in person. At first the prosecutor received his petition coldly with all formality, but then the conversation expanded and warmed. They talked about the situation and books and people they knew in common. Ghaly was able to offer some advice for a medical condition that the prosecutor was suffering from.

On March 22, the investigating prosecutor filed his recommendation that the plaintiff's case should be upheld and that Nora should, by court order, be permitted to take repossession of the apartment. On April 1, the general prosecutor endorsed this decision and the file was passed to the office of executive administration for implementation.

One afternoon much later, I sat with Akila Mohammed as she explained the varied layers and stages of Egyptian jurisprudence. Nora brought more tea and more cookies for my aching, grappling brain. The Egyptian justice system was an old machine that had broken down many times and was now patched and jury-rigged with gaffer tape and soldered together with recycled batteries that were wired through competing circuits . . . a temperamental set of levers: the complainant pushed, the prosecutor pulled, the police gear turned with its cog teeth and the mechanism wound, or more often jammed, and the judge coughed and adjourned the case. Akila Mohammed was the diligent engineer who knew the mood of the machine intimately, knew when and where and how much to oil. A prosecutorial judgment in this type of case often took several months, even a year.

"Of course we had to use a lot of *wasta* to speed things up," Akila Mohammed said. Connections, favors, envelopes with cash. "This did not influence the court's decision," she emphasized, "this was just to speed things up." Her mouth made an upside-down smile. It was, she explained, carefully, a little rueful, but not abashed, a matter of $500 to the official at the executive administration, just to move things along.

During the year and a half that I lived in Cairo after the revolution, I went to the courthouse in Abdeen several times. Once I accompanied Nora to a hearing in the case she had filed against her aunts for the theft of items from her apartment. A couple of times I went to the courthouse looking for a lawyer to talk to about a client arrested in a demonstration. It was a grand cavernous building, dusty and bustling inside. Its long corridors were lined with prisoners waiting for their court appearances, sitting cross-legged or slumped on their heels, their hands chained and clasped in their laps. It was difficult to walk past them knowing you were free and they were not. They had sunburned faces and skinny frames; they wore a loose garb of frayed tracksuits, grubby shirts and plastic sandals; and they gazed at the floor of trash mixed with cigarette butts and rags of plastic bags and yellow Cairo dust. Lawyers swept through with black robe wings left behind by the British—although the judicial system owed more to the Napoleonic code; there was no trial by jury. "Funny," Adrien once remarked through his cigar smoke, "the French were here for only a very shortest amount of time, but their influence seems more than the British."

In the courtrooms, three judges sat on a dais, below scales of justice held in balance by a sword. Plaintiffs, witnesses, defendants all sat in rows of wooden pews, some fiddling with their phones, others tracing suras in the Koran. When a new case number was called, a bundle of people approached the bench and the lawyers argued in turn. Sometimes the defending lawyer would shout passionately: "This is a case brought by nefarious means, the tale of an unhappy family according to the rancor of such disputes long harbored and which should not prejudice Your Honor." Sometimes the defendant would say something in a small voice to show humility before the court. Then the judges would announce an adjournment until the afternoon, or next month or after the Eid holiday or some distant time to be announced in accordance with the schedule not yet set for the month of October. Then the next group of supplicants would press forward, only to be dismissed on a piece of procedure, and the court registrar would call out, "Case number four thirty-five!" and a new group would shuffle forward and the people waiting for case number 436 would begin to agitate in anticipation of their turn. Then for some unexpected reason there would be an interruption and one of the court police would whisper a word or two and the three judges would remove themselves back into their chambers.

In the halls and corridors, case numbers waited in family clusters, crying cooing babes in arms, milling, weight shifted from one leg to another. The women hiked their heavy shoulder bags, adjusting their weight under a fall of veil. The sound was a submurmur of the stretched tension of waiting. November 16? So far away? No, not next week, there was a judges' strike called for tomorrow and no one knew how long it would last. The lawyers told their clients to be patient, but it was difficult to be patient when there was nowhere to sit. A bent old man hovered with a broom, and with jagged arthritic movements swept the cigarette butts and rags of plastic bags into the corners. The bristles of the broom made stripes in the dust like a comb.

People sat on the steps of the stairwells. They took their *foul* sandwiches out of their plastic bags and picnicked while they waited. No matter the weather outside, inside Abdeen Court it was always gray and thick with cigarette smoke and waiting.

"What I managed to finish in two months," Akila Mohammed said proudly of her navigation, "could have taken a year."

The case file of Tewfik House was passed from the prosecutor's office to the Office of Administrative Execution. According to procedure, a witnessing magistrate had to then file a request with the police station to deploy officers to oversee reentry to the apartment. This required a triangular coordination between the plaintiff's lawyer, the witnessing magistrate and the police.

In the meantime—and the meantime was a long time, a while
of whiling, an elastic wave toward some kind of maybe deadline—
possession was nine-tenths of the law. Which meant, meantime,
that possession, the de facto, was a state that became more and
more immovable as the weeks months years went by. In the meantime the evil aunts rented Nora's apartment to a secretary from the
embassy of Liberia.

At this development, all Nora's friends told her to give up on
the legal process—too long, too complicated—and to hire her own
baltagea, for God's sake, it was the only way.

"My mother's brother had the same problem with his estranged
wife over his father's house on Ibn Zanky Street and now it's the
Libyan embassy and they have not paid rent for fifteen years."

"Once I went to Luxor for the weekend and I came back and
my sister had thrown all my clothes onto the street and my father
was too ill then to stop her."

Talking to Nora's father, Ghaly, one day, I stumbled over the
word *baltagea*. I said *Beltegi* instead and Ghaly laughed because I
had mixed up the Muslim Brotherhood politician's name with the
Egyptian word for "thug."

"Do you know the origin of this word?" he asked me. I shook
my head. "Ah!" He leaned back in the sofa. "A long interesting
history! The Ottoman Empire was a vast area, far east to the Eu-
phrates, to Tunis in the west, from Lebanon to Saudi Arabia. And
there were too many revolts and mutinies and treasons and be-
trayals, so they got used to employing the *baltagea*. *Balta* is the
Egyptian word for 'ax' and *geya* is the Turkish word for 'carrier.'
So *baltagea* is the man who carries the ax. The *baltagea* became the
Ottomans' favorite enforcers. They killed instantly, with a slash to
the head or the chest. And so the word became synonymous with
violence and aggression and repression."

Nora was torn between her American half, which cleaved
to the rule of law, and her Egyptian half, which said: life is not

fair and you must make what you can of it. If the secretary from
the Liberian embassy was allowed to move into the apartment,
he would be a sitting tenant with diplomatic immunity. Luckily
Akila Mohammed had speeded up the waittime and had managed, by dint of persistence, wiliness and a little cash, to set a date
for repossession between the witnessing magistrate and the police
commander.

On the morning of Monday, April 18, three police officers and
the witnessing magistrate, a small neat man with a raisin prayer
callus in the middle of his forehead, crowded onto the third-floor
landing with Nora and Akila Mohammed. Nora began to explain
that her key did not work because her aunts had changed the lock.

Then Jou-Jou and Tati appeared, still in their dressing gowns,
disheveled, pulled out of their beds or their toilettes, coiffures
awry. They inserted themselves between the opposing judicial police group and the door and folded their arms across their chests.

"What court order?" Jou-Jou declaimed, pointing her arthritic
knuckled finger at the witnessing magistrate. "This order is no
longer valid. The apartment has been rented to an embassy. You
cannot implement a civil order against an embassy, the case must
be referred to the Ministry of Foreign Affairs." For added emphasis she brandished an official-looking brass plaque.

The witnessing magistrate asked if the new tenant was at this
very moment inside the apartment. The aunts conceded that he
was not.

"Has he taken up residence?"

"Not exactly residence, yet, but his belongings are already inside!"

The witnessing magistrate had the measure of the situation
and remained unimpressed.

"So, if I understand correctly, during the period pending a
judgment in this case, when the apartment was sealed by order
of the general prosecutor, you let a tenant in to see the apartment,

signed a lease with him and allowed him to move his belongings in. Please show me the lease."

Tati waved a piece of paper at him. The witnessing magistrate took the lease and carefully entered its details into his notebook and slipped the original into his case folder. Jou-Jou was dialing furiously, to husbands, to lawyers, her mouth working a hurried staccato whisper behind her clawed hand.

"Give me the lease back!" Tati demanded, realizing a little too late that the lease was technically unlawful and, in the hands of the general prosecutor, possible evidence of criminal intent or endeavor. Jou-Jou had bought the brass plaque from a stationery store.

"What lease?" replied the witnessing magistrate, feigning disinterest, regarding the little balled fists studded with bands of gold and glittering rubies with an almost smile.

"The lease I gave you. It's mine!"

"No it is not. It is now the property of the court and you may apply to the court for a copy."

Jou-Jou continued to jab at her mobile phone, rallying, railing.

Tati, her blond hair gray at the roots, ranged around her livid face like a wild bird's nest, trilled invective. Her cheeks were spotted crimson.

"Give me the lease now!" She drew her dressing gown tight around her, squashing a collapsing bosom. Against the pink of the lipstick her teeth looked yellow. She repeated her imperious demand, the demand of a ruling class to their hired underlings.

"Give me the lease right now!"

The witnessing magistrate allowed the faintest smile to play around his lips. Tati thrust her arm out to make a grab at the buff-colored folder in his hand and he was forced to retreat two polished mahogany steps up the staircase. Tati continued her lunge. The witnessing magistrate stretched his arm out and held the file aloft. Tati pulled at his forearm with her bony bird hand. The police sergeant had to step across and forcibly unclench her grip.

"Do you know who I am?" Tati fixed her black-bead eyes on the police sergeant. "I'll call my husband and you will be sorry for this outrage!"

"If you assault me again I will have you arrested," the witnessing magistrate told her evenly.

"Now," said the police sergeant, stepping forward with a demand of his own, "give me the key to this apartment."

"Oh, we don't have any key," Tati announced triumphantly. "Only the Africans have the key. The embassy has changed the locks."

The witnessing magistrate looked at Nora and shook his head. In order to gain access to a locked apartment a judge had to sign a warrant, an order of breaking. "We will try," he promised. But the window of time was closing; witnessing magistrates were only available to effect repossession orders on Mondays and Wednesdays, and the following week was a holiday when all state institutions would be shut for several days. The aunts, mollified, turned their backs and ascended to their own apartments. As they were leaving Jou-Jou turned to the witnessing magistrate.

"Oh, you, the religious one! The righteous one!" She spat on the ground in front of him in derision. "Praying and fasting!"

In the *meantime* Ghaly had hired a porter he knew and trusted from his old medical practice to stand watch on the third floor in case his sisters tried to move the Liberian diplomat into the apartment. The twins had hired their own thug, who stood guard all night in case Nora tried to break in. These two offset guardians had slept several nights facing each other across the stairwell. At eight o'clock on a Tuesday evening, Nora met her father's old porter coming down the stairs, his head hung against his breastbone.

"I am sorry," he mumbled, "your aunts told me I could not stay in front of the apartment anymore or they will call the police."

A precious twelve hours would pass before the next morning. Nora went straight over the road to the guards on the gate of the Gezira Sporting Club. They knew all about the disastrous lockout and the battle against her aunts and had many times offered all in their power to help.

"I need the *baltagea*. Right now!" Nora told them. "My aunts are going to move their diplomat in tonight!"

Half an hour later Nora opened her parents' door to a very large man with a bald head who introduced himself as Mr. TV. His handshake was firm, his smile fleeting and professional. He was already apprised of the situation and now assumed control.

"Don't worry," he told Nora reassuringly. This is what would happen: two of his men would arrive shortly; they were to be paid a thousand pounds each. Nora nodded. Then he went upstairs and talked to the aunts' *baltagea*. When he returned he gave her a thumbs-up sign.

"I've talked to him. Everything will be fine. He is with a group I know. You are in the right with the judgment of the court; all of this I explained to him. I know his boss—I don't think there is going to be any trouble."

Two thousand pounds' worth of *baltagea* arrived, large as pylons, well muscled, with thick corded necks and giant forearms. Nora was pleased. They were twice the size of the aunts' *baltagea*.

"We'll break your knees if you try anything," they told him.

Jou-Jou and Tati were not to be outwitted so easily. They called the police, and the police came and found Nora waiting in the hall. "What *baltagea*?" she asked innocently as the two big pylons hid in her parents' apartment. Then the next morning Akila Mohammed found Jou-Jou at the courthouse when she went to collect the witnessing magistrate.

Jou-Jou waved her lease with the secretary of the embassy of Liberia at the judge, threatening a diplomatic incident if he signed a breaking order for the apartment. The judge told her lawyer to inform his client of the law and that his client should have thought about diplomatic incidents before she illegally rented an apartment to a diplomat. He looked over the lease. Yes, he agreed, if the agreement had been signed with an embassy he would have been powerless to enforce a civil judgment against it, and the case would have to be referred to the Ministry of Foreign Affairs. Since the lease had been signed only with an individual, he would let the original judgment stand. Down came the gavel.

Jou-Jou called her sister Fussy. Red hair, red mouth, her tortoise neck twisted around as she clamped the telephone to her chin with a bejeweled hand.

"Make every effort!" she hissed. "Call your big husband! We have to do something now. Because I am standing in the court and they are going to get a warrant and I tell you we don't have a chance here!"

Akila Mohammed saw her put the phone away in her crocodile bag and lean against a railing, rubbing her kneecap and wincing with arthritis. Akila Mohammed reached out her arm to help her, but Jou-Jou barked, "I'm fine!" and set off hobbling away down the corridor, the heels of her Ferragamo pumps making an uneven limpy click against the early-hour echo of the tiled floor.

The police commander at the Garden City station had agreed, as before, to lend them three police officers to effect the breaking order, but when Akila Mohammed and the witnessing magistrate arrived, he kept them waiting more than half an hour. Finally he admitted them into his office and without offering them tea or coffee said that he had no men he could spare them today after all. Akila Mohammed threw her hands up in the air. The commander could barely meet her eye. Finally after a long awkward silence he looked up and admitted the truth.

"I have just received a phone call." His mouth compressed into a single line. "You have no idea of the pressure on me! This is above my head. I have been ordered not to send any officers."

He spread his hands wide in apology and helplessness. "I simply cannot do this."

Akila Mohammed called Nora. Nora called her father. Her father called his old friend who was a general in State Security. The general had a son who was born deaf and as a small boy was prone to hitting and screeching, diagnosed with psychological problems and prescribed tranquilizers. Nora's father had operated on him, implanting an artificial cochlea. As soon as he could hear, the boy was transformed into a happy, healthy, responsive child. The general said he would call the police commander directly.

Half an hour elapsed. Akila Mohammed and the witnessing magistrate waited outside on the steps in the lemon-colored winter sunlight, exchanging pleasantries. Eventually the police commander emerged. His face was caught between a grimace and an apology. He held up his palms to the sky.

"There are two sides opposite each other; both are strong and I am in the middle!" he said, releasing a whistle like a squeezed balloon. Akila Mohammed stepped forward and reminded him gently that her client held a lawful warrant; the judgment was in her favor. Shouldn't a good policeman uphold the law? The police commander shook his head slowly and a little sadly. Then he slapped his hand against his thigh as if to wake himself up.

"No, you are right!" he declared. "It is the law after all. You are right. I signed this two days ago and there's no reason not to sign it again. If I did not implement this judgment I would be in contempt of the law." Akila Mohammed watched as the commander's shoulders grew a little wider and his head stretched a little taller as he said this. "*Wasta* be damned. I am going to order thirty of my men to go with you and I am going to come myself!"

And so Nora and her father watched with some incredulity as a whole regiment of police decanted from a tiny blue metal police truck in front of Tewfik House. All the *bawwabs* came out onto the street to see the commotion. The witnessing magistrate stroked his raisin prayer callus. Akila Mohammed smiled broadly, proud, and the police commander, now extremely pleased with himself, grinned at the locksmith who had been engaged to drill through the lock. Jou-Jou and Tati made no appearance.

Inside the apartment all of the furniture had been upended and pushed against one wall. In the bedrooms clothes had been dragged out of the closets and piled in heaps onto the beds. The children's drawings had been ripped from the walls, leaving scraps of paper marked in Alexander's favorite pink felt pen and tears of clear tape. Nora walked through the mess, silent, fingering the rumpled rainbow rug that the kids played on and the warped Wendy House tent broken down in a corner between an overturned sofa and the blue silk Ottoman with the stain where Zoo had once spilled his Coke. She opened drawers and ran her hands through piles of disarranged sweaters, a jumble of boots, papers and bills strewn on top like giant confetti, but her red suede jewelry case was gone.

Many times in the months that followed I sat with Nora on her balcony, watching the blue flashing police lights at the edge of the demonstration across the river or remarking on a strangely calm week that meant something was bound to erupt tomorrow. Ghaly would come up from downstairs with papers to sign. Nora was back in her apartment but fourteen suits and countersuits between aunts and niece were filed over the next year. One day Ghaly said, "A lion in his cage is a nice and kind and amiable animal. But when the lion comes out of his cage he becomes the beast that he is. So now we have come out of the cage and we are all lions in the jungle now."

Everyone was protesting: the fishermen and the textile workers, nurses in the hospitals, teachers in the schools, students on campuses against their appointed chancellors, journalists in the syndicate against Mubarak-era editors, longshoremen at the Suez Canal, lawyers over the privileges of the prosecutors and the prosecutors over the privileges of the judges. Villagers blocked a high-way to protest the deaths of their children because there was no safe crossing point; passengers refused to let a train leave a station until the air-conditioning had been fixed.

One day Hassan and I found the police themselves protesting. They were wearing elements of their uniform, leather jackets over their winter navy blue, asking for their rights.

"We need money and health care!"

"We are paid less than a hundred dollars a month and we have to pay tips to our superiors from this and now nobody respects us and this is not good for the country."

"The officers treat us like slaves!"

"The officers have apartments, money allowances, cars. We're not getting anything."

"I have been a policeman for twelve years and receive seven hundred pounds a month, and no health care. The officers have two hospitals reserved especially for them, and there's nothing for our kids or families."

Sometimes Nora would see Jou-Jou or Tati in the lobby of Tewfik House; once or twice they spat some nasty invective in her direction, but most of the time they carefully ignored her. The story of their perfidy became supper entertainment and Zoo would pipe up: "Are you talking about the evil aunts again?"

KOSHARI

TAHRIR KOSHARI IS A BLOCK AWAY FROM TAHRIR SQUARE. IT HAS been open for fifty-five years, owned by the same family. Kamel Kamel has been cooking there for thirty-one years. He doesn't cook at home. When he gets home his wife spoils him! He works from seven A.M. until midnight six days a week. He stands every day behind the counter by the window where the great metal tubs of macaroni are displayed.

"You first fry the brown vermicelli," he said, explaining the recipe. "And then add the rice and the water and leave it to cook and add some salt and pepper. Then the second part is the pasta: you cook the spaghetti first and then add the macaroni and boil it until it's cooked and add oil—it feels really fattening! Then the lentils: First boiled until they rise to the surface and then steamed and then put in a pan for a few moments on a low heat with nothing else. This dries them slightly. The chickpeas have to be soaked the day before and then boiled until cooked. And when you do the lentils you mix them with the chickpeas."

Lunchtime rush, delivery boys hovering for orders to be filled. Kamel Kamel shoveled spaghetti macaroni into plastic takeaway tubs. He shoveled fast, a flick of his heavy corded wrist, a heap of pasta, a layer of rice, lentils, a few chickpeas.

"The sauce? It is oil, then onions and garlic, and then you squeeze fresh tomatoes and add salt and some black pepper and celery spice and leave it to cook for ten to fifteen minutes."

The tomato sauce went on top with a ladle slop followed by a dump of crispy fried onions. Hassan and I always liked extra chili oil and garlic vinegar added too. "Carbo-bomb," said Hassan, equally happy and depressed, resigned to the fleeting happiness that came with *koshari* eating and the deadweight tummy coma that followed.

"What makes good *koshari*?" I asked Kamel Kamel.

"It is from God," he replied modestly. "Well, it is the quality of ingredients. For example, the tomato sauce. Some people add water but we don't."

A customer wanted his tomato sauce separate. Kamel Kamel said it would cost fifty piastres extra for that.

"Why would it cost an extra fifty piastres?"

"The plastic bag costs me!"

"But how much does the plastic bag cost you?"

"Look, it costs what it costs."

Another customer became impatient: "I want two chili oils and two vinegar ones."

"Okay, so take the bag and don't pay! Because we work here from seven in the morning 'til midnight and you're making me lose money over plastic bags!"

WHEN PLATON
MET WAEL GHONIM

I DON'T LIKE HAVING MY PICTURE TAKEN," THE SUBJECT SAID, WAVING her hands in front of her face. "I am not at all photogenic." The feminist revolutionary was perched uncomfortably at the edge of the upturned crate against a plain white backdrop. Platon's camera clicked. I sat in the corner, back against a coffee table that had been pushed out of the way, at my observation post. Isherwood; I am a camera too. I watched her hands come down. Protesting seemed, for a moment, a bit silly.

Platon came over and knelt down in front of her. He held his camera in his lap, thumb at rest and snug against the viewfinder—a gesture, a weight, as familiar a corporeal extension as prayer beads.

"I promise I will take the most beautiful picture of you," he told her gently. The feminist revolutionary fluffed her hair out and wondered if she should take off her jacket. "I don't see any of that stuff," Platon assured her. "I just see the beautiful person behind that. No one is going to be looking at your clothes or your hair, just let it go. They'll be looking at a young woman fighting for history." He raised the camera. "Chin down a little."

Platon was a diminutive figure, a funny little guy, small and serious. He carried a calm intensity, the eye of the room. Around him in the makeshift hotel-suite studio, his assistants wordlessly clicked light meters, flashed flashes, replaced batteries, loaded and unloaded film, passed cameras back and forth, looped and spooled cable, reangled lighting. Platon stood. No mobile phone, no newspaper. One arm across his waist, the other hand propping up his chin. The technicals fussed; Platon was a statue. He was thinking. When he picked up the camera again I saw that the feminist revolutionary had mirrored his stillness. She had surrendered to a kind of catharsis. Her face relaxed to Sphinx repose; her chin was strong and square and her eyes seemed to fathom a far-off rain-washed vision. Her soul shone from her eyes, a profound reflection of a deep interior pool.

"You don't understand, but that was just beautiful," Platon told her, smiling now. Platon turned around from his lens and said to me, "Something happens here."

The heavy concentration broke. Platon consulted the schedule with Minky Worden, Human Rights Watch coordinator, who had commissioned the portfolio of revolutionaries. This was the last day of the shoot. The feminist revolutionary picked up her bag and said good-bye and thank you. As she was leaving I noticed that her face had returned to its original shape. Blunt forehead; heavy jaw. She had large pores; her skin looked thick and coarse. Under her eyes were blue semicircle shadows I had not noticed before. She was tired. Everyone was tired in those weeks after the eighteen days—day jobs and then in the evenings meetings, more meetings, groups committees, parties forming, unforming, trying to form something . . .

Platon finished the roll and then Wael Ghonim arrived for his appointment. He was wearing jeans and a blue button-down shirt and had a black backpack with a *January 25* sticker and another that read *Dubai Baggage Screening*. He held a mobile phone in his hand. He was distracted, busy; his mobile bleeped. He looked at his watch. He had to be somewhere; he didn't know how much time he could give. Minky, the Human Rights Watch coordinator, nodded, trying to hide her disappointment. Of course, of course, she understood. But she had hoped that he could come out to Nasr City and shoot some pictures with Khalid Said's mother and sister. Wael said he very much would like to, but Nasr City was far. Perhaps he could shuffle a meeting or two. "But I have to be in Mohandiseen at five," he said, and began texting.

After he was released from prison, Wael Ghonim gave six interviews over the next two or three sleepless days, but then he stopped. He tried to disappear from the media's radar. He continued posting on his Facebook page, he had one hundred thousand followers on Twitter, but he recused himself from the position of figurehead. This had been thrust upon him and he didn't want the mantle. His natural caution had been honed into savvy and wariness.

Platon had been hovering in the background and now he came forward to introduce himself. Platon said how honored he was to meet him and how humbled he was to be in his country. Wael Ghonim did not seem impressed; perhaps he felt the sentiment was a little overblown, but he was certainly curious.

"Yes, well I Googled you," he told Platon, making a joke.

Platon, finding his gracious magnanimity rebuffed, explained himself further.

"You guys are changing the world in a very humble and honest way. Everyone I've talked to has deeply moved me with their courage. Everyone has their own point of view, their own character, their own history, their own faith and politics. It's very rich. I've treated everyone in their own way; I am just trying to honor them. It's very important to understand my level of respect. I am documenting your role. And I need your help. I am only one side of it."

Wael Ghonim nodded and tried to make himself accommodating.

"Do you think if I held the laptop it would be a good idea?" he asked. Platon said yes, they could try that. Wael Ghonim stood in front of the white paper scroll backdrop as the assistants measured his face with light meters. "Just as long as you don't make my nose seem as big as it is!" he joked. He stood straight to the camera and held his hands together in front of his stomach. "What about my belly?" Wael Ghonim gave in to a pang of vanity.

"Don't worry about your belly." Platon used smooth tones, trying to talk a racehorse out of a stable. "Haven't you heard of Photoshop?"

Wael began to worry about the apple logo on his laptop being visible, in case of inadvertent advertising, and he balked at the way he had been asked to hold his laptop.

"But I don't hold my laptop ever like this."

"It's not a prop you're presenting to me," said Platon, explaining, "it's just in there."

"Okay," said Wael Ghonim, still unconvinced. "It's a pose but I'll go with it."

"It's all a bit of a pose," agreed Platon, perhaps trying to mollify him, "but as long as there's authenticity—"

"Do you want me to smile?"

"Not smiley, not serious," said Platon. "Neutral. Just kind of honest."

Platon took a few photographs. "Just with your eyes," said Platon encouragingly through the viewfinder. Wael Ghonim's face remained masked in a mixture of helpfulness and reticence. He asked if Platon could count down three-two-one so that he could keep his eyes open because he was worried about blinking with the flash. "Don't worry," said Platon, trying to soothe him. "Relax. Don't anticipate me. Be in slow motion. I'll dance around you. The most exciting thing for me is slow-motion honesty." Wael tried to oblige by keeping his face still, but his expression remained occluded, awkward, pressed onto a stage.

"Now imagine you're a child," coaxed Platon. "A child looks out at the world in such a beautiful way, before all the scars, before the . . ." The camera clicked and clicked. Wael Ghonim stopped trying to hold his mouth somewhere between smile and hope and sought to remember something from his childhood. "Let it all fall," said Platon. Wael Ghonim seemed to catch a thought and for a split second—"That's all it takes, one five-hundredth of a second!"—his expression reflected something inside himself instead of projecting the public persona he was inhabiting. But then he shifted his weight from one leg to another and the physical present reasserted itself with a constrained expression.

"Are you bored?" Platon asked him. Wael Ghonim made an acquiescent grimace. "Stay with me," said Platon as he took another camera and tried not to let the changeover interrupt the flow and concentration. "Stay with me; if you lose it I'll go crazy!" He finished the roll and an assistant handed him another camera. Wael Ghonim could see that Platon was serious; he respected the intent, but he didn't know how to meet it. He still wore his celebrity like an itchy suit.

"You're worse than my dentist!" he said. Platon laughed and said a lot of people felt like that about having their picture taken. Yesterday, it was funny because he had shot Alaa Al Aswany, the novelist, in his office. Al Aswany was still a practicing dentist and Platon had made him sit in his own dentist chair to take the picture.

Wael Ghonim continued to stand as carefully as he could, face neutral and stiff, his eyes registering one moment duress, another pretense, another a wan half-hoped-for smile. Platon cajoled and clicked. Finally, he was finished. Wael Ghonim gave a little mock bow to show that the performance was over. "I've got it!" Platon told him. "You're free!"

The plan was to take a van to Khalid Said's mother's home in Nasr City. While the assistants broke down the studio, Wael Ghonim stood around and made calls rearranging his afternoon and chatting. He asked which other people had been invited to the photo shoot and nodded as Minky listed names, pursing his lips. He said they should also try to include Islamists and Salafis because the revolution wasn't only made by people with laptops. He was concerned that the world was focusing too much on the bloggers and he didn't want the religious people airbrushed out of the story.

"There's a sense that the liberals are excluding the Salafis; that is completely unfair, they were there on the Day of the Camels and in the front row fighting. You shouldn't exclude people because you see the world from a different point of view—" Then he grinned as he corrected himself. "Well, then again the Salafis want *sharia*, which is exclusionary as well. Both have same problem . . ." And the army? Minky asked.

"They are just as scared as we are." Wael Ghonim's totem status meant that he was, from time to time, called in by generals. He had told them of his fury about the virginity tests, about the hundreds detained under military prosecution on the ninth of March. He was sympathetic to the generals; they were trying, maybe, in their own way. They had announced an investigation into the virginity tests—"Just the fact that they have a Facebook page now is something unimaginable!"

We went down to wait by the van that would take us to Nasr City. Recognizing him, the doormen came out from their posts and gathered around Wael Ghonim. More questions and uncertainties: what about the tourists who had stopped coming and what about the stock market and what about the police who were nowhere anymore, what should happen to the police, because it was getting to be a problem; you need police, don't you, against the robbers? Wael told them that those in the police who were forced to attack protesters should be forgiven but those who were shooting from rooftops should not. Wider economics, he said, demurring, these were harder to opine on . . .

It was a blustery overcast day and it was raining. Cairo is a desert city and it doesn't function well in the rain; intersections flood, traffic slows even more. Stopped in the starburst grid of downtown, Wael Ghonim started to wonder aloud why Human Rights Watch didn't have a good reputation in the Arab world. It was a shame, he thought, that they had not communicated their political independence well enough. They could do more to publicize, for example, their criticisms of the Israeli government and the fact that they took the American government to task as well as governments in the Middle East and all over the world. Grassroots opinion, collecting forums, making and shaping movements, this was his professional expertise and his impassioned hobby. When he had first set up the "We Are All Khalid Said" Facebook page, he explained, there was already a competing page and he had won the audience by deliberately creating a concept that was easy to identify with and by encouraging participation. He had asked people to send in pictures of themselves holding up signs that read *We Are All Khalid Said*. The response had been amazing, he said. Even a young mother had sent in a picture of her toddler with the message spelled out in Lego. Wael was convinced Human Rights Watch needed to have a much stronger strategy to win over the Arab press. "Media," he said. "I know this."

We inched through honking downtown onto the highway. The traffic was solid. In the next lane the passengers in a bus recognized Wael Ghonim and waved and gave thumbs-up signs.

"I don't want to be seen with foreigners," he said, drawing the curtains of the van. "No offense." Apparently there were smears across the Internet that he was an American agent because he used an Apple computer and worked for Google.

A group of five or six workmen, dressed in ragged tracksuits and grimy shirts, one with a turban looped over his head, were trying to jimmy a broken streetlight pole out of the concrete lane divider. Three chipped away at the concrete base, one stood under the falling arm as if he could catch it and another was trying to wave at the traffic to stop (it was already stopped) and back up (where?) because the pole was about to topple onto the road. They made a comic little group of mechanicals. Everyone in the car was laughing at their bumbling effort. Platon loved the absurdity of the scene. Wael Ghonim wanted to run out and take a picture of it. The light pole leaned over, but remained rooted. The cars swerved into a bottleneck around it and the three workers continued to chip away with their crowbars. The traffic crawled.

We had been on the road for perhaps forty minutes when Platon, who had been sitting in the front seat next to the driver mostly quiet, began to talk.

"I'm not an intellectual," he began, "but this whole experience, this revolution, must have been full of moments of intense joy and intense pain." Platon has an estuary London accent, but he doesn't speak like an Englishman. He makes effusive, formal pronouncements, emotional appeals. Wael Ghonim might have dismissed this as flattery at first, but Platon is very sincere in his intent, and his intent is to make a connection with the person he is photographing. This is what allows people to open themselves to his lens and this is what creates and captures a moment of genuine truth on a piece of paper. We had discussed this process the first time I had seen him work a couple of days before. He had been photographing the family of a martyr who had been killed by a bullet fired from a police station the day after the Day of Rage.

The mother of the martyr held a portrait of her son in her hands and looked into the camera. Unlike the feminist revolutionary, unlike Wael Ghonim, she did not seem at all concerned with the idea of herself as an image. She simply was herself and inhabited herself without regard for reflection or perception. Her face did not carry an expression of strength or sadness or pride or humility or dignity, and yet it was the sum of all these things, collected in the vessel of herself. The room fell quiet. Platon eschewed his usual patter, no "great, yes, like that, there, beautiful, wicked." For several silent moments, the mother collected what she had known, what she felt, what she yearned for and dreamed and the bitterness she understood, into a focal point. Afterward Platon said that he was sure I had seen the strongest shoot of the trip. I told him I had never witnessed anything quite like it. He explained that he tried to strip everything away. The studio wasn't artificial so much as it was meant to be a neutral space, shorn of context and situation so that nothing would distract from the emotion. He said that in order to get such honesty he had to be very open and bring no judgment. I told him I had been very touched by the complicity between photographer and subject. "It was something magic," I told him. "Yes," he agreed, merging his humility and his arrogance in this word. "That's what I've always thought."

Wael Ghonim listened as Platon told him he thought it must be very difficult for him to live in this strange new state of fame. Platon said he thought it must be particularly hard for him because he was such a natural communicator and at the same time an expert in communication, which made him hyperaware of how perceptions could be twisted. "I understand, I think," said Platon. "You feel like you have no room to move."

"Yes, I need to be politically correct now, which I hate," said Wael Ghonim.

"You have a very powerful skill," replied Platon, warming. "Creating and understanding people en masse and how they operate with each other. I don't think it's an accident that your web page tapped into a communal consciousness. Do you somehow feel trapped?"

For the first time I saw Wael Ghonim loosen his grip on his constructed persona a little. He nodded.

"The worst time was Thursday night, the day before Mubarak stepped down," he said. "I was told by an army officer that whoever went to the presidential palace would be killed." The situation was confused. Mubarak had been expected to resign on Thursday night and instead delivered a rambling speech about duty and responsibilities. State Security was still trying to manipulate the situation; they had put out a fake Facebook page under Wael Ghonim's name urging everyone to leave the square and go home. Friends and activists were looking to him for leadership, but he was scared about what to tell them.

"I couldn't figure out what to say. Those words could be like bullets. A friend called me and said, 'You are going to kill people if you send them to the presidential palace.' He had tried to conduct an Internet survey to find out what to do, but there was so much traffic the survey site had gone down. A friend of his had looked at him, red eyed, sitting on edge of history. "He told me: 'Are you crazy? You've been in prison, you haven't slept for three days. You need to go to sleep! And you don't have to say anything. People will go to the presidential palace whether you tell them to or not.'"

Minky leaned into the conversation, maternal. She had worked as a human rights activist in many countries. She knew very well the guilt of dissidents, the ones let out of prison when so many were left behind inside. She explained to him, very carefully and gently, that he carried no moral responsibility. If people had been killed it would have been the government who killed them and the responsibility lay clearly, she told him, with them. Wael Ghonim listened to her very carefully and then shook himself, like a dog coming out of a river, announcing: "You're too emotional for me!" trying to deflect his undoing with a joke. His laptop was open in front of him. He had been periodically glancing at it, updating, tweeting. Platon explained why he was probing him.

"I felt you came in a bit vulnerable, like you felt you had no room to move," he said. "I could see your struggle."

Wael Ghonim looked up from his laptop. "It's interesting," he replied, now open and won over by Platon's clear sincerity. "It makes me believe photography is not as simple as it seems to be." He asked if Platon minded that anyone could pick up a digital camera these days and be a photographer. Platon said he did not pay too much attention to what other photographers did.

"I believe when I take pictures," he said, "I believe in the process of meeting you and deeply searching for answers about you."

Wael was scrolling through a slide show of Platon's photographs online.

"So you photographed Ahmadinejad?" Wael asked him.

"Yes I did," Platon replied without false modesty. "And Gaddhafi." Wael Ghonim now turned the screen to show Platon his portrait of Putin. Platon had shot Putin, seated in a chair, at an upward angle so that his hands, both resting on the arms of the chair, appeared massive; his expression was derisory, imperial, defiant and cruel. It was a stark illustration of power.

"How did he agree to have his photo taken like that?" Wael Ghonim was fascinated.

"Oh no, he knew," said Platon, and went on to describe how he had managed to bond with Putin over the Beatles and music, how Putin had sent everyone out of the room and how Putin was basically a tough guy who wanted to be portrayed as a tough guy. "He likes the picture!" said Platon.

Wael Ghonim considered this for a moment.

"I don't want to be seen as someone posing, as someone above others." Platon nodded; he understood this.

"You don't want it to look like you are showing off, everyone is looking at you and that you are getting carried away with the media, which is pulling you to be a superstar. That's why I understand, it's not about vanity. You're nervous because you have a responsibility to do the right thing; you're dealing with life and death. I get it, man," concluded Platon, "I get it."

Wael Ghonim was overcome. "I love you!" he said simply.

Platon had broken through. "I love you too!" he replied. "You know what Putin was very frightened of? What his issue was, like your equivalent of not wanting to show off? He didn't want it to look like a photographer was coming to give him the Hollywood treatment and make him look glamorous."

"I am going to tweet," said Wael Ghonim, "I am going to tweet that I am sitting in the car with the most creative and weird person I have ever met!"

"I don't understand Twitter," said Platon as Wael Ghonim commenced tapping. "I've never done e-mail!" he admitted. Wael Ghonim was deeply shocked. He made a cartoon recoil. Seriously. No e-mail? Not one? Ever? "Dude, get out of the car!" he cried.

"I have dyslexia," Platon told him. "I can't look at a computer screen and I struggle with information on paper so I work with very simple shapes and feelings."

Wael Ghonim reconsidered. "No, I won't tweet it. People will say: 'You're having your portrait taken and you should be working for the country!' One hundred thirty-seven thousand people follow me on Twitter and about twenty percent of them hate me."

"Who hates you?" Minky asked.

"Some activists, because I got too much light shed on me. I

never claimed anything, but some are jealous. It's perfectly fine. I understand it. But I never claimed credit for anything."

For a moment the traffic eased forward in a slow flow and we came alongside the main State Security building, where Wael Ghonim had been held for ten days during the revolution.

"Is this where you were a guest?" Minky asked.

"Yes, well I was hosted . . ." Wael Ghonim didn't seem to want to dwell on his incarceration. He returned to the list of people that hated him. "And people who were part of the old regime. I hate people hating me," he said. "But I have to accept it anyway."

"Yes," counseled Minky wisely, "you have to accept some things that are beyond your control and be yourself."

To pass the time, Wael Ghonim opened up a video package his group had made commemorating the martyrs. Platon craned his head around to watch. The rally in a school hall flickered in jumpy video. A small boy, perhaps eight years old, walked across a stage to a microphone. "My dad wanted to go to heaven," he said in his clear child voice, "and my little brother told him yes, because there are good things in heaven and bad things in hell. When my father was martyred my little brother said to me: now I wish I had never told Dad that there were good things in heaven so he would not want to go there."

"It's an amateurish video," Wael Ghonim noted, a little despondent about the corny violin background music. "Oh look!" he exclaimed, pointing out of the window at an advertising banner strung up across the road. *For the Youth of the Revolution: 30% discount on furniture!*

We had been on the road for more than an hour. Time was running out of the afternoon and Minky apologized to Wael Ghonim, whose plans had obviously been completely destroyed.

"I am going to tweet that I have kidnapped Wael Ghonim!" Minky joked.

"Yes, detained against my will!" Wael Ghonim concurred.

"That's going to look really great, detained by Human Rights Watch!"

Finally, eventually, we arrived in front of the apartment block where Khalid Said's mother lived with his sister and her family. The assistants carried the equipment up and Wael Ghonim lingered on the stoop. Soon enough a small crowd gathered and pointed at the famous face. Oh you, the foreign agent, why have you done these things to show Egypt in a bad way and make everything chaos? He patiently explained himself to them. In return they complained there was no work nowadays, no income, things were hard. And look at all the violence at the Zamalek football match last night!

"This is all because of the freedom!" one man said.

The Saids' family apartment was spacious and well appointed. His mother, wearing a black gown and a black head scarf, greeted Wael very warmly, kissing his hands and saying over and over, "You are like a son to me." This was only the second time they had met. The first had been hurried and emotional. They had met by chance on Tahrir during the revolution, in the days after Wael Ghonim had been released.

Wael Ghonim had kept his identity as the administrator of the "We Are All Khalid Said" Facebook page anonymous. He had felt weird about this, perhaps a little disingenuous in keeping it from Khalid Said's family, but even from his home in Dubai he was scrupulously paranoid about security. When he met Khalid's mother he had held himself back, abashed, apologetic, but she had cried out and embraced him. He felt comforted, close to her, a moment of virtual to flesh, of transubstantiation. "I feel my son is not dead when I see you, because you are just like Khalid."

Khalid Said's sister, a modern blonde, wore a pendant with her brother's picture around her neck. Her daughters ran around chasing kittens. The assistants set up the lighting and unrolled a backdrop. Khalid's sister told us the night before she had dreamed that she opened a door and Khalid was there and he came inside and spent time talking with her, just as if he was alive. Then her mother had woken her up in the morning and she had been angry at her for interrupting his visit. Platon arranged sister and mother together. Sister rested her head on mother's shoulder, mother held her daughter's face tenderly and together they made a pietà. Khalid's mother retained her expression of gentle bereavement, but his sister's face showed everything: pain and loss and sadness and hope and pride and future and past and everything the revolution was and all its sacrifices and all the uncertainties to come.

When the time came, Um Khalid and Wael Ghonim leaned their heads together and held a cushion with a picture of Khalid Said's photograph stitched into the center. Khalid's mother's face rested, beatifically sad. "Now, every ounce of emotion," Platon said as he bent over his camera. Wael Ghonim let his expression fall where it might. Now his eyes seemed to see everything and to be looking at it from a distant perspective. What did this look like? It's hard to say. At that moment he was relaxed, he was loved, but the affirmation of Khalid's mother was bittersweet.

"I look really hurt," he guessed out loud, between takes. But that was not quite accurate. His expression was between pained and proud.

Afterward Platon came out onto the balcony as his assistants were packing away the equipment. He hung his hands over the edge of the rail. He confessed he was emotionally exhausted. "I am at the edge of what I can do."

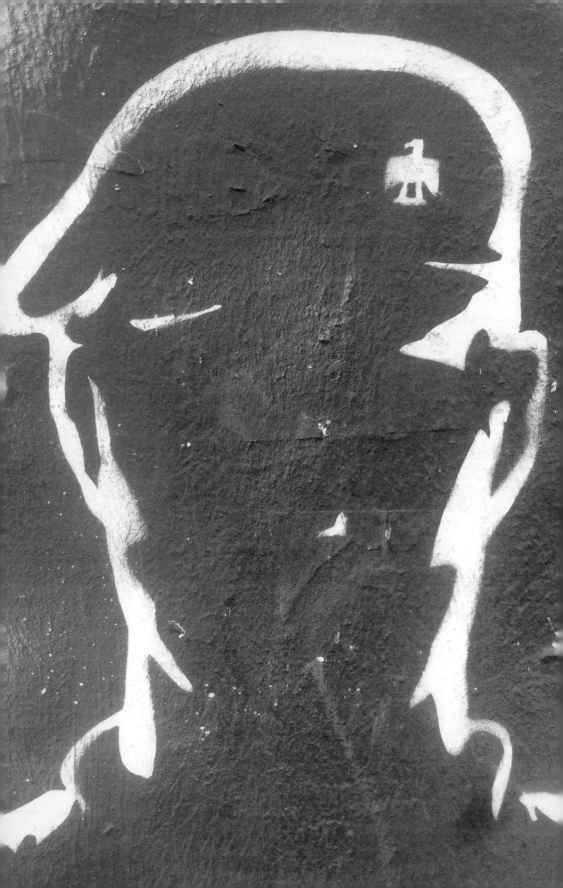

THE ARMY IS A RED LINE

FRANÇOIS EMPAIN WAS A BELGIAN BARON WHO BUILT HELIOPOLIS, Cairo's first desert suburb, at the turn of the twentieth century. The architecture is a mix of Ottoman arches and Moorish columns and Italianate flourish. Vaulted colonnades for shade, wooden balconies, garden squares planted with palm trees and hibiscus. There was a country club and churches and mosques and synagogues for the well-to-do civil servant class, a hippodrome for weekend horse racing, art deco cinemas and the grand Heliopolis Palace Hotel, with four hundred rooms and a vast domed lobby filled with gilt-edged Louis XIV furniture. Nasser lived in a villa on the edge of Heliopolis and after the 1952 revolution-coup the Free Officers of his new regime settled around him in the area. There was plenty of spare land and proximity to the airport, and over time the military took up residence in the vacant lots along the highway. This was the district where Hassan lived, not far from the Big Pharaoh. When Mubarak became president he refurbished the Palace Hotel as his presidential palace.

Friday morning was the only time of the week when Cairo slept and there were no traffic jams. Hassan protested at the early hour, but then again, Hassan, a not-atypical Cairene, considered anything before four in the afternoon the morning. "Eleven o'clock?!" He looked at me, crestfallen. I bribed him with lunch that would be his breakfast. "Whatever you want."

In the front seat of the taxi he hung his head, quietly grumpy. There were no traffic lights in Cairo, and on Friday mornings no cars, and so we flew above the city over the elevated highways at sixty miles an hour and arrived, barely jolted, in Heliopolis in ten minutes flat.

The urban highways that ran through Heliopolis were well kept, their grassy medians planted with spiky bougainvillea and watered by workers in corporate overalls and networks of automatic sprinklers. On either side, walls. Walls and gates. Walls that shielded the compounds of the Egyptian military-industrial-business complex. White walls topped with shallow pitches of red-tiled roofs, walls decorated with brick swags or wrought-iron carriage lanterns, concrete walls, stone walls, blank walls posted with *No Photography!* signs, walls topped with broken glass, iron spikes, rows of barbed wire, walls guarded by concrete watchtowers with bored soldiers watching the traffic from underneath the brims of their metal helmets.

We drove slowly so that Hassan could read the signs above the gates.

"But not too slowly," Hassan cautioned the driver. "And we can't stop; they'll shoot at us."

"They're not going to shoot at us," I told him. "Don't be melodramatic."

"Okay. But did you see the red lines they painted on the road outside the Defense Ministry?"

We drove suspiciously slowly. Hassan read:

"'The Central Security Forces Communication and Vehicles.' 'Training Facility of the Ministry of Interior.' 'The General Administration for the Central Security Forces of Cairo.' 'The House of Weaponry and Ammunition.' 'Military Vehicles Department.' 'Ministry of Petroleum.' 'The Egyptian Mineral Resources Authority.'" We passed a lump of pink-painted cement, concrete balconies angled like wings.

"That's a hotel. Owned by the military; only used by the military. You can tell by the guard on the gate," said Hassan as he kept reading:

"'The General Authority for Transportation of the Ministry of the Interior.' 'The Administration of the Central Military Area.' 'The General Authority for Investment and the Free Zone.' 'The Administration for the Infantry.' 'The Military Technical Institute.' 'The Military College for the Science of Leadership for Military Officers.' 'The Club for the Officers of the Presidential Guard.' 'Air Force House.'" We passed a grand Ottoman palace behind a wall surmounted with swiveling security cameras, of anonymous use and ownership except for two wrought-iron eagles on the gate.

"The army is a black box," George Ishak told me once. "We don't know anything about the army," Alaa Al Aswany told me. "An Egyptian person could live and die after doing his military service without knowing anything about the army." Hassan had lived in Heliopolis all of his life and he pointed out things that I had driven past a hundred times without seeing. A block of empty desert scrub in the middle of a residential neighborhood surrounded by a chain-link fence and signposted: military zone. The brick-faced block of a cemetery mausoleum, padlocked because this was the Mubarak family plot. The Armed Forces Mosque, three flattish sky-blue domes and an armored personnel carrier (APC) parked outside. Another unused rectangle of barren land, trash dumped, with a lone conscript sitting on a bench under an umbrella guarding it. The sign read: *Future Project Land Belonging to the Armed Forces.* From the balcony of Hassan's apartment we could see over the wall of the Air Defense

Officers Club, tennis courts and handball courts, tables set out
on an adjacent lawn, a mosque attached to a marble-clad hotel
with an external glass elevator. Hassan said there were weddings
there every night in the spring.

The army was an army but it was also a vast corporation and
a giant welfare umbrella. Every Egyptian eldest son with a male
sibling was conscripted for three years of military service, but
despite the numbers of Egyptians who went through its proce-
dures, the Egyptian army was opaque. Its budget was secret, its
business interests undisclosed. It was against the law to mention
the army in a newspaper or talk about it on television. Crimes
committed against army personnel or property were subject to
military courts and military prison. Egypt had been under emergency law for thirty years. This emergency law was not rescinded
after Mubarak fell.

Officers and former officers and their families held special
military national ID cards that gave them access to military hospitals, military hotels (when the Big Pharaoh went to London
he stayed in an Egyptian-military-owned hotel in Paddington,
thanks to his father's service thirty years before), military clubs,
preferential mortgage and loan arrangements, military-owned
apartments and real estate developments. All the public land in
Egypt was by default owned by the army. The Egyptian military owned and operated countless businesses and factories left
over from Nasser's nationalizations: National Chicken, macaroni, bottled water, supermarkets, seaside resorts, real estate development, cooking oil, washing machines, soap powder. When
an officer reached the rank of colonel it was said he was made
golden. Pensions were very generous, retirement was often early,
positions for former senior officers found among the network as
directors of factories or investment portfolios, provincial governors. In Egypt the army was engine room, ballast, star chamber,

puppeteer. The army was all these things and a hundred more no one understood.

Hassan and I drove out further to the edge of the city, toward the airport: walls, walls, and tall things glimpsed behind them—arc lights, radio towers, flagpoles. Along the road were new billboards with a picture of a soldier cradling a toddler and the slogan *The People's Revolution Protected by the Army*. The child was a big heavy baby and the soldier carried him with one arm—his other held his gun—so that the child dangled awkwardly. This was the army's only PR effort. They put this image up on billboards all over the city and made stickers out of it and stuck them to the front of their APCs. The soldier was swarthy and had a heavy chin; the kid looked like a sack of potatoes that might slip from his grasp at any time. Hassan and I started calling it the pedophile picture.

"'The al-Maza Military Hospital.'" Hassan continued to read the signs above the gates. Officers and former officers and their families who held military IDs were treated at military hospitals, separately from the general population. "'The House of the Officers of the Tank Corps,' 'The Presidential Guard.'" The walls were decorated with bas reliefs of bronzed plasterwork or epic mosaics or vast murals, scenes from a victorious history: charioteers and archers, Mamelukes on horseback, Egyptian tanks mounting an Israeli berm. Eagles and palm trees, crossed scimitars, crossed rifles, crossed tank barrels and antiaircraft guns. The Infantry Institution's entrance was flanked with polished cannons. "'The Chemical Warfare Institute.' 'The Chemical Warfare Administration.'" Across the road was strung a banner proclaiming: *The Armed Forces, the Hand That Builds, the Hand That Carries the Weapon. The Armed Forces: All of This Effort Is for Egypt.*

The military had an engineering corps that, from time to time, built civil engineering projects, out of apparent largesse. One of

these, a road bridge toward the airport, was known as the Army
Bridge. It was high and smooth and solid. A sign announced:
Bridge of the Egyptian Army. Subsequent signs, in clean reflective
white on blue, were posted at regular intervals and displayed the
following refrain:

> Egypt
> The Homeland
> Egyptian Homeland
> Egypt First
> Egypt Forever
> Egypt

Hassan and I looped around and turned back toward the city.
Under an overpass decorated with a montage of Egyptian might:
wheat sheaves and guns and Mubarak's portrait. Mubarak's face
had been chiseled off. As we came near to the compound of the
Defense Ministry there was indeed, literal and recently painted, a
thick red line across the street.

Hassan's stomach was rumbling. "Feed me," he reminded me
plaintively. Hassan ate like an American teenager and looked like
a starving refugee.

"There's no way you are twenty-two," I told him. "You have
the appetite and sleeping habits of a seventeen-year-old."

In the center of Heliopolis, beside the baron's grandest colon-
nade, I got out of the car to take a picture of some new graffiti
martyrs I noticed stenciled on a doorjamb. Half a block further
along we were stopped at a police checkpoint. Hassan was nervous
and extra polite. I was his friend; he was just showing me around.
The police wanted to take my iPhone because it was a camera. I
said I was a journalist and then they wanted my ID. One of the
policemen took it away; his sergeant held his hand out, *stop*, to

prevent my following it. Another motorist was pulled over and a second scene of interrogation was enacted. I watched the sergeant walk over to a police car parked at the other side of the intersection, say something to the plainclothes policeman sitting inside and point in my direction. An officer came up and demanded my iPhone again. I said, "No. What's the problem? I was taking a picture of a wall."

"It is forbidden to take photographs," the officer stated, mustache implacable.

"Photographs of what?" I remonstrated. "Are you telling me that no one can take any photographs anywhere in Egypt?"

"Yes," repeated the implacable mustache. "Everything is forbidden since the revolution."

Lieutenant Colonel Gamal Abdel Nasser and then Air Marshal Anwar Sadat and then Air Marshal Hosni Mubarak had taken off their uniforms and put on the civilian suit of president. Nasser was pan-Arabism and the voice of the Arabs, a secular socialist dream, part of the nonaligned movement. Sadat was "open-door" economics and the Camp David Accords before he was assassinated by an Islamist officer during the Sixth October parade in 1981. Mubarak was stability and sclerosis and an ally of America and played a swing-door trapdoor game with the Islamists. Each president had ascended from the appointed right hand of the vice presidency. Each had fought a power battle with a popular defense minister and won.

Rewind a little, pick up a piece of the puzzle that has fallen on the carpet. It is two days after Mubarak fell. Adrien and I are sitting on the balcony of the hotel and talking.

"Since 1952," I said to Adrien, nursing another theory, "the army has been responsible for each transition of power."

"Yes, that's true," said Adrien, taking a draw on his cigar and looking out over an empty Tahrir, where teams of volunteers were enthusiastically sweeping up the garbage to make everything clean and tidy for the new Egypt.

We had just returned from interviewing a former Military

Intelligence general. The former general had smiled like a big salmon and talked in elaborate paragraphs. Between the lines he seemed to suggest that the revolution (so recent, so searing-soaring, so grand and celebrated!) had been in fact nicely orchestrated by the generals. There was an undeniable logic underpinning this theory. Mubarak was old and ill and had never appointed a vice president who could be seen and understood as a successor. Instead he had supported the project of his younger son, Gamal, to take over. Gamal had smoothed-back hair that was a little long at the back of his neck and had emerged as the chief economic agent of the country, promoting privatization and foreign investments and along the way aligning certain interests and business connections. Gamal had never been in the army and the generals hated him for being oily and soft. It was a point of particular pride among the officer corps that the army was the only efficient and clean institution in the country. The army built the best roads, the army dealt with the worst terrorists, the army was upright backbone and brain. Egypt needed the army to save it from itself.

So according to this version of events, the army had acquiesced to the demands of the protesters on Tahrir because they had dovetailed with the interests of the generals, to secure the succession and to get rid of Gamal. The big-salmon general paused for a moment to allow a silver-scale smile. I kept writing furiously in my notebook, trying to make sense of his elliptical coruscations.

"But what happened?" I asked him, and then ran through the bones of what we knew: "Mubarak never actually resigned. He never ceded power of his own volition. In his great disappointing speech on Thursday night he said he would continue to rule until new presidential elections were held in six months' time. Everyone thought he was going to step down! But he didn't. He went off message. Then on Friday Omar Suleiman stands in front of a microphone with that funny twitchy man behind him, looking right left, right left. And then Mubarak was bundled onto a helicopter!" I was extemporizing, imagining the scene. An urgent conversation in a palace corridor, phones ringing in the background and not being answered, gruff threatening tones, hand on shoulder to steady, to push, to shove—*It's enough, Mr. President, there are eight million people on the streets, the workers are on strike, the navigation of the Suez Canal is threatened. It is time to* go. And then in an aside to an aide (perhaps to the man in a uniform standing behind Omar Suleiman, the man whom no one knew but who had become a great Internet joke, looking this way and that), *Get this sick old man and his wailing wife out of here.* "So Mubarak and his family were pushed out onto the tarmac and

flown away to his private villa in Sharm el-Sheikh and locked in with a guard on the door."

The former intelligence salmon interrupted my scenario. "How do you know it was a helicopter?" he asked, eyebrow cocked.

"I guessed," I admitted. "It's the most convenient form of transport for the distance." He stopped smiling for a moment and gulped as if he had swallowed a fly. I did not say anything into the silence. At length he regained his fish grin and allowed, "There is a big difference in what can be said and what must be done."

BREAD, LIFE

SUMMER 2008: IN THE DISTRICT OF BULAQ THE BAKERY WAS AT the center of the neighborhood. Hajji Hussein's family had owned the bakery for a hundred years. They had baked bread for the British soldiers when they came to Egypt to train before Gallipoli. The bakery was on the ground floor of an old elegant corner house, long since dilapidated, twisted wrought-iron balconies, tall green shutters awry or missing, the floral swags decorating its lintels clogged with grime and spotted with spiders' nests. Hajji Hussein was tall and white haired with a kindly, harried air; his teeth were ivory at the front, stained yellow and red from tobacco further back. He wore a long gray *galabia* and spent his days on his feet, traversing the few-steps route from the window grille that gave out to the customers on the street to the cubbyhole office behind—with a lumpy floor, a rickety table and a large and ancient iron safe—"Empty now! No money!"—to the heat of the orange-glow oven in the interior.

All day the customers massed and clamored and all day the oven cranked and roared. The regulation 120 grams of dough was formed into a flat circular pocket and dusted with bran, and then traveled along the conveyor belt through the fire-breathing oven to bake into *baladi* bread. The room was a furnace and I pressed myself between a skeletal tower of proofing racks and the floury plaster wall. A lone bead of sweat dripped from my nose onto my notebook. The brothers and cousins of the Husseini family bakers held themselves a little proud as I talked to them. *Baladi* means "country," did I know that? Did I know that the Egyptian word for bread, *aish*, meant "life"? The little circular loaves emerged from the dragon, scorching, tipped onto a table, spread out to cool for half a moment, because already the crowd was baying for the next batch. The runners for the falafel sellers who bought the bread for sandwiches hung impatiently by the half-open door. A stout man came in and picked up a sack of flour and left. The women waiting in the street pressed forward and knotted their fingers around the metal window grille.

Hajji Hussein passed through the loaves, back and forth, bread and five-pound notes, creased and softened with finger grease or tinkly brass coins, the smallest of which, twenty-five piastres, bought five loaves. *Baladi* was so cheap there was no denomination small enough for a single loaf. The quotidian sum of Egypt, cheap bread, was the contract between people and government and had endured decades. Bread, country, life, government, people. I watched the women elbowing forward.

"Give me five loaves."

"There are ten here."

"Five. God bless you."

"Take the money."

"Me first!"

A little girl, no more than four, with hair spun gold in the sunshine, took ten loaves and crouched down on the stoop to blow on them and cool them down, balancing each hot rim in her fingers, careful not to let them fall into the dusty street. She was so immersed in her task and so diligent that the mothers in the crowd by the window clucked at her affectionately.

"Here's a pound."

"Hajji, you gave me five, I want five more!"

"I need change—"

A woman complained that he had not given her all the bread she had paid for. Hajji Hussein patiently counted it out for her, twenty, twenty-five, but she laid all the little rounds out again recounting them herself to make sure, twenty, twenty-five, before she was satisfied.

The batch of bread was finished and in the bread queue the women slumped back into waiting, shifting from one leg to another, no shadows in the midday sun.

"And rice has gone up again," one woman began.

"It was four and a half, even five!"

"That grocer is a thief! He has no concern for the people of his neighborhood!"

"Why should he when he's sitting nicely in his air-conditioning!"

"I have been busy trying to get my pension. They were giving me a very hard time about it. They want every document, marriage certificate, the birth certificates of all my children, so many things I don't have. I finally got it today! Every time I went there they would send me away. My neighbor came with me and I was lucky to have him there. Thanks be to God. But there are still so many steps!"

A small boy tugged at his mother and asked her for some money. He wanted to buy some *koshari* from a street vendor.

"We've got food at home!" she told him kindly, refusing.

Next to the bakery was a vegetable cart owned by Ramsi and his brother Sopi. They sold potatoes, tomatoes, cucumbers and eggplants and had a small bag of okra, which was expensive and so not much called for. Ramsi was thin and hollow, but the women of the quarter who shopped there were shaped like eggplants.

One picked up an eggplant and asked Ramsi, "I bought it yesterday and it was a pound and now today two pounds. Why are you charging tourist prices?" Ramsi demurred; she managed to get a kilo and a half for two pounds.

"Give me a lemon, just one, for free."

"Potatoes?"

"Two and a half pounds."

"That's a lot. Okay. Give me half a kilo."

There were three piles of tomatoes, good quality, medium and a pile that were half-rotten, bruised, oozing and covered in flies. An old woman with a cane picked through the box of the cheapest tomatoes, carefully discarding those whose skins were cracked.

"How much is this?" another woman asked gingerly about the expensive okra.

"Five pounds," Ramsi told her.

"Only because you've got a foreigner standing here!"

"I'm telling you the okra is five. Everywhere else it's six." She walked off muttering. Another women came along asking about the okra. This time Ramsi told her, "Five and a half."

"No, I don't want it," she said, and began to stroke an eggplant, thinking, calculating, and then asked about the potatoes. Ramsi told her the price; she looked away, withdrew her hand from the vegetables and left, shuffling heft and an empty string bag.

Another batch of bread. A little girl in an orange head scarf tried to inveigle her way to the front of the jostling women and jump up to the window, but the women said no, wait your turn. I had seen her come three times in the past half an hour to collect bread. She had a red welt birthmark in the middle of her forehead and her face was set to her task. She stacked the rounds on a bamboo pallet and loaded it into her arms, heavy enough, and I followed her as she wove back through the lanes. On either side was her familiar slum. The houses were, like the bakery, left over from the time when downtown was built to rival Paris. Now their balustrades were cracked, plaster had fallen to expose brick, what might have been a stone cherub was weathered into a nub, multiple families lived on every floor and roofs were given over to chickens. Now the streets of Bulaq were filled with sand dunes drifted with fragments of plastic bags and bottle tops, doorways partially buried. The girl in the orange head scarf continued her progress, darting past the ground-floor workshops soldering banging clanging and the cubbyhole shops dark as caves, skipping around the ten-year-old grease monkey balancing a tray of tea glasses, tripping over the cracked wooden chairs of a café and two old men playing dominoes on a piece of rough-hewn Formica pitted with cigarette scars.

I followed her out to the main road, squat and dark under the elevated highway that hummed above. I lost her orange head scarf for a moment among the rainbow racks of secondhand clothes. But then I saw her again. She was bending down to deliver the pallet of bread to her mother, who was sitting on a low stool in the gutter with plastic bags of *baladi* for sale in front of her. Her mother bagged the bread and sold it at a small markup to passersby who didn't want the bother of waiting in the throng at the bakery. Her husband was an invalid and this was her only income. Blue flashing lights suddenly interrupted the gloom. Like a wave, the racks of clothes turned into fluttering flags as the shop boys hurried to move them out of the street and hide them in doorways or the chinks between buildings, until the police car had passed.

For lunch I bought fried shrimp sandwiches in *baladi* bread from a food stall and went to sit in the café opposite. My sandwich was crunchy and salty, the *baladi* good, rough and chewy, gritty on the outside, with a sour taste. I sat at a rickety table on the sidewalk of the café opposite. A glass of tea arrived, green mint speared against the acrid black. The café owner sent a boy for a bottle of cold Pepsi for the foreigner.

The men at adjacent tables were eating bean sandwiches and sharing a water pipe. By and by we talked the afternoon away. Things were better now than in the spring, when there were shortages of *baladi* and everyone had waited in bakery queues for hours and the country people came into the city to buy cartloads of *baladi* because animal feed had gone up and *baladi* was cheaper to raise livestock with and Hajji Hussein rationed down to ten loaves per person . . .

"And if you have many children? How will you feed them all with only ten little round loaves?"

"Oh, we would have liked to go out and demonstrate on April 6, but you know the streets were full of police and we were afraid." They leaned their grizzled heads together toward the water pipe, better to talk quieter that way instead of broadcasting to the whole street. "We were afraid. So many people disappear, you know, you can disappear behind the sun. They can arrest you and you disappear like that." One man clicked his fingers together and made a sign of the cross. Bulaq was a mixed quarter, church next to mosque. "We're all neighbors here, we all know each other, there's no difference between us."

"Why were there shortages?" I asked. "What caused them?" The men of Bulaq harrumphed, everything rolled up in the same ball of wax.

"These prices! The corruption!" Thick ridged fingernails, callused palms, grimy tactility of hand to mouth.

"Pah! This country has been corrupt since the time of the Pharaohs."

Later in the golden hour of the late afternoon, when the baking was finished for the day, Hajji Hussein sat in a wooden chair pulled out onto the street, cigarette in one hand and a glass of tea perched on the corner of an old bookcase. The doorway was framed by a heavy lintel covered in thick black paint like bubbling tar. He was exhausted, thirty-five years of baking bread and the last two of them more demanding, more difficult, shoving, shouting.

"The hardest part is the crowds," said Hamdi, a fourteen-year-old cousin, coming in from the back oven room, wiping his floury hands on his apron. Hamdi was working during his holidays; in term time he was at technical college, doing well, his uncles proud of him. "You get angry and they get angry and it's hard to keep your temper." When it had been bad with the shortages a couple of months ago, some people filed complaints against them with the police. An accounting cousin, clean shirt and pressed olive-green trousers, came in and began to count a brick of soft mulchy five-pound notes, leaning his elbow on the empty safe. Another baker cousin, with a lumpy growth on the back of his neck and a frayed collar, pulled up a chair and we began to sort through the piastres and pounds of the shop's economics.

Each day the bakery received seventeen fifty-kilo sacks of flour at the subsidized rate of nine Egyptian pounds. They produced eighteen thousand loaves a day and sold them at the government-fixed rate of five piastres a loaf. And then the complications began.

"The production cost is basically five piastres per loaf, basically the price we have to sell it at," explained Hajji Hussein. "And costs have risen. Gas is not subsidized anymore. So we play around, but it's not a living." This was the sack of flour I had seen the stout man take. They sold a sack a day, off the books, for its market rate, ten times the subsidized rate they paid for it, to a private baker. They couldn't sell any more because demand for bread was so great and the shortfall would be noticed by the inspectors. A fine was fifteen thousand Egyptian pounds. And the bakery inspectors, Hajji Hussein said, rolling his eyes, "just want to show you who has the power; they are a bunch of ignoramuses, really unkind." Either they wanted a bribe or they were under pressure from their boss to file a certain number of complaints to make up a quota that would show that they were doing their job.

"Obviously we smuggle, it's the only way to make money."

The oven inside whistled a tune as it cooled. A woman came late to ask for bread and they tried to send her away, but then Hajji Hussein relented and went back to find five loaves to give her.

MILLING

THE SECOND TIME I WENT TO EGYPT WAS IN THE SUMMER OF
2008. I had an assignment to write a story about bread
prices. Global commodity prices had spiked in the spring
and there had been riots and demonstrations all across the world,
from Senegal to Indonesia to Mexico. In Egypt bread queues had
stretched six or seven hours long; fights broke out, and there were
reports of stabbings. In the industrial city of Mahalla the textile
workers asked for time off because there was not enough time
to stand in the lines and wait for *baladi* bread after a day's long
shift, and when the factory bosses said no, they called a strike.
Mubarak's government had been worried: they engaged military
bakeries to ease supply and the Ministry of Social Solidarity set up
special kiosks to ease distribution. On April 6 workers and their
families marched in Mahalla and the government cordoned the
town with roadblocks and sent in the police with batons and tear
gas and shotguns.

Something had happened in Egypt, or had nearly happened,
or was about to happen. Wasn't this how revolutions began? With
hungry masses and bread riots? (Ah, the delicate academic irrel-
evance of *theory!*) Mubarak put down the demonstrations. By the
summer, everything had subsumed to an apparent normal.

I spent that July trying to figure out the relationship between the global wheat trade and bread queues and civil unrest. I was accompanied by my friend Lina Attalah, who drove me around in her scratched-up Honda. Lina was a journalist, small, smart, tenacious. She was one of a triumvirate of Arab Linas I knew and loved and admired. One in Beirut, one in Damascus, and one in Cairo. They were all journalists, indomitable and single. Whenever I had to parry the question of women in the Middle East, I thought of Lina in Beirut, bringing up two daughters as a single mother, working, brilliant at her job, every telephone number you would ever need in her phone, and Lina in Damascus, who loved to wear sundresses in the Old City in the summer and had to fight her mother and every leering taxi driver just to dress the way she wanted. They shared an extraordinary strength of will and purpose just to be themselves every day in a society that would spit and hiss and whisper vulgar slanders behind their backs for wearing immodest clothes, for not being married with children, for working with men who were not their relatives. The Linas were not the only Arab women who strove against the fastness of quotidian slights and insult. Almost all the Arab women I met did this in some way or another. The women went out into the Arab Spring to shout for their freedom too.

Lina Attalah was fascinated by Sinai and spent a lot of time in the desert among the Bedu, trying to understand the tribes and smuggling and undercurrents of rebellious Islam. And it was Lina Attalah who first took me to Café Riche on a Friday. She had been working on a history of the café and its role as intellectual and political entrepôt. We walked in, and there, sitting at one of the long tables, was Dr. Hussein. I had not seen him for eight years, since my first time in Egypt, and we embraced, long lost, and celebrated coincidence. He kissed Lina hello and said, "You know Lina too!" and Lina said, "You know Dr. Hussein too!" Sometimes, often, Cairo, for all its twenty million inhabitants, felt like a friendly village.

Lina was amused at my earnest attempts to figure out the bread price story. We talked to wheat experts at the Agricultural Faculty of the University of Cairo, to the head of the Bakers Union, to traders in the warehouses at the central grain market. I wrote down figures in my notebook: tonnages, costs, markup. The Egyptian government was the largest single buyer of wheat in the world; the bread subsidy was 5 percent of the national budget. Seventy percent of the bread consumed in Egypt was subsidized *baladi* bread. In May Mubarak had announced a 30 percent pay increase for all government-sector workers. The trade minister announced that an export ban on rice would be continued for another year. I noted in my margins numbers that slipped their balance-sheet moorings: I learned that when wheat is washed before milling it absorbs water, and weight before and after can be adjusted to allow for a discrepancy that can be sold on the side; there is a difference too—did you know?—between flour milled to 82 percent extraction or the coarser 85 percent or 90 percent, and sacks were filled with half and half or rounded out with sand.

We went back to the beginning of the supply chain. Lina and I drove into the delta along narrow lanes that ran alongside irrigation canals. We sat in the Bible villages, with donkeys, palm trees and ragged children, and talked to farmers about land redistribution and fertilizer subsidies and middlemen grain buyers and this year's seed price. Last year they had planted onions, which was a risk because onions needed a lot of fertilizer, but when the harvest came the trader from town offered such a low price that they decided to store their onions to wait for a better market, but then half the crop rotted when it rained. This year they had planted rice, because the price had gone way up, but then the government banned rice exports and the price went down. The government said that instead they would pay twice the price for wheat as last year, but this announcement had come only after the fields were planted with rice. And now everyone had planted rice and there was not enough water for all the fields and the local agricultural officials were fining farmers for excess water use.

I remember one afternoon sitting on a sack of rice in a trader's warehouse, trying to understand the impact of imported wheat on the domestic market. The trader was a kindly man with a prayer callus on his forehead. Behind his desk was a portrait of his father, a grain trader before him, and next to it his certificate of candidacy for the parliament of 1953, a token left over from when Nasser had promised elections that never happened. I carefully copied columns of numbers into my notebook but I could not make them add up.

"So the traders are holding back rice supply now, because of the export ban?" I watched three flies land on a grain of rice and begin to probe with proboscis tongues. The trader gave me a quizzical expression and patiently tried to explain something I could not grasp. My brow knit. I put my two hands out, measuring a fish. I extended my index fingers for calibration and brought them close together, but their tips missed each other.

The Muslim Brotherhood MP on the movement's agricultural committee was convinced the price of food was connected to larger geopolitics. Food security: Egypt should be self-sufficient in wheat production. "We have enough land, enough water. We can clear the minefields in El Alamein and plant that area!" He was clear enough about the real problem: Egypt was run by a dictator; presidential elections were a farce. The dictator had no need to follow popular opinion but instead had allied himself with foreign interests, which were closely tied to his own personal interests. America paid the regime money so that they could have their peace with Israel, their first Gulf War, their invasion of Iraq, but then America pressured Egypt to buy American wheat and use American shipping companies to transport it. "Australian and French wheat is cheaper, and the American shipments sometimes arrive spoiled, and Americans have also been pushing Egypt to buy yellow corn recently—yellow corn? We have no use for this. Imported food has been used as a weapon against Egypt!" These were higher injustices. The Muslim Brotherhood MP leaned forward. "And why does Egypt sell its gas cheap to Israel?"

The head of the Agricultural Committee of a national business association was an NDP man, with an office on the twenty-fourth floor, well air-conditioned and hermetic with a view of the Nile. My feet slid on the delicate gray silk Persian carpet; my gilt-edged teacup rattled against the saucer. He had a polite, well-assured manner. We talked about government export subsidies and oil subsidies.

Export subsidies, he explained, were used to support things like air freight. For example, he cited the fact that EgyptAir receives about five million dollars a year.

"Above the subsidy for oil?"

"Yes, separate from that subsidy."

I wrote down "$5m."

"Which is indirect support to allow Egyptian farmers and their products to compete abroad, which otherwise would be a high cost because of the costs of energy and fuel."

"Which are already being subsidized—"

There was a knock on the door. A businessman came in carrying a briefcase and a worried expression. He was sorry for the intrusion, could he have a word? He nodded for a cup of tea, which was brought for him, and he began to explain his problem:

He had bought thirty million pounds' worth of alfalfa to export to Jordan, Kuwait, Cyprus and Dubai. This was the first time forage was being exported from Egypt. But on June 13, the Ministry of Trade, under pressure of rising meat prices, because of rising animal feed prices, had suddenly banned forage exports. Now he had twenty-three containers of forage waiting dockside in Suez. He had already paid the export tax! No—he shook his head—he didn't think he would be seeing his 180,000 Egyptian pounds again.

"When you give something to the government, you don't expect you'll get it back!" He unfolded a contract with a Cypriot trader, pointing out the penalty clause for nondelivery. He had been to see the Minister of Trade, but the minister had said, "It's a force majeure!" to be covered by insurance. The businessman held his palms heavenward in exasperation. "But it is not a tsunami or an earthquake!"

"He's not God, the minister of trade!" I put in, and we all laughed.

"Yes, Mr. Rashid is not God!" they agreed.

Opposition bloggers had created an April 6 campaign calling for national demonstrations to support the textile workers in Mahalla, but in Cairo only a few people turned out to gather on the steps of the journalists' syndicate. I interviewed Ahmed Maher, one of the founders of the campaign, in a street café downtown. He had been arrested in the early summer and held for two months and had only recently been released. They had wanted to intimidate him; they told him, "You are an insect, we are the masters." They demanded names and structures of party membership. His interrogators seemed intrigued by this new Facebook thing; who were these people who did not seem to belong to a party that could be banned? Two weeks after we met, Maher was arrested again.

Far above the noise of the street, high up in the leafy elevations of Zamalek, I sat and talked to a wealthy man who someone had told me was somehow connected. He wore a pair of jeans and a button-down shirt with brown suede loafers. I asked him what line of business he was in, but he waved away any answer. We sat in his large and comfortable reception room lined in beige silk and soft chenille, and admired the view of the green lawn tennis courts of the Gezira Sporting Club through his picture window. Again I tried to prize the tangled subsidies. The wealthy man with the soft shoes was a member of the NDP but seemed to regard himself as above politics. He told me he had tried to tell the ministers last year that global food prices were rising—now, of course, they were beginning to implement his suggestions. He opened his palm in a gesture that said: wasn't this the way of things everywhere? But he was not overly concerned; the government was doing the right thing, a little slowly, but that was to be expected. And one must remember, they were dealing with the Egyptian people and the Egyptian people were very difficult to deal with. "Everything comes from them with a political agenda. Shaking in the streets." He mentioned the bread riots of '77 with a shudder. "This is the wolf head. The ministers don't want chaos in the street." The people? He turned down the corners of his mouth with distaste; they were hostile and grasping, they no longer deferred to better judgments. There was something not right, he thought, musing on the plebeians, in their mentality. "Something has happened to them," he told me. "It's as if there are no Egyptians anymore."

The wealthy man described for me a complicated interim solution for tackling flour smuggling. Instead of five piastres a loaf, *baladi* bread would be sold at ten piastres, but they would use 82 percent extracted flour instead of the current 87.5 percent and that would squeeze the black-market millers' profits because they were now extracting at 90 percent or 92 percent . . .

"So it is the speculators, it is the traders," I said, still grappling for a villain, for a cause, for a reason.

"The people who get rich from wars, the millionaires who have not even completed their high school education," said the wealthy man mysteriously.

"Who are these people?"

He looked away from me, thinking somewhere else, casting his gaze out across the green lung of the Gezira Sporting Club to where the tower blocks began again, Cairo's sand-blown, dense tessellation.

"Now they are much more powerful than even the government. They own newspapers, even state security."

Who are they?

"Ghosts," he said quietly.

I railed against my confusion to poor Lina. "The answer is ghosts?" Lina sympathized with my frustration, but I could see she thought it was the frustration of a Westerner. When the frustration was everyday, there was little point in being actually frustrated by it. "You've worked hard, don't kill yourself about this. Let's go and get some lunch."

When I came to write my story I found it impossible to thread a thesis. I could not connect Ahmed Maher, with his brave and quiet determination, with the baker Hajji Hosseini. I had no idea how the numbers had added up to a shortage, nor what had caused it nor what had eased it again. I did not know where to put the paragraph about the doctor I met in a clinic next to a slum who described cases of anemia and childhood stuntedness and used the words *obesity* and *malnutrition* in the same sentence. I did not know how to stretch an Egyptian bread queue into a global context nor how to tie it to domestic politics. I struggled, knitted facts, made something, but could fashion no conclusion.

When I returned to Egypt during the revolution, I found Lina, not surprisingly, editor of the English version of the independent newspaper *Egypt Today*. She had a stable of young reporters under her and they were writing stories they could only have dreamed about in 2008. The door had opened a fair crack in terms of freedom of the press, and although she had her run-ins with certain interests that intersected with the owners and editors of the main paper, the English-language edition could get away with good critical reporting—sometimes even on the army.

Once a month or so Lina and I would meet for lunch to talk over scraps of quotes and gossip or Facebook proclamations by the military authorities. One hot afternoon in late August, after the summer sit-in had dissolved into Ramadan, we sat in an empty Lebanese restaurant that was open during the day because it was in a hotel.

"Do you remember that summer, driving around trying to find out the connection between wheat prices and bread queues and protest?"

Lina shook her head at me. "Don't go back to that!"

"Because there was never any answer to the question."

"You tried to find it. It didn't work."

"Yes, that was my lesson. "

"Exactly," said Lina, "the explanation was never in the numbers or the figures. The explanation was somewhere else. We have a saying in Arabic that the explanation lies in the belly of the poet." She clapped her hands. "So good luck in finding that!"

Lina told me she had known all the time that bread prices were never the real story.

"I felt the story should have been about the wit of survival, how people were forced to navigate the limitations when the limitations were so incumbent. It was the most interesting for me when we talked to families. And you would sit there and ask them how much do you make and how much is your rent and how much is cooking oil and how much do tomatoes cost and the numbers wouldn't add up. And so you would ask, 'How does this work?' and they would answer in different ways: solidarity, or someone's father gave them a little money every month. The story was in this zone, and this was even maybe the beginning of a revolution that we could not yet imagine."

I had expected to be able to draw a line between cause and effect, action and consequence. But Egypt defied objective, defied analysis. Eighty million people and eighty million versions of a story. I thought back to that summer of bread and numbers and red herrings and ghosts in the machine. Life, bread, Egypt; but no truth, no answer to the question of why and how. "In Egypt," I said to Lina, "in Egypt," I said again, on the precipice of a grand generalization, and then I stopped myself, realizing that I was extrapolating, even as I spoke, from Egypt to the whole world, as history itself had once done. And even as I articulated the rest of my sentence I was thinking to myself, *This is a bigger notion than only Egypt, this is perhaps a new theory to cleave to* (for a while at least; at least until it too dissolved like all the others into an ironically italicized *theory*) *that could explain my life and everyone else's too.* "In Egypt there is no such relationship between something that happened and the word *because*."

LET'S GO FOR A WALK

LIKED JON ARGAMAN IMMEDIATELY ON MEETING HIM ONE EVENING, at dinner with friends. Open face widened by a high domed forehead and thin blond receding hair; heavy chin balancing a big-toothed overbite; blue goggle eyes blinking behind Coke-bottle glasses. His whole personality eagerly pushed itself forward. He told me that he was a PhD student studying urban planning in Cairo. Urban planning in Cairo?

We became friends and we went for walks together. Argaman said he needed to walk to strengthen his legs because when he was a teenager he had a bad curvature of the spine and an operation to straighten out his hunchback.

"Ouch," I said sympathetically. Argaman shrugged. Each time we went for a walk he revealed a new teenage affliction—he had been badly overweight; he had worn braces, which made him lisp; he had asthma and carried an inhaler with him at all times; he was gay—and each time, he shrugged it off in the same way. At the end of several walks the full litany of sufferance of his growing-up years was revealed, and I saw, behind the mask of friendly geek, a titanium spine, literal and figurative. He helped me download movies from the internet. He knew how to unplug cookies and rearrange volume differentials.

"So you're a techno as well! How on earth did you survive high school as a fat wheezing hunchbacked metal-mouth teenager coming out of the closet?"

Argaman shrugged. "It was even worse than that. I was a mathlete."

Walking in Cairo was parkour, jumbly hopping, dodging. There were sometimes pavements and sometimes not; sidewalks slid into the road or were blocked by corrugated iron fences or by a widow selling bags of *baladi* or by a tree or a truck or a parked car or a puddle of blood from the butcher's shop, or else thronged by café chairs or a whole market that had tumbled out of an alley. Zigzag through the handcarts and pushcarts and horse carts and chugging *tuqtuqs* and *baladi* bicycle boys who slalomed through the traffic in elegant parabolas balancing long bamboo trays piled with bread on their heads. Trip curb, hexagonal paving stones, potholes, black greasy car parts laid out on a blanket, blind man's tapping cane, a pile of sheep jawbones, cat squawk, a crate of iridescent pink nectarines—eyes veering, jagging: caught on flies clustered on the strips of dirty yellow tripe hanging from hooks, or the flitting shadows of street boys hustle-running, flapping broken sandals, a tea boy with his tray of glasses aloft, dead pigeon in the gutter, an old bent woman shuffling her hands through a pile of garbage.

Cairo's streets were humped with sand as the desert blew over to reclaim its territory; sidewalks crumbled into mud verges of re-membered floodplain when it rained. The city was girded with the diesel grind of overloaded trucks circling on the ring road. Inside this loop the city was crosshatched with to-and-fro and noise: the drumming din of an iron pedestrian walkway above the highway; screeching railway cuttings that divided neighborhoods between villas and slums; rumbling bridges over the Nile; a slice of humming elevated highway that ran between canyons of dust-grimed office windows; the old aqueduct to the citadel, its gradient gently descending from cathedral to hovel niches stuffed with bales of hides from the tanning towers. The only quiet place in all the city was at the very southernmost tip of the island of Roda, a five-minute walk from Dr. Hussein's maternity hospital. The traffic petered out because there was nowhere to go, and the river was wide and muffled the noise from the cars stuck in traffic along the Corniche. There was an old abandoned palace there and you could walk around its rotting veranda and wonder at the low-slung silver surface view—water mirror to sky and thoughts—and then visit the well-preserved nineteenth-century pagoda that housed an ancient Nilometer. The vertical column ran deep and silent down, calibrated to measure the annual inundation and thereby to calculate taxes, boring down to the past.

Cairo was one of those cities that had borrowed the Soviet preference for urban highways and U-turns instead of crossroads and traffic lights. Adrien thought there might be a correlation between dictatorship and traffic police. In Cairo the traffic policemen, with white arm gaiters and whistle, were of no practical application in the teeth of the monster honking mass of traffic. Ah, the honking! It was traffic conversation and it never ceased. I could sit on my balcony at three in the morning and there would never be a quiet second without a honk. Beepity beep tootity toot. Call and response. A Cairene drove with one hand on the gearshift and the other on the horn. Some of them drove while honking a constant refrain: *I am here! I am driving! I am alive!* Hassan taught me the vernacular: beebeep, *I'm turning left,* beebeebeep *I'm right behind you and I want to push through.* Bepbep, *Hi!* Beebeebeebeeep: *You asshole!* There were nuances and variations for more complicated communications, like: *Slow down because I want to ask you directions through the window while we drive in tandem* or *What's happening up ahead?* or *I know it's after the curfew, but it doesn't matter if there are many of us on the roads because they can't arrest everyone!* Interestingly there was no honk for frustration. If a driver was really angry he would stop and get out of his car (without pulling over) and take issue directly with furious arm-swinging gesticulations. Then the other man would yell back, and, honor satisfied, each would go his separate way.

There were no pedestrian crossings in Cairo. I learned to cross the road in the local fashion, by stepping purposefully off the curb and pushing my body in front of the cars, forcing them to stop. Mostly they stopped, but even if they didn't it was important not to hesitate or to dart suddenly backward. Whatever happened, you should not show any fear, because the only thing keeping you alive was a blind faith in the invisible antimagnetic repellent force between corporeal body and metal chassis.

Walking in Cairo was not a restful experience, but every so often curiosity would rise above the level of residual trauma from the last time and Argaman and I would "go for a walk."

"Let's start from Hardee's in Tahrir, because it is the easiest place to meet." That particular afternoon, the traffic on the square was stationary.

"Which way are we going?" A man's head stuck out of a driver's-side window to talk to a crumpled face crunching sunflower seeds. The traffic was stuck, Talaat Harb was closed off, Qasr al-Aini barricaded, and instead of an anticlockwise flow around the roundabout, two lanes were pushing through clockwise. Drivers were honking and sticking their heads out of the windows and asking each other, "Which way?"

"Which way to where?"

"To where I want to get to."

"Ah. Well to get *there,* keep going."

"Straight?"

"Around!"

Argaman and I skipped through the cars and took a random route through downtown. Past Magdi, nestled scowling in his office den in the window of Café Riche; past the clean expanse of the Air France office and Groppi's, echoing vault of something half-forgotten with a scrim of Lipton yellow tea-bag tea, empty except for a few Muslim Brotherhood youth and their girlfriends trying to decide an old NDP problem: whether to split from the movement or to stay and try to reform it from inside. The statue of Talaat Harb had been measled with *NO TO MILITARY TRIALS* stickers; the bookshops were quiet and quaint, the old bars shuttered for privacy. Flotsam around these islands of nostalgia (or what Alaa Al Aswany would recognize as nostalgia: remnants of a cosmopolitan past that no one else paid much attention to) was the Perspex signage that had grown over the stone like the encrustations of a garish coral reef, smooth, plastic, multicolored, diamante shoes and sequined head scarves.

After a while we came, by chance, to the Ministry of Planning, an unremarkable block, rows of windows.

"What do they plan in the Ministry of Planning?" I asked Argaman.

"Nothing, as far as I can tell. Every five years they publish a five-year plan." Argaman spent his days making phone calls to set up meetings with civil servants. From time to time, after several weeks of unanswered calls, deliberation, cancellation, rescheduling, he managed to actually meet one. Every so often a certain kind of elision in their conversation gave him a certain kind of insight. "I think I am not the first to be fooled by the existence of the Ministry of Planning," he said. "The Germans opened a slum upgrade project in the ministry, thinking it was the center, but it turned out that everything was really handled by the Ministry of Housing." Overlapping jurisdictions and ministries. "And then there's the famous elusive Cairo City Plan." Argaman rolled his big eyes in his big head. "Apparently it does exist but I can't find anyone who will admit to having seen it."

Argaman had a theory that was one of my favorite Egypt theories for a while: Each ruler of Egypt had built a part of Cairo in the image of the future he wanted to project. Ismail Pasha built downtown as a showcase for the new modern Egypt that would open with the opening of the Suez Canal in 1869. Downtown was modeled on Paris, the greatest city in the world at the time, with boulevards that radiated from a central hub like Haussmann's starburst from the Arc de Triomphe and six-story apartment buildings decorated with concrete fruit swags and marble lintels and ascended with German-engineered electric elevators. Nasser built the district of Mohandiseen, which translates as "the City of the Engineers," for his new class of technocrats. High concrete blocks as dull and regimented as Moscow, built for the great new middle class of socialism. Sadat's open-door policy in the seventies saw five-star hotels rise along the banks of the Nile, built as fortresses of a foreigner archipelago, with rooftop swimming pools like strategic cisterns in case of a siege. Mubarak's reign saw the new satellite desert suburbs spring up, the Fifth Settlement, Sixth October, American-style gated-living developments, villas and golf courses, shopping centers strung out along the highways.

"They each built the city of the future that they wished Egypt to become," Argaman said. "But each time they built their vision, they built it anew, on a virgin plot, something totally separate from anything that had gone before." The minarets of Islamic Cairo were left to rot and crumble in the middle of an Abbasid slum. The Coptic garbage families grazed their pigs in the lee of the Mameluke aqueduct until the global swine flu epidemic, when all the pigs in Egypt were slaughtered. Downtown emptied of its polyglot denizens during Nasser when the Jews and the Greeks left and was taken over by a rash of cheap clothing stores and hostels camped in grand old apartments.

We continued to walk, past the closed-down department store heyday from the thirties, rotundas, overgrown plazas, dry fountains, broken balustrades. After grand downtown came an area of low-slung streets crowded with trucks piled with loads of over-hanging rebar or scavenged scrap metal or crates of giant cauliflowers. Alleys and lanes ran off from the roads into an interior maze, overrun with children. After this was a highway to cross (we held hands and sprinted) and a low quiet dusty brick settlement, the City of the Dead, tombs and walled enclosures, some lived in by guardian families or squatters, some locked, cupolas and orange-blossom firework trees, yellow dogs, no cars. The sun striped against the ocher walls, the dense absorptive color of egg yolk mixed with desert, and here and there were daubs of original graffiti, the naive stencils that commemorated a pilgrimage to Mecca, black-cube Kaaba, minarets, crescents and stars, or the blessing of habitation in blood handprints.

Rising ground-up toward the Moqqatam cliffs, which bristled with military encampments and spiky communications antennae, the large quiet oblong of the City of the Dead bordered dense slum. Gray concrete skeleton structures filled in with raw redbrick walls, some with timbered window frames, some without windows at all, satellite dishes like ear-shaped mushrooms sprouting from the flat roofs, washing strung between ledges and narrow juts of balcony. Dirt tracks rimed with ragged tribes of kids playing in the sand, digging holes, playing tag and bang-bang-you're-dead, gathered in an audience around a little stall selling the basic necessities: soda and chips and cigarettes.

This was the Cairo median, most of Cairo. Grown up with the population explosion of the previous twenty years, 60 percent of the city had been built off-plan on pocket handkerchief squares of farmland. You could sometimes see a stand of green wheat or a field of onions or a flock of sheep grazing on the garbage in between the housing blocks. This was the greatest irony of all, the *unplanned* city. A strange phenomenon that in a dictatorship so much of the city had been built beyond state control.

"The builders build the buildings and then the people move in," Argaman explained. "Sometimes someone comes along, usually the army, and knocks something down because it was built illegally, but most of the time they leave it. At first people steal the electricity from the pylons and hook everything up jury-rigged. But after a while the municipality seems to accept the reality and the electricity comes through and strings up proper lines and the sewage companies come and dig pipes in."

"So how do people vote?" I wondered as we walked through the redbrick alleys, meandering on the edge of somewhere around the next corner. There were going to be parliamentary elections soon, September or October or November. "If the address doesn't exist, how do people register for a constituency?" Argaman said he didn't know. A question for a Saturday afternoon, wondering about the disenfranchisement of millions of people. For a while I thought I had stumbled upon a serious issue. But a week later Argaman told me he had asked around and it turned out that people voted in the local schools according to the normal procedure. In Egypt there was always a gap of formal and informal, legal and not legally recognized, ownership and tenancy, living and living in. Somehow everything muddled through.

Later Argaman showed me a book by an urban planning academic that compared two aerial photographs of ordinary Cairene neighborhoods, one taken a hundred years ago, the other recently. Each was the same image, cubed flat roofs along the curving grids of alleys so narrow that sunlight only reached the ground at midday, mapped as veins on moth wings. An eternal pattern, almost organic, apart from any government or greater vision. Cities grow into their own physiognomy like people do, lines and curves etched with time and disposition—upturned, downslope, rough, smooth, scarred, open, guarded—into a personality. In all the cities I have lived in I can feel the architecture holding past and present and future aspirations in one street scene, history laid down like sediment, or foundations blown up and razed or shame covered up in flashing neon strip clubs. Space and shape: walk between the upthrust majesty of the Sixth Avenue steel skyscrapers in New York, through the serried lanes of old Jerusalem, where a staircase leads to a walkway roof that opens into a covered market and looks over a hanging garden that leads, spiral descent of rock-cut steps, into an ancient cistern. Puff up the mountain in Tehran in a shared taxi, cough cough blech, from smog to clearer upper air, from the poor southern suburbs of the Islamic Republic to the northern climes of Persia. Beirut: heart ripped out by civil war, tied off and surrounded by a highway and then rebuilt ersatz on landfill made from the rubble of conflict into a Gulfie shopping center.

Cairo was a city where the past was for the tourists and the orientalists. The pyramids were surrounded by the encroaching fly-ridden trash pile of Giza, village lanes full of stables for horses rented out for desert safaris; ride, if you like, up a sand trash heap of waste ground, alongside a chain-link fence through the grit whipped with fragments of windblown black plastic bags and back past the piles of festering garbage and a dying horse thrown on top, its ribs heaving, flies all around. Twisted Abbasid minarets, locked up with a giant rusted lock by order of some long-dead pasha, flagstone mosque porticos polished over centuries with barefoot footfalls and the gentle carpeted ministrations of kneeling prayer. Crenulations and wooden-grille balconies and elegant pillared courtyards—but all around and in between and piled on top, hawking carts and running-around kids and the pendulous gait of women carrying laundry loads on their heads. Get in a taxi and fly overhead on an elevated highway, look down and glimpse blurs of life in the interstices between the buildings: chicken coop, advertising hoarding, school playground, rail yard . . . and land in the newer suburbs, wide roads, large apartment houses, parking on the ground floor. Further out into the desert there were billboards illustrating future perfect: green lawns, villas, blue-water swimming pools. But the billboards were furred with blowing sand and the developments they heralded were faceless concrete shells, stuck in sandlots and surrounded by the scurf and detritus of an abandoned building project.

Cities and societies fashion a shape for themselves, as does the relationship between a government and its people. These arrangements are made up of conscious unconscious norms. Laws may be written down, avenues designed, but their implementation, their practical contours are a function of complicity—a communion of will. In all of the revolutionary welter that followed Mubarak's fall there was never an articulation, either by a political leader or by a protesting group, of a rule or an ideology or a clear template. No address, no maps. Cairenes did not perceive their city as a two-dimensional diagram: taxi drivers navigated by landmarks, the Sheraton, the Blue Mosque, the zoo, and then asked directions at many points along the route. Arrival was achieved, eventually, by consensus. Instead of manifesto and plan there was a deeply held understanding of the revolution. It was as large and simple and intricately explicit as the shape of a city. There was an accordance that there should be better, fairer governance, that there should be justice instead of corruption and general opportunity for prosperity instead of vested interests.

Argaman and I walked and talked, through the myriad streets, stumbling over the uneven ground, stopped by unexpected awe in front of some forgotten facade or cul-de-sac. Theories wound through the traffic, through the afternoons, through the convulsions on Tahrir and the implacable everyday continuing all around it. Theories wound like spools of string we used to find our way and then were snagged or cut, leaving us lost. Stop then, and sit for a moment on a broken-down chair in a café and take a swig of Coke fizz up your nose and scratch the dust from your ears and wish, like Adrien, for a moment, that you were a cat so that you could wander unconcerned and observe the follies of men from a superior plane of disinterest.

EVERY FRIDAY

EVERY FRIDAY PEOPLE RETURNED TO TAHRIR. THE FRIDAY OF DEmand, the Friday of the Popular Committees, the Friday of Cleansing, the Friday of the Martyrs. Hassan and I would go to the square after prayer time, walk and talk and bump into people. Some Fridays were quiet, some were full of knots of people debating whether there was any point in standing on the square anymore, some were riots.

Here is an extract from my notes:

> April 8th 2011.
> And so I return to my earlier theme of unpredictability. Just when it seemed the Tahrir fervor was over and the

army had taken over road mapping the country's future, just when it looked like politics were polarizing between liberals and Islamists: today was an even bigger Friday protest than last week. It was called ostensibly, the "Day of Purge" and called to demand the trials of Mubarak and other leading corrupt former regimists, but I have a feeling that many were on the square to demonstrate that they could still demonstrate.

Among the square that day was a group of army officers in uniform who had joined the protesters. I thought their presence might indicate a crack in the army, younger officers frustrated with the old generals. The field marshal, Tantawi, who was head of SCAF and de facto ruler of the country, was over seventy, yellow with rumored hepatitis, slow-footed, old guard. He had never addressed the nation, and the revolution was beginning to chafe at SCAF's Facebook declarations and the thousands of protesters in military detention.

"After all," I said to Dr. Hussein, sitting in Café Riche with the din of demo outside, "remember how Nasser came to power. He was a lieutenant colonel. The Free Officers were the young officers, angry at being let down in Palestine in 'forty-eight, fed up with their superiors."

A few hundred protesters had stayed on Tahrir overnight on April 8, for a sit-in. In the early hours the army came and beat everyone off the square, smashed down the tents and arrested two hundred or more. I went to see the aftermath the following day. The late-afternoon light fell into alternate stripes of gold and gray ash. Burned cars smoldered and set an acrid tang in the air. The ground was littered with the detritus of fighting—rubble and cartridge casings—and the square was full of angry young men, slum kids, skinny toughs, bruised, defiant, hands clenched in fists, kicking at the rubble. There were no police or soldiers to be seen. A stuffed military uniform was paraded around the square on a stick and I heard anti-SCAF chanting for the first time. In the middle of the dusty traffic circle, among the rags of torn tents, I found a blond woman weeping. She had a small photograph in her hands, the headshot of a man in military uniform, and she was holding it out, imploring someone to help her. The photograph was of her fiancé, a first lieutenant in the special forces who had been on the square the day before. The military police had come to his parents' home at midnight and taken him away. "His father is a retired officer, they put a gun to his head when he tried to stop them. They dragged him away like a criminal."

A couple of days later I saw the army clear the square again, this time in daylight, chasing the lingering clots of skinny, tough kids away and removing the burned cars. Hassan and I watched the cleaning crews sweep up all the trash, and soldiers plant the central traffic circle with bright green grass turf. Then a ring of military police cordoned the new lawn and didn't let anyone step on it. "Red line," I said to Hassan, looking at the red berets of the military police. "Regimes fear most the precedents they themselves have set."

In May a group of Salafi thugs burned two churches in Imbaba, the neighborhood across the river from my apartment, and a second Day of Rage was called to protest against SCAF and military trials, but the crowds on the square were almost celebratory and the afternoon passed with no trouble.

In June Hassan and I were out one evening with friends when it came over Twitter that there was fighting on Tahrir. A friend of Hassan's drove us straight there and we parked in the lee of Mo-

gamma on the far side of the tear gas. Hassan's friend put a cassette of funk music into the stereo and we stood there listening to Marvin Gaye and watching the kids running and hurling rocks and pulling their choking friends out of the gas. A man standing behind us accused me of being a spy. After some time we managed to convince him that I was not and it was funny because the next day we bumped into him on the square again and he greeted me like a long-lost friend.

The violence had been triggered by an awkward incident at a memorial service at the Balloon Theatre on the Giza Corniche when some kind of altercation occurred between police and a martyr's family. The rocks and tear gas continued for a couple of days and then everyone decided to have a summer sit-in. The sit-in went on for a month. Hassan and I used to go at around midnight when the summer heat had relented and the crowds were at their peak. There was a list of thirteen demands and a sprawling tent city served by hundreds of street vendors—tea and Turkish coffee brewed on the spot, popcorn, roast sweet potatoes, sour tamarind juice and fried liver sandwiches, flags and T-shirts and plastic Tutankhamens and SpongeBob SquarePants cuddly toys, sunglasses, postcards of great figures like Nasser and Um Kalthoum and Saddam Hussein; I remember a bookseller with a stall of self-help books and noted titles: *The Pathway to Excellence, Team Work, Self-Confidence as Power.* People came with their families, and the children had their faces painted with the Egyptian flag and they took a tour or stopped to watch the open-air cinema set up next to the Arab League where they showed footage from the eighteen days. There were Syrian and Libyan and Yemeni and Bahraini flags for solidarity with Arab

Spring battles not yet won, and flags of the old royal Egypt and Hamas and Palestine too. The Freedom Motel tent went up again, next to a tent of Salafis who were very friendly. The graffiti guys came and painted anti-SCAF messages all over the Mogamma facade. When one general appeared on TV and told the people to go home and calm down and shook his finger like a stern headmaster, they painted his cartoon with a big military cap and a big pink wagging finger. But the summer sit-in carnival had withered by the start of Ramadan and then the army went in again in the middle of the night and cleared lingering protesters with batons.

In August protesters marched to the Ministry of Defense. They were met with birdshot and thugs and local gangs in the neighborhood of Abbaseya, even before they made it anywhere near the military compound.

In September there were protests outside the Israeli embassy after several Egyptian soldiers were shot by Israeli forces in a confused

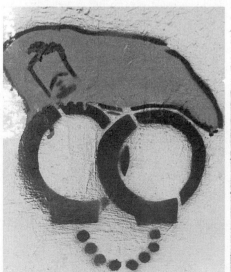

incident on the Sinai border.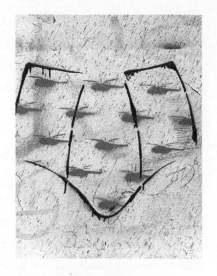
The Big Pharaoh and I went
to see the commotion at midnight. Protesters had already
broken into the embassy office
suite on the thirteenth floor,
and the sky was full of fluttering paper documents thrown
out of the windows. There were
scuffles with the black-clad
State Security police, burning
bushes in the adjacent Cairo
zoo. The Big Pharaoh and I left uneasy about it all, wondering why
a line of armored personnel carriers stationed on the Corniche
were doing nothing. I remember, after the lights were smashed,
how dark the night was as the Big Pharaoh and I walked away
across the empty University Bridge, as a long rumbling column of
armored personnel carriers drove toward us.

MASPERO

I N OCTOBER I WENT TO PICK UP MY JOURNALIST ACCREDITATION AT
Maspero. The Maspero building housed the Egyptian state
media. It was designed in the sixties, a circle stabbed with
a square tower. Forty thousand people worked inside Maspero:
several TV stations, cable channels, radio (where Hassan's father
worked) and the minister of information. Adrien said that after
traffic police the giveaway of dictatorship was a Ministry of Information. Apart from the American embassy, Maspero was the
most visibly defended building in Cairo. Even in the age of social
networks and a thousand satellite TV channels, the instrument of
state mass media remained as powerful a totem as it was in 1952

when the Free Officers took over the airwaves and proclaimed Communiqué Number 1. Even before protests gathered at its rim, during the eighteen days, the army had built a tall barbed-wire wall around its base. The ground-floor windows were boarded up; steel mesh was fixed to lower balconies; the side roads were garrisoned with soldiers.

Inside, Maspero was like an ashtray, gray dust and gloom, the sense of something crushed. Blank computer screens, partitioned walls; overhead fluorescent lights flickered with the carcasses of flies and cast a dull greenish glare. It did not change, not after Mubarak fell, not after Morsi became president either. Machine gunners were stationed on the first-floor balconies. I used to feel sorry for the poor guy, heavy and hot in full battle fatigues in the summer interior fug, bored, leaning on the gun barrel that was fixed to a tripod, pushing his helmet back from his sweaty forehead, cadging a cup of tea or a cigarette from the secretaries.

"I'm afraid Mr. Islam is working in another department."

"And when is he coming back to this office?"

"Tomorrow maybe. I cannot say exactly. Because of the troubles." An arm swept to indicate the machine gunner, on this occasion standing in the window with his feet apart, alert to the chanting outside. "The man who was supposed to bring the new plastic ID cards has not been here for a week or more. His brother had an accident. It is a matter of fate."

"Should I come back tomorrow?"

"If you want."

In the foyer, a group of desultory employees stood peering out through the grimy window at the demonstration ten feet away on the other side of the barbed wire. The chanting ramped up, louder and more forceful.

"Are they ever going to shut up?"

"They're paid to stand there and shout lies at us!"

"Who knows if they are paid to shout or paid to shut up?"

"Look at them! They're all sixteen-year-old kids. Look at the one who is leading them. He's a thug. Don't these kids see that we are their brothers? That we are all Egyptians?"

"This isn't a coffee shop to stand here and watch the show. Pull the shutter down!"

"And who are you to give the orders? Who is boss around here?"

"Close it!" the man repeated. Perhaps he was a little more frightened than the others, because he said insistently, "I'm not kidding," and reached over and pulled the shutter halfway. The others ignored him and bent over a little to continue watching the crowd underneath it.

"How can you stand this? Did you get caught up in it yesterday?"

"No, it wasn't bad, it was just some kids from Bulaq."

"Aren't they going to shut up?"

"It was like that yesterday and the day before yesterday."

In October I was working on a profile of Alaa Al Aswany. Hassan and I went to absorb the atmosphere of forgotten nostalgia in a hole-in-the-wall bar around the corner from the Yacoubian Building. It was barricaded from the street, and against time it seemed. The windows were boarded up for discretion, the walls stained the faded nicotine yellow of old newspapers. Four tables, shelves of  green bottled beer, a half-empty bottle of Johnnie Walker, *arak*, no ice. It was early evening. A man sat beside the bar, half snoring, flubbing his lower lip against gray stubble, legs stretched out, napping. When he woke, he put his hand over his face before opening his eyes, before he could bring himself to reenter the world again. The only other patrons were two men who sat at different tables but had begun a conversation about how making *hajj* was such a rip-off these days.

One of the men was better dressed than the other. He wore a pressed blue shirt and was cleanly shaved around a rakishly well-combed mustache. He winked in our direction with a lascivious twinkle.

"I like to drink!" he announced by way of introduction. "I don't know why." He began to tell a story that turned out to be long. He concluded it with the line "and everyone knows you shouldn't bring a Koran into a bar!"

"Do you know Alaa Al Aswany?" I asked.

"Yes, I know him. He used to sit right over there." The lascivious mustache pointed to a corner table with the neck of his beer bottle. "He had a big mouth and curly hair and wore flip-flops." He made a sneering sound like a screeching wind-up toy, so I asked him: "You didn't like how he described downtown in his book?"

"He didn't live it. I live it every day. He just wrote about it. It's not the same."

He looked into the depths of his green glass, and in the pause came a bang as a young man suddenly burst in from the street, rushing with news.

"There are tanks at Maspero!"

Hassan and I looked at each other. We were tired; we had planned to have a drink and then call it a day. But without saying anything we put money on the table and left, walking quickly. It was the going-home rush hour, traffic-jammed cars and in between them young men running to a halt to catch their breath, breathing hard, waving their hands at people who were walking toward the bus station on the Corniche next to Maspero. No, not that way, go back, it's dangerous! Tanks! The army is shooting!

I retied my shoelaces. Hassan held my hand as we ran through the highway traffic, dodging veering taxies around the looping access roads that embraced the bus station. Jogging through the underpass, up steps, stumbling over broken paving stones. People were sheltering behind pillars or standing on low walls craning for a better view. The kids held their heads cocked toward the trouble, venturing forward one at a time, curb to corner.

"Let's get up on the bridge for a better view," I said. But the protesters were suddenly running back now, smashing into us.

"Here!" Hassan jumped onto a bus and hauled me in after him. The bus was full of people and closed its doors and trundled unconcernedly up the bridge, diesel heaving. We pressed ourselves against the grimy doors to see. Protesters were running away from Maspero along the Corniche, taking cover around the corner of the Hilton. The bus hauled, lurching stop-start, bumper to bumper. Hassan banged on the door for the driver to let us out.

The Corniche in front of Maspero was full of black State Security, police in riot gear, army, plainclothes; clumps and groups, some standing, idling their truncheons, some walking backward, walkie-talkie in hand. A platoon of soldiers in camouflage fatigues lined up on the narrow central reservation. Two or three cars were burning already; elsewhere patches of flame glowed bright orange in the dusk. Molotov cocktails arced flares that crossed over white trails of tear gas and crosshatched with the zooming red tracer. We stood at the top of the road ramp and watched protesters throwing stones down at the shapes of uniforms. I could hear the sizzle of Tasers, cracking gunfire. A couple of protesters led a vanguard down the road ramp to throw stones closer. Figures wearing the same jeans and T-shirts of the protesters emerged from the military throng on the Corniche

and darted forward, picking up rocks from the road and throwing them back. Behind them came the police, slowly advancing.
Hassan and I moved back a few meters, checking behind us for
our exit route. Then the police were charging and we were running back across the bridge all the way to the Zamalek side.

The protesters on the bridge scattered and the police pulled
back to the road ramp. After a few minutes, panting, catching
their breath, the protesters regrouped and crept forward, raising
their fists, taunting the police. Hassan and I followed them back
across the bridge. Everywhere below us, along the Corniche, in the
plaza in front of the Hilton, underneath the access ramps, around
the pillars of the bus station, was chaos. People were running or
fighting or standing, some collapsed, others hauling wounded
friends, motorbikes veering across the sidewalks. We leaned over
the railing and saw a blue police van, its doors open and flapping
like hinged wings, accelerate wildly into the confused and milling
mass of people, then reverse, and ram again.

"Let's go," I said. "I'm scared."

"Yes."

And we ran all the way back across the river and all the way
to Tewfik House. Nora opened the door with a big hug, David

gave us a couple of beers and we
all stood on the balcony watching
Maspero on the other side of the
river. We could make out only the
flashing lights and hear wailing
sirens. Zoo craned up to see. "Are
the police being bad again?" Nora
nodded. We scrolled furiously
through Twitter for news. Soldiers
had invaded the studio of a satellite TV channel live on air and cut
their broadcast. State TV was call-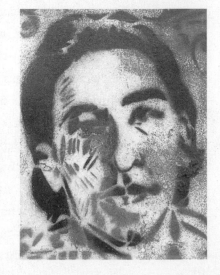

ing for "honorable citizens" to defend Maspero against thugs with guns. The Coptic Hospital was under attack by a mob. Profile pictures turned black. The activist Mina Daniel was dead.

Twenty-four people were killed that night at Maspero. Almost all Coptic Christians. It had been a Coptic march to protest a dispute in Upper Egypt about the building of a church, and to press, in these uncertain times, when the Islamists were emerging as a political force, SCAF to protect Christians throughout Egypt. "The Copts are freaked," said the Big Pharaoh. He had been in the march and when the shooting started he asked a female protester he knew who wore a *hijab* to walk with him as camouflage. Agit thugs were hunting the crowd for protesters with *Christian* on their ID cards or crosses tattooed on their wrists.

The next morning at the Coptic Hospital Hassan and I watched the coffins arrive stacked up on the back of a truck. The crowd wailed and held up pictures of the martyrs. In corners kids were squatting and sobbing into their bloodstained T-shirts. A dispute broke out about whether to take the bodies to the morgue or to release them for autopsy. The police wouldn't let us upstairs to the wards to interview the wounded. A doctor pulled us aside at the bottom of the stairs and told us that State Security officers were roaming the halls, barring access, especially to TV cameras.

In the days that followed there was a lot of confusion about what had happened.

The march had come under attack by thugs even before it reached Maspero. Shots were fired, but by whom? Police State Security army agent provocateurs thugs on the Interior Ministry payroll local shopkeepers defending their property "honorable citizens." There was footage of military armored personnel carriers running over people in the crowd. The army said that protesters had stolen the armored personnel carriers and run amok.

Z

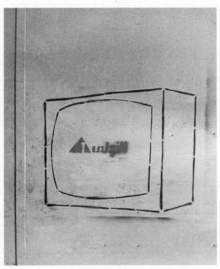

THE PROLOGUE TO THIS 1969 MOVIE READS:

> *Any similarities to real persons or events is not coincidental.*
> *It is intentional.*

Z is set in an anonymous European city as it tips toward a military dictatorship. The director, Costa-Gavras is a Greek filmmaker who made French films. Z won an Oscar, absurdly ironically, as the Algerian entry for best foreign film. It is probably the best political thriller ever made.

The leftists stage a meeting. They are worried about a confrontation. "It will mean agitators, baton-wielding cops, injured," says one with a familiar dismay. Outside the hall where the leader is giving a speech, the square is crowded with an angry mob yelling against them. A line of police stand to the side and do nothing when scuffles break out. When the leader finishes his speech and walks out onto the street the crowd shouts at him and then falls silent for a moment, stilled by his authority and his presence. From nowhere a three-wheeled delivery van appears, driving wildly, gunning for the leftist leader. A man in the back of the van reaches out and bludgeons him with a baton. He dies the next day.

It all happens very fast. Afterward, the chief prosecutor and the police want a speedy investigation to conclude it was a traffic accident, but the investigating magistrate begins to unravel the plot. His investigation is sabotaged at every turn, by false witnesses and fake alibis, collusion, lost evidence, character assassinations, allegations of doctored photographs. Slowly, despite all the obfuscation, the magistrate pieces together certain connections. The chief of police held sway over the men in the three-wheeled van because he issued their work permits and he is linked to a right-wing group of petty merchants used by the police to break up demonstrations. The driver of a VW Beetle that arrived on the scene suspiciously soon after the incident turns out to have been the personal chauffeur of the chief of security.

The colonels have gold stars on their shoulders and military caps with gold-braided rims and wear sunglasses. Their boots clip smartly on stone-lined corridors and the soundtrack echoes drumbeat, heartbeat, and jangles a tattoo that sounds like sticks on metal railings. The investigating magistrate is warned off. He is told the case is a matter of national security, that public trust in the police and the judiciary must be maintained; his own career, he is reminded, hangs on his discretion. But the dogged investigating magistrate will not be deterred. The decorated colonels and generals splutter their indignation and declare they will commit suicide (none does) if they are dishonored by indictment. They look preposterous without their power. The hero investigating magistrate remains firm. Four senior officers are charged with murder.

The leftists are overjoyed. There will be elections! The extremists will be toppled!

Nothing of the sort happens. The epilogue makes that clear. The generals engineer a coup; parliament is dissolved. The investigating magistrate is dismissed. The witnesses in the case die one after another of suicide or heart attacks, in car accidents, by falling out of a seventh-floor prison window or suffering a seizure while being transported between prisons. The leftists and journalists are arrested and deported.

All of the story is true. The Greek leftist MP Grigoris Lambrakis was killed by a thug wielding a club from a three-wheeled delivery van after he had delivered an antiwar speech in 1963. Scheduled elections in 1967 were preempted by a military coup and the "Rule of the Colonels" lasted until 1974. The magistrate who had indicted police and security officers as part of a plot to kill Lambrakis was indeed dismissed from his job and then imprisoned. The composer who wrote the score to Costa-Gavras's film was placed under house arrest. Z was the graffito that appeared all over Athens. It means "He lives."

ON THUGS

KAMAL DROVE A TAXI THAT HE RENTED BY THE DAY FROM A FAT
Salafi neighbor who owned three taxis. That's how Hassan
met him. Kamal picked him up the night of the Abbaseya
fighting in August and drove him to downtown through clever
back ways, avoiding the barricades. Hassan was so impressed that
he took his mobile number and whenever we needed a driver we
called him. Kamal lived in Shubra, one of the higgledy working-
class neighborhoods along the river. It was a neighborhood of clans
and boys on motorbikes. Kamal was the youngest son of a family
of many brothers—"We are big around here," was how he put it.
His eldest brother was a one-eyed graybeard known as "the Fixer."

Their house was situated on a lane just wide enough for a car to scrape its wing mirrors through. Four nephews, eeny meeny miney mo, all with the same round baby-ox eyes, came out to greet us. The littlest was Salah; like Kamal, everyone doted on and indulged him. His older seven-year-old brother hoisted him over the lintel and up onto his hip and solemnly introduced him. Salah waved his little fist and received us as a smiling prince. The Fixer stood on the balcony above like a general on a battlement and gave a wave-salute. Four brothers and their families shared this house, two stories off an open-air staircase that went up, without any guardrail, to the roof. The roof sloped over a ruined wall and a waddle of ducks picked their way over the litter of cast-away metal pipes and broken wooden things. "We don't eat the eggs," said Kamal, "but I like duck very much."

The house had been built in the time of his grandfather. Its lopsided facade was painted Roman terra-cotta and decorated with suras from the Koran and "Yes to Mubarak!" slogans. Kamal smiled a little ruefully; it was like Eid lanterns left up long after the holiday. During the eighteen days he had joined the pro-Mubaraks marching to Tahrir, but when he saw the men on the camels attack the crowd he changed sides. "The regime was revealed to us. Brother to brother, this was not right." This was all he ever offered of his political views. Kamal had two strong arms and was not much given to pontification or introspection.

Kamal was a taxi driver; he was also *baltagea*. "Do you want to see my gun?" A neighbor had made it for him, Kamal said, smiling shyly, "in a hidden way." He brought it out and held it out for me to hold. A heavy toy, fashioned from a solid wooden handle riveted to a short length of shotgun barrel. The trigger guard was welded with fat caterpillar joints. It looked a little like a piece of plumbing. "It's like a devil in my hands," Kamal commented, but as usual he would not be drawn except to say that he helped people who were on the right side of justice. The revolution had not made much difference to his family or his tight-knit neighborhood. "The police disappeared, but we can take care of things," was all he would say. One of his brothers told us the local police station had been recently attacked by a drug gang who wanted to free their leaders. Kamal snickered, "The government doesn't touch us much."

On the ground floor of their family house there were two rooms; stooped ceilings, dirt-tamped floors laid with patches of linoleum. One was a soot-dark kitchen where Kamal's mother made us supper, the other was smaller and lined with bedding wadded up against the walls. Kamal slept on a mezzanine shelf. We sat on a bench lumped with horsehair cushions around a small table laid with a plastic tablecloth, thimble glasses and spoons and ate chicken and rice and *molokhia* and *foul*. It was all delicious. Afterward Kamal and a brother brought some chairs outside and we sat in the lane and drank tea.

The next-door women came out in a cluster carrying babes in arms and clucking to say hello. The neighborhood men came by, sitting two or three on the back of revving motorbikes. They liked to skid to a stop for effect and they cradled their mobile phones, hip to hand, like gunslingers. Several of them had Tasers. This was the cool new street accessory. "You plug it in and it takes the electricity and makes the electricity," explained Kamal.

Brothers, neighbors, childhood can-kicking friends: it was a friendly and familiar cocoon. Kamal, handsome, young and strong, held himself among them with the confidence of a favorite son. He slapped his palms together: "What I want is to get married and to own my own car," he said, and took out a small pink album and proudly showed me the engagement portraits of his fiancée. Hassan looked away politely, because her shoulders were uncovered in the pictures and it would have been unseemly for him to admire another man's fiancée. She was sixteen with a dimpled smile, a plump girl trussed into a red sparkly ball dress with red fishnet gloves and henna tattoos drawn around her arms. Her face was heavily made up with purple eye shadow, her hair striped blond, sprayed with glitter and lacquered so that it framed her face with carefully coiled pin curls. "We went to a professional studio," said Kamal, boasting. "Ah, look, here's her younger brother!" A tubby twelve-year-old came forward and hovered at his elbow. Kamal laughed at his chaperone. "I call him Radar," he said, "because he always finds me."

When we had drunk our tea we went around the corner to a kind of clubhouse where they had set up a boom box and an old pool table in an empty lot with a tarpaulin roof. The nephews and the motorbike friends all piled in; Kamal hospitably insisted on buying us bottles of Coke and sent Radar to fetch some. Two boys were playing Premier League Football on a dusty terminal, thumbs toggling, legs swinging clear off the floor.

"Have you been to a real neighborhood wedding?" Kamal asked. I shook my head. "Oh, it's really something!" He showed me video on his mobile. A bareheaded, bare-bellied woman was dancing, undulating, ululating, swinging her long hair in circles like a dervish. He promised to take us along when there was next a wedding—and he had many cousins, so there was often a wedding. A couple of weeks later he called Hassan and told him we were invited.

The party was held in the open air of an alley cul-de-sac. Colored lights had been strung up along the walls, and a few tables were laid out with platters of kebab and cans of Stella beer. The festivities were divided between men at one end and women at the other. The bride wore a giant white satin puff-ball strapless gown over a white long-sleeved turtleneck; her hair was carefully wrapped under a jeweled turban. The groom was skinny and slight and could not have been more than seventeen years old, a sliver of new blue suit amid a voluptuary of female relations, padded in layers of silver and purple taffeta. A DJ was set up on a platform with two drummers. The noise was unbelievably loud and smashed all conversation into shouted fragments. The women danced inside clapping circles, hip sway, shoulder dip, laughing at their half-remembered younger selves, throwing their toddler daughters into the air and catching them again so that their ruffled party dresses made little parachutes. The young men stood at the other end, smoking, drinking beer, passing a joint between them, and watched this display while pretending not to. Kamal pulled out his homemade gun and fired two shots in the air for celebration. Banging thudding beat, fireworks cracking. Hassan put his hands over his ears and complained, "What's wrong with Egyptians and their sense of *volume*?" Every so often the music halted and a portly uncle took the microphone and announced a generous cash donation to the couple, and then he would throw wads of small-denomination notes from the stage so that the little kids ran about to retrieve them. Sitting on an oil drum next to me was a man with a huge scimitar scar that curved from his temple to the corner of his mouth. It was such an extraordinarily perfect cartoon scar, even down to the dots of scar stitches on either side, that I found it hard not to stare. The women whipped their dancing faster, raucous stamping, and Kamal and his friends poured lighter fluid on the ground and lit it into a smoky bonfire and jumped over the flames, egging each other on, cavemen against firelit shadows.

But that first afternoon hanging out in Shubra we played pool and shot the breeze some more and then—I am not sure why—Kamal took us to the mosque. It was evening prayer time and green neon lights lit up the minaret like a birthday-cake candle. I waited outside during the protestations and pulled my scarf over my head. When the prayers were finished Kamal led us inside to the office of the imam. He was an emaciated man with wide-spaced eyes, a desert ascetic cowled in a white linen robe with a frizzy black beard that fell in two points to his breastbone. I touched my hand to my heart in greeting. He called for tea to be brought and asked me what my religion was. I said I was a Christian. The imam nodded his accession. There were many Christians in Shubra; Christians were permitted as people of the book.

"Do you believe that Jesus was a prophet or that he was the son of God?" he asked me, carefully looking over my left shoulder, so as not to look a woman directly in the eye.

I demurred. This was a conversation I was used to having with imams with long beards; it never came to any satisfaction. I tried to deflect him by asking what direction Egypt should take now.

"The country should follow the right way, the *sharia*."

"But what about those, Christians and Muslim, who don't agree with this idea?"

The imam's certitude was masked with beatitude. He answered:

"These are the people who don't know Islam or don't understand it. Christians will be happier under Islam, as they were in the ages of the caliphs."

I frowned at this formula. It denied the validity of another view and was wrapped up in an old shibboleth, hankering for the past glories of Arab civilization. The Andalus argument, left over from when the Arabs ruled Spain. The imam saw my frown and misinterpreted it.

"Are you worried about having to wear the head scarf?" he asked me in a tone of avuncular admonishment. Ah, the head scarf. A whole religion reduced to a flag.

"I have worn the *hijab*," I told him. "In Iran I was forced to by the government, in Iraq I wore it as a disguise from kidnappers. I am wearing it now out of respect. I don't care about having to wear a head scarf," I told him. "The future of Egypt is not about a head scarf, it is about how a government makes laws. What laws will govern Egyptians? God's laws or man's laws?"

The imam began to describe the greater efficacy of God's laws.

"And what should happen to the adulterer?" he asked rhetorically. I tried my best not to roll my eyes. Head scarves and sex.

(What Hassan and I would come to call the alcohol and bikini conversation.) Why were debates with Salafis always chained to these two hooks? Neither was one of the five pillars of the Islamic faith. Their emphasis had reduced all dogma into shorthand for the things that separated our societies into East and West, in fundamentalist eyes, into morality and a licentiousness that we called freedom.

I did not answer him. He persisted: "What happens to the adulterer in Christianity?" The twin forks of his beard twitched with conviction and indignation.

"Prayer, atonement, forgiveness," I offered. The imam shook his head.

"The woman should be buried in a pit in the earth and then stoned. And when this happens there is practically no adultery in society."

"But what about those who do not believe in these precepts?" I countered.

His response discounted all dialogue and negotiation: "They must be forced."

The imam stopped talking. He had come to the conclusion that I was not worth it. Foreign, woman, infidel, whore. *Yes, all of these things*, I thought, and bristled at his condescension. His cheeks unpuffed their volume of air and fell slack and wrinkled. While we had been talking the Fixer had arrived, and now he stepped forward. He had come to the mosque, it transpired, as a neutral space in which to find a solution for a difficult incident.

The story was a little confused, but it began with a slap. A man had slapped his five-year-old nephew in the street. His brother, the boy's father, had remonstrated and a fight had ensued. This was how the Fixer explained it to the imam: his brother had tried to restrain the man and the man was injured and bleeding from his head. But then when the brother went to visit him to apologize and make amends, he was beaten for his trouble.

Angry at this insult, Kamal and several other brothers had gone to beat the offending family back. Now the offended family wanted compensation.

The imam held out his hands and murmured something in prayer and then made his excuses and removed himself from the room and the judgment. The rest of us, Kamal and the Fixer and other brothers, went next door to a café, where the discussion about what to do was reconvened. The nephew's father wanted to pay the compensation and have the bad blood over with. But the Fixer was against this, especially as Kamal had now been charged with attempted murder and an arrest warrant had been issued. The nephew's father and the Fixer argued furiously, fingers jabbing. Another brother stood by with his arm in a sling.

"What do you think about what the imam said?" I asked Kamal, turning away from the argument.

"It is my religion," he replied automatically, "so I agree with it."

A skinny kid in a red shirt on a red moped went past. Hassan went out and flagged him down and bought some dope from him for his Syrian roommate, who was from Homs and depressed.

TREES GROW

ALONG THE ZAMALEK CORNICHE, IN FRONT OF TEWFIK HOUSE, IS a row of ficus trees. They must be thirty years old or so, saplings when Mubarak came to power. Cairenes favor ficus trees, maybe because their leaves are glossy enough so that the dust slips off easily, maybe because their branches grow thick like a hedge and can be shaped with topiary haircuts. Each tree was planted within a cylindrical metal cage to support it against the wind. The ficus trees grew slowly year by year, putting on wood, fattening millimeter by millimeter, until they had filled out the circumference of their metal supports. But no one came to remove the supports and the trees kept growing so that the iron bands cut into their bulking bark as if cinching a waist and their trunks began to bulge. The trees continued to grow despite their restrictions, growing around the rebar struts so that the metal was now enveloped with wood. Wood stronger than metal over time. In some places, I noticed, lower branches had pushed the upright iron bars so far back that they opened like the petals of a flower.

NOVEMBER DECEMBER JANUARY

N NOVEMBER SCAF SUDDENLY ISSUED A CONSTITUTIONAL PROCLAMA-
tion.

The constitutional process was a balloon animal. Full of
air, twisted into a sausage-dog shape, it made a screeching whining noise when rubbed. When Mubarak fell the constitution was
suspended. But the emergency law that had for thirty years superseded it remained in place. Then, in March 2011, there was
a referendum to ratify several constitutional amendments. The
Constitutional Court never decided whether amendments to a
suspended constitution were constitutional. Still, the amendments provided a vague transitional road map. There were to be
parliamentary elections. The parliament would then choose a constitutional assembly. How this committee was to be chosen and
according to what criteria was never made clear, and when the
time came, the process was negotiated behind closed doors. The
constitutional assembly would then write a new constitution. How
this was to be ratified and by whom was never made clear either.
Then there would be a presidential election. None of these steps
were timetabled. No politician or party ever discussed publicly

what their constitutional policies were and there was never any national debate about constitutional issues, for example whether a parliamentary or a presidential system would be preferable.

New rules were grafted onto precedent—what had always happened in the past—and this made a hobbled creature, lacerated with lawsuits and bandaged with spur-of-the-moment compromises.

Parliamentary elections were to begin at the end of November. Nora was campaigning for the new Adl Party, which was trying to encompass young Islamists and revolutionaries. Dr. Hussein was running around trying to register paperwork for Egyptian Social Democrat candidates. The Muslim Brotherhood, still the only political party with a national network, smelled imminent victory. If they won a majority in parliament they would be in a position to control the process of choosing the constitutional committee and therefore the drafting of a new constitution. SCAF issued a constitutional declaration to preempt an Islamist one.

Everyone went back to Tahrir. This time not a summer carnival sit-in but a winter one, angry and defiant. The police tried to clear the protesters from the square in running barrages of bird shot and batons and tear gas, but each time, the protesters beat them back. The front line coalesced by the Hardee's corner of Mohammed Mahmoud Street. Tahrir was so full that volunteers made lanes through the crowd out of string to let the motorcycle-ambulances whiz back and forth ferrying the wounded from the front line. Further up Mohammed Mahmoud Street, at the tax office crossroads, black-uniformed State Security police stood in a line with their shotguns. This was the First Battle of Mohammed Mahmoud, a battle of bird shot, of the blinded. Of the eye-patch revolutionary Ahmed Harara, who had lost one eye to police bird shot on the Day of Rage and now lost the other in the same way. Ahmed Harara went on TV with two silver eye patches that crossed over his forehead, each inscribed with the date of his blinding, and spoke with great humility and fortitude. One of the generals went on TV and declared, irritated, "Egypt is not Tahrir Square. We will not relinquish power because of a slogan-chanting crowd." Everyone on Tahrir thought this was the second revolution. The people against the army.

I t came over Twitter that my friend Jehane Noujaim had been arrested filming in the demonstration. I tried to call Karim, her second-in-command, but he had no news. They didn't know where she had been taken. He was worried. He said he had to go, there was another call . . .

I had met Jehane a couple of months after Mubarak's fall. We happened to leave a party at the same time and walked together, talking, along the Zamalek Corniche. Jehane was a filmmaker, half Egyptian, half American, black voluminous hair and Cleopatra eyes. This was her country and her revolution and I could see she felt the weight of documentary responsibility. She worked at all hours all the time, hundreds of hours of tape, surrounded by a crew of friends, cameramen and collaborators. Dr. Hussein and I used to laugh at the fact that she always came to his balcony parties very late—even by Egyptian standards (two A.M.)—and always with a posse. She and I commiserated about the exhausting and overwhelming, relentless news cycle. "It's a washing machine!" said Jehane. We shared our confusion, and I felt better that I wasn't the only one to admit it.

Jehane had been separated from her crew in a cloud of tear gas in Mohammed Mahmoud and ended up across the police lines. She was coughing and blinded. At first the soldiers helped her but then an officer appeared, seized her camera and smashed the eyepiece. She was bundled into the back of a blue police van and they took her mobile phone away. It took until the next morning for Ragia Omran to find her held in military detention. Jehane was okay, not beaten, charged with throwing Molotov cocktails and released, case pending. I went to see her a couple of days later.

I found her sanguine about the arrest and consumed with the task of editing. She was living with her crew in a grand old building downtown; the lift juddered and the doors opened a foot below the floor level. They had rented a neglected penthouse with plaster bas reliefs of hunting scenes on the walls. In the corners of the entrance hall there were camp beds set up with rolled-up sleeping bags.

Jehane went from room to room, relaying with editors and audio engineers, hunting for adapters and leads, coordinating phone calls and Skype sessions. Her hair fell over her face; there were gray rings under her eyes and brown coffee-stain rings on the table. "It's chaos," she said, apologizing. Karim came loping in from the street, face caked in ghostly white flour-water used as an antidote to the tear gas, shaking his head. Yeah, it was still going on.

"We're trying to get a cut ready for Sundance," said Jehane.

The deadline was in a week.

Jehane disappeared into an editing suite with blacked-out curtains. Have another cigarette, another cup of tea. Jehane's parents arrived near midnight and we waited together a little longer. Jehane appeared again, running her hands through her hair, pulling it up into a ponytail.

"Okay, finally! I'm sorry, guys. We had to overdub the new ending."

So we settled into the black vinyl sofa and watched the gathered-so-far sum of the revolution. The camera jumped over protesters running, focus tumbled. Urgent voices, cracking outrage, cracking ricochets; marches, chanting, forests of placards and fists, another sit-in, more tents, again marching, chanting and white trails of tear gas arcing overhead.

"What do you think?" Jehane sat back, twirling in her office chair. It was late now. The film had unspooled its reel over the last year, a continuous white noise of protest.

"We have no idea what the story is," I said. "But we can't know, because we're still in the middle of it."

CIRCLE OF DECEIT

VOLKER SCHLÖNDORFF'S FILM *THE TIN DRUM* WON THE OSCAR FOR Best Foreign Language Film in 1980. For his next project he decided to take this directorial currency and make a movie about a journalist in a war zone. He wanted the action to be contemporaneous and he shot the movie in the no-man's-land ruins of Beirut in the winter of 1978. He brought German actors to play the principals, but all the other characters—gunmen, victims of massacres, inhabitants, street kids, other journalists—came as they were. All of Schlöndorff's films have a sense of intense authenticity, but *Circle of Deceit* plays both sides of fact and fiction, each a mirror unto the other.

On Adrien's DVD version there was a special feature documentary of the making of the film. Schlöndorff narrates his reflections standing in a burned-out street in Beirut, wearing a baby-blue sweater. He grapples with the effort and experience of trying to tell a story within an unfolding story of itself.

"Everything was so real and so contradictory around us, and so I felt the real challenge would be just to confront a piece of fiction with reality." He looks behind the camera and points to illustrate. "For instance there is a crossroads down there where snipers from the east are able to shoot at us."

In one scene, the German reporter shelters from artillery in a vaulted basement with dozens of Lebanese. "The explosion is fake but the panic is real," explains Schlöndorff, trying to separate fact from fiction, which seemed to be proving, as he continued to talk through the process, impossible. "Because these people"—the extras, the inhabitants of Beirut—"were so traumatized by six years of war and massacres . . . our filmmaking was too close to the reality." In another scene the German reporter is walking on the beach when he comes across charred body parts. The production designer had brought special anatomical models from France, but local boys, hanging around the film set, were not convinced by the dummies, so they went away and returned with their own contribution, a plastic bag of actual severed limbs.

Schlöndorff didn't have to make anything up. "Because everything looked so real we decided not to use any handheld cameras to make it look documentary-like but quite the opposite—to use cranes and tracking shots to show the operatic side of it. It should look like a strange beautiful nightmare dreamed by the journalist. . . . It was never clear where the movie really ended and the reality started. Often we would come back from shooting to the car park where our cars were and they were riddled with bullets."

His lead actor found the proximity almost unbearable; his leading lady ended up trying to adopt an orphan just like her character in the movie. Schlöndorff cocks his head, squinting. Standing on his set, which is a real bombed-out Beirut street, he realizes he has caught, and been caught between, something real and something invented.

"I tried to be as open as possible to all the influences around us, even though they often collided with the fictitious story we were telling. But I thought: *This is the reality these people have lived, this is their experience. Why should we stage anything if we can just observe them and show them? Circle of Deceit*, or *The Falsification*, in French, is going to be another circle of deceit anyhow. Our picture is not going to be any more real than any of the pictures journalists have given before us."

What does he mean? He is a storyteller beguiled by real life. And I am laughing because I am the journalist beguiled by the greater truths of fiction. Several times I have put an imaginary tape recorder inside the mind of someone I encountered on Tahrir: What is the captain sitting on top of his tank thinking? Is he thinking about his wife who no longer wants to make love to him, the possibility of *koshari* for lunch, about how many tightly packed people a tank shell would actually kill? What does the fourteen-year-old slum kid think with his hair gelled into spikes and a concrete brick in his hand? Is his heart filled with the great joy of revolutionary fervor or is he calculating how to steal my mobile phone?

But I am not allowed to imagine and sometimes I am frustrated because it seems that imagination and empathy might be the same thing.

Schlöndorff's musings reflect mine, mirror inverse. And then he concludes a very sweet and simple sentence that I borrowed for a while as my own tenet:

"So I just tried to keep my eyes open," he says. "To show it. I don't know who it will interest. *I* was very interested."

I had the flu and a fever that week of the First Battle of Mohammed Mahmoud—burnt out, exhausted with work and the trampling and the noise and the rumors of political maneuvers. Everything blurred behind my swollen eyelids. I went down to the square every day but it was difficult to move in the densely packed crowd hemmed and pushed between the motorcycle lanes and the wafts of tear gas, and I could not see what was happening. I was trying to finish my story on Alaa Al Aswany and I kept trying to call him because his name had come up among various liberal figures connected to a mooted revolutionary committee known as the National Salvation Front. My head pounded, my eyes scratched. My editor e-mailed to say that they wanted a comment piece on the latest developments. Whither Egypt? Even the great commentator Hisham Kassem had stopped trying to make sense of it. "I am only observing things," he told me, "I have given up analysis." For three days I clunked sentences and then deleted them. The force of the street . . . the revolution . . . the deep state that snagged . . . the relationship between the army and the Brotherhood . . . I was updating the story with new paragraphs even as the revolution rewrote them.

The army built a wall out of concrete blocks across Mohammed Mahmoud, and Tantawi, the head of SCAF, replaced the prime minister with a new prime minister who had once been an old prime minister under Mubarak. The army kept to their road map. When the parliamentary elections began everyone (except for a few of the revolutionary youth who boycotted) stopped protesting and went to vote.

I n December protesters tried to stage a sit-in outside the cabinet office just off Tahrir. The army went to clear them out and there was another round of fighting. The Institute of Egypt caught

fire, with all its Napoleonic man-
uscripts, and the soldiers went
through the square with sticks.
They pushed a woman wearing the
niqab to the ground and pulled off
her scarf and her veil and pulled
up her shirt, exposing her blue
bra underneath, and they kicked
her. This picture went around the
world's front pages. Black boot
raised above a bare female body,
her cobalt bra like a red flag.

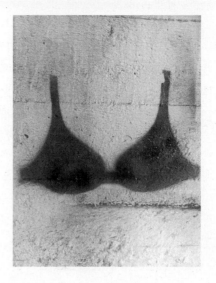

In January the new parliament convened.

A PARLIAMENT

ON THE FIRST DAY OF PARLIAMENT EVERY EGYPTIAN TUNED IN. The Muslim Brotherhood had won the election—they had by far the largest share of seats, 35 percent; the Salafis came second with 25 percent; the liberals were a motley collection of factions in third place, among them Dr. Hussein's Egyptian Social Democrats (Nora's Adl Party had barely managed to get its leader elected). In the *shisha* café downstairs the tea boy thrust a rag into the tea glasses to dry them as he kept an eye on the TV on a corner bracket. In the Salafi money exchange the big-beard tellers carefully fed the banknote counting machines, listening to the live coverage. In every taxi the radio was tuned to the proceedings, and the usual banter between driver and passenger halted; the fruit seller on my corner set a little TV on a tomato crate and passersby stopped and stood and watched with him; children were herded into classrooms with the TV on a wall turned up loud. Hassan and I watched in my apartment with a McDonald's sofa picnic between us. The city hum seemed muted, but probably I only imagined this. For once we did not scroll for Twitter commentary. We all sat patiently and paid attention, because this was the first parliament Egypt had ever freely and fairly elected.

The new parliamentary deputies took their seats in the circular parliamentary chamber. Excepting the four head scarves of the Muslim Brotherhood sisters, the new deputies were all men. Most wore dark blue suits and ties with enamel party badges in their lapels in the American fashion. The liberals wore a yellow sash that read *No to Military Trials* and sat together in a bloc; elsewhere there were beards of every length and every degree of mustache trim, one or two Salafis with their heads devoutly covered in white cowls, a Bedu in a red and white checkered headdress and the red *tarboosh* wrapped in the white turban of an Al Azhar scholar.

The chairman of the session asked each of the new deputies to swear their oath of office:

"I swear to God to faithfully protect the peacefulness of the nation, to look after the interests of the people and respect the law and the constitution."

There was not yet any constitution to respect.

From the outset the deputies had their own agenda.

"I swear to God to faithfully protect the peacefulness of the nation, to look after the interests of the people and respect the law and the constitution, *and* Hosni Mubarak must be tried according to a revolutionary court!"

"Nothing extra!" admonished the chairman. "Just the oath; please perform the oath correctly. Dear member, my friend, my colleague, please stand up and repeat the oath." But the new deputy refused to do so, referring instead to an obscure procedural point.

The next deputy stood up and recited: "I swear to God to faithfully protect the peacefulness of the nation, to look after the interests of the people and respect the law and the constitution, *but* even now the constitution does not specify if we are a parliamentary or presidential system!"

"Please!" The chairman held up his hands in remonstration. "We cannot begin discussions until we elect the speaker of parliament!"

The next deputy, who had a thick black beard, swore: "I swear to God to faithfully protect the peacefulness of the nation, to look after the interests of the people and respect the law and the constitution, *and* apply the *sharia* of Allah."

The next deputy swore: "I swear to God to faithfully protect the peacefulness of the nation, to look after the interests of the people and respect the law and the constitution, *and* the martyrs of the twenty-fifth January."

"Please!" The chairman held up his hands again, calling for order. "We are beginning a new era. There is a script we must stick to!"

The next deputy swore: "I swear to God to faithfully protect the peacefulness of the nation, to look after the interests of the people and respect the law and the constitution, *and* the goals of the revolution!"

The chairman became exasperated and wagged his finger. "Please! Brothers! Everyone has something to say and you will all have the opportunity to do so later on. Let's get on now. For my sake, please, respect the constitution for this first session!"

The next deputy said: "I swear to God to faithfully protect the peacefulness of the nation, to look after the interests of the people and respect the law and the constitution, *and* I will obey it unless it contradicts *sharia*!"

Several other Salafi deputies echoed him. The chairman stood up, angry now.

"Read article two! It says what you are saying already, so stop referring to this. This is a procedural session. We respect all of you. We ask you to respect the law, nothing more nor less."

It was the turn of a liberal deputy with a yellow *No to Military*

Trials sash: "I swear to God to faithfully protect the peacefulness of the nation, to look after the interests of the people and respect the law and the constitution, *and* bread, freedom and human dignity and the blood of the martyrs."

One deputy did not repeat the oath but said: "I swear to uphold the constitution that I am going to write."

MOGAMMA

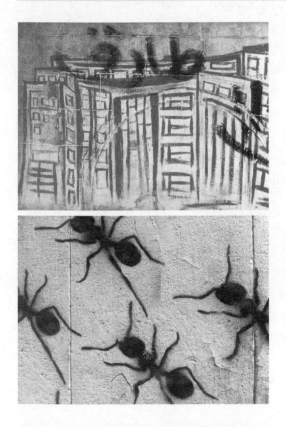

WENT TO RENEW MY VISA AT MOGAMMA. IT WAS STILL THERE AND just the same gray toad. The plaza was crowded with a mini market sprung up on trestle tables and laid out on squares of cardboard: nut crackers and saltshakers and stainless steel mixing bowls, piles of new socks and packets of pink sugary wafer cookies. There was no grand entrance to Mogamma, just a stream of people funneling between the bored guards through a narrow door.

Blink from bright sunlight to the gloom of the interior. A mass of people pressing in several directions, a queue for the slow shuddery lifts and a Sisyphean trudging column climbing the stairs. The corridors appeared to be straight but in fact were curved arms embracing a central airshaft garbage pit. Their length and subtle ellipse made for an optical illusion; you would walk a long way and then look back and not be able to see where you had come from. On either side, doors—some open, some closed, others closed off with wooden partitions. And at the end of the corridor the crowd surged against a row of official windows.

They said a million people visited Mogamma every day, which seemed an impossible, apocryphal number until you were inside its clutches, pressed into queues and up against wads of people ferrying documents between photo booth and photocopying concession and window number thirteen and come back at two P.M., because, of course, the whole building closed at two P.M.

The foreign press visa office was down a side corridor, opposite a tea seller. The police general, wearing civilian dress, tan jacket, tan trousers and tan shoes, sat behind his desk. Perfect official Egyptian repose: a cigarette, a glass of tea, mobile phone to his ear. His assistant sat at an adjacent desk copying out information from a stack of passports into a ledger. Beside his elbow was a blue ink stamping pad and an official seal. Hassan and I sat waiting patiently.

The police general was on the phone with his nephew. The nephew, it became apparent, was in another part of Mogamma; he had recently enrolled in the police academy and needed to change his national ID status from student to police. His uncle told him, "*Habibi*, just give the phone to whoever is in charge and I'll talk to him." Hassan and I continued to eavesdrop as the police general adjusted the tone of his voice into brightly collegial.

"General X. Hello! It's General Y! Yes, this is my nephew, he needs to change his ID, what should he do? . . . Yes yes, I see. Very good." Then his voice became soft and familiar again. "*Habibi*, you need to go and see General Z and he will sort it out. Yes, yes, just give him the phone when you walk into the room."

A few moments elapsed.

"General Z? It's General Y! Yes! And how are you and how is everything and how is your wife? Can you help my nephew out? He needs to change his ID to policeman. Yes yes, of course. Could you send a police officer with him, so that it all goes smoothly? Thank you! . . . Okay, *habibi*, he's going to send an officer with you. Give me a call if there's any difficulty, and I'll talk to them directly."

I noticed there was a portrait of Field Marshal Tantawi hanging on the wall behind his desk. Military hat with a black patent-leather brim, gold-braid epaulets, medals. In Mogamma, they were all for hierarchy and the status quo. I once overheard a conversation between two of the ladies who collated the forms for tourist visa extensions, complaining about the crowds and the mess on Tahrir and when was the army going to come and finally clear everything up.

Hassan and I waited patiently. The assistant did not look up from his copying. Columns of blue ballpoint names and numbers grew slowly. The police general Y lit a cigarette with his gold lighter and made another call. There were two telephones on his desk, one red and one white, the old-fashioned kind with heavy plastic shoulders and curly cords, but he used his mobile.

"Well there are two Bradleys," he began, this time using a formal clipped reporting-for-duty voice.

"He's talking to intelligence," Hassan whispered to me. "I can tell by his tone."

"One of the Bradleys is an American," the police general continued. "He is decent, very pleasant, polite. He is a journalist, all good. The other . . . I have my doubts about. I am not sure he's a real journalist . . . yes, that's why I am telling you. Perhaps you should conduct further checks."

"I think I know both those Bradleys," I whispered to Hassan. Hassan gave me a hard stare to shut up.

"Yes, and now, how can I help you?" The police general put his mobile down and was leaning forward toward me. "Another visa?" He took my passport and passed it to his assistant, who took it without looking up and put it on a pile of several other passports.

"Tantawi," I said, pointing at the wall behind him. "In some places they still have Mubarak up." The police general smiled wanly with a certain warmth in the shared surreality of the times and lifted up something hidden in the gap between his desk and the wall. It was Mubarak's portrait. He made a funny sort of guilty grin.

"I couldn't bear to throw it away," he said.

ANNIVERSARY

ON JANUARY 25, 2012, THE ANNIVERSARY OF THE REVOLUTION, WE marched from Mohandiseen to Tahrir. We were several hundred thousand strong in high holiday mood. The kids spray-painted anti-SCAF graffiti and Tantawi's crossed-out face all along the walls. When we marched across the Qasr al-Nil Bridge our footsteps made the structure vibrate. Marchers converged on Tahrir from every part of Cairo, and by the time Hassan and the Big Pharaoh and I arrived in the late afternoon, the square was so packed we couldn't push any further than the statue of Omar Makram. The crowd was larger than it had ever been during the eighteen days. I was happy. The Big Pharaoh grinned from ear to ear.

Unfinished, *transitional,* messy messy—but—but, still we had hope. Editors would ask, "What has changed since Mubarak's fall?" and I would grope for an answer because I didn't want to admit that nothing had changed. Instead I would come up with:

"Politically everything is still up in the air. But. There has been a change in people's awareness and expectations. The state cannot dictate anymore. Whenever they—SCAF—overstep the mark, with their heavy-handed military trials or trying to force through a constitutional declaration (a perfect oxymoron, by the way), the people go back to Tahrir and they have had to back down. Tahrir is a shared and sometimes violent space, but it still carries the legitimacy of the revolution and SCAF needs to accede to that legitimacy, even if it's just lip service, in order to allow them to hitch their interests to the revolution . . ."

I could go on like this for an hour or more. I could talk about popular people, populism, checks and balances; Egypt as a new paradigm, a revolution without guns

or demagogues or leaders or parties. Tahrir as an everyman parliament subject to constant referendum by means of demonstration. (*Demo-cracy.*)

It sounded perfectly plausible. I remember a group of visiting Scandinavian MPs on Dr. Hussein's balcony being impressed with my "excellent analysis." Dr. Hussein had become the foreign policy adviser to the Egyptian Social Democratic Party and was often called upon to brief ambassadors and play host to visiting European social democrats.

"And what effect will the Muslim Brotherhood's majority in parliament have?" asked a flaxen-haired Swede. He looked about twelve.

"Impossible to say," I said, falling back on my other analyst trick. "You can't predict anything in Egypt right now. Parliament is a blank slate, but it has legitimacy. The MB can make of it what they want. But at the same time, they have to pay attention to the street too."

The flaxen-haired Swede nodded earnestly.

"It is all very interesting," he said, thinking no doubt of snowbanks in Trondheim that slowly grew larger and thicker all winter and did not move.

Parliament was two days old; already there had been demonstrations at its gates. The Brotherhood called on the police to garrison the surrounding streets and there had been fighting. Squashed in the anniversary crowd, I tried to climb up on Omar Makram's plinth to catch a back view of the stage that had been set up. It was a Brotherhood stage; everyone on it was wearing green team baseball caps. The loudspeakers boomed Koranic incantation, but the crowd was yelling over the blare. People jeered and whistled, held up their shoes in contempt, flipped their middle fingers and threw empty water bottles and tangerine peels at the green baseball caps, chanting, "Traitors! Traitors!"

The green baseball caps put out their arms to appeal to the crowd but the crowd continued to yell and push against the stage so that the structure of lashed planks and scaffold seemed to sway like a shipwreck. The Koran recitations stopped and the national anthem came through the loudspeakers. The sound was tinny and lost amid the catcalls. No one sang along. One of the green baseball caps took the microphone and started to chant, "One hand! One hand!" a revolution call, a prompt, to co-opt, just as the protesters had chanted to the tanks a year before. "The army and the people are one hand!"

"Dirty hand! Dirty hand!" came back the response. "The square is already full! We don't need the Brotherhood!"

I watched two green baseball caps pull up a ladder propped against the stage like pulling up a drawbridge. The microphone sounded desperate now, lying to save its own skin: "We are the youth of the twenty-fifth!"

Boys in the crowd climbed up the traffic lights and began to unwrap the wiring that held extra speakers in place. The speakers fell with a crunch. I watched one kid shimmy out onto the far overhanging horizontal of the traffic lights and begin to unpick the cables fastening a cluster of loudspeakers, like he was picking berries. He overreached and revolved, almost in slow motion, around the pole and fell into the crowd. No one seemed to notice. The moon rose in the lavender sky, a strange upside-down moon that was smiling like a Cheshire cat.

THE SECOND BATTLE OF MOHAMMED MAHMOUD

ON THE FIRST DAY OF FEBRUARY, ONLY A WEEK LATER, SEVENTY-four Zamalek Ultra football fans were killed in a riot during a match against Port Said. The Ultras were the fighting vanguard of every protest and they immediately marched on Tahrir, furious that the police had stood by during the carnage and done nothing. The revolutionaries joined them. This was the Second Battle of Mohammed Mahmoud. Hassan and I put on our five-pound plastic gas masks and went down to the street again, resigned to the familiar. The scene had become repetitive. My notebooks filled with the same words—*rock throwing tear gas bird shot running motorbikes*—but I could no longer articulate the meaning of it, and when I asked them, neither could the rock throwers or the boys choking on tear gas.

Morning, quiet time, clean blue canvas stretched overhead for the start of a new day. Only a faint miasma of tear gas hung over the breakfast cease-fire. Hassan and I picked our steps through the rubble at the tax building crossroads, where the fighting had been fiercest overnight. A middle-aged man walked toward us, circumventing a pile of smoking garbage. He announced his good morning to a global audience: "The Egyptian revolution inspired the whole world!" Then he shook his head at the dozy apocalypse around him. "This is not a revolution. What is this? I don't understand this . . ." In the mornings after the battles the kids with homes had gone home to sleep and the street kids lay in the gutters, one arm across their eyes against the waking sun, filthy cracked feet curled under. No one was awake to answer his question. The middle-aged man paused and pointed for us. "There's blood on that kiosk on the corner if you want to see."

The middle-aged men had families and worries, furrowed brows, receding hairlines, bowling-ball bellies, big hands that held their chins, steady, tired, over a glass of tea. The middle-aged men wore shirts with collars that were frayed and carefully mended with small stitches by their wives. They debated in circles and when the conceptual got too highfalutin they broke off with a joke and everyone laughed and remembered that they were Egyptian and whatever happened they would still be Egyptian. When the tear gas and running would start up again they retreated to the verges and cracked sunflower seeds between their teeth and saw spies and foreign hands everywhere and blamed everyone equally: the youth and the police and the army and Tantawi and that idiot Baradei who never does anything useful and only sits in his garden giving interviews to American TV cameras and Mubarak and Nasser—no, not Nasser!—Well you have to go back to the beginning—Well you might as well include the Pharaohs because that's what we've had for seven thousand years and you can't expect a country to change in nine months even *inshallah*, God willing.

The kids were more numerous; there were literally millions of them. Demographically Egypt was theirs and the future was theirs, but the view was obscured by the rubble—well, no matter, the rubble was theirs too! And they picked it up chunk by chunk and hurled it forward. The kids were skinny and lithe and jumped and ran and scattered with the speed and tactile tread of street cats. The kids liked to climb on walls and rev motorcycles and to Twitter Twitter Twitter. Most of all they liked throwing things. The kids congregated in groups, egging each other on, cuffing, joshing, sparring lion cubs. It occurred to me that their battling with the police was a kind of playact fighting and not meant to harm. In their pockets they carried mobile phones and their national ID cards and nothing else—not keys, not money. Most had sneakers, but some were so poor they wore only plastic sandals. Their hair was slicked with gel and oil and sometimes carefully coiffed into spiky curls. The nice boys were smooth skinned; the rougher ones carried knife scars from the slums. These were the legions of the revolution.

Below the kids were the little street boys who reached only as high as an adult waistband, urchins with thin bones and frail shorn skulls. They ran everywhere, swarmed barricades as if they were climbing frames and poked long sticks into humps of garbage rubble in case they found some treasure there, a coin or perhaps a brass cartridge casing. They darted about like goldfish, through the long reeds of adult legs, selling packets of tis-

sues or holding out dainty hands to beg. They fought each other
in the flower beds, ganging up to steal the sandwich the shop-
keeper had given, out of pity, to the littlest one, and chase trails
of spilled booty when the roast sweet potato and the corncob
vendors threw out their rotten wares. No one paid any attention
to the goldfish boys except to brandish a feigned fist in their direction to shoo them away.

A morning lull in the midst of a sleepy riot scene: Hassan
and I dutifully went to inspect the blood smear and then we
sat down on a couple of white plastic chairs dragged out on the
sidewalk to have our morning coffee. A tear gas canister streaming white smoke came lobbing out of the sky and Hassan got
up and kicked it away. There was not much to say. The routine
of the violence had become only familiar. Hassan was naturally
liberal but too cynical for activism. Hassan reacted to events only
inasmuch as they meant more or less work for us and whether he
had to get up early in the morning. He was one of the kids in
that he instinctively bristled at authority, at those who would tell
him they knew better: father imam Brotherhood politician military officer policeman bureaucrat, the university administration
professor who failed him every year. But he thought the violence
was stupid. He never picked up a stone—although he did fashion his own graffiti stencil in the outline of a duck. He spray-
painted several ducks on walls in Zamalek and underneath, in
English, the alliterative allusion *What the* . . . (One what-the-
duck? was opposite my all-time favorite tag in giant cloud letters,
impossible to tell whether it was naively misspelled or knowing:
FREE-DOOM!) This was Hassan; funny and looking for the
fun in something. He wanted to live; he wanted to live happily.
He espoused no grand ideas and was not remotely interested in
them. His moral compass was kindness, respect, decency. I loved
him for this—for his dogged friendliness, big smile, frizzy halo

like he had stuck his fingers in a cartoon electrical socket. He was the same polite to everyone we met, beggar or general.

We drank our coffee and after a while the Big Pharaoh appeared from around the corner. Big tall grin. "Look!" he said proudly, pulling up his trouser leg. "I got hit with a rubber bullet!"

The sun ascended, warming, hotter. By midday the rising heat haze from the soft molten tarmac made peering toward the frontline barricade like trying to see through the watery tremble of a shower curtain. At the tax building crossroads a small crowd was awkwardly penned between a large lake puddle and an island of barbed-wire tangle. A canister flew over and burst open with white smoke, breaking the crowd into pieces. Hassan and I retreated a block backward, through the frontline kids, to stand with an outer ring of middle-aged men observers.

A cloud of white smoke engulfed the tax building crossroads, and from out of it came a motorcycle with a sidecar and a middle-aged man with a pair of goggles perched on his forehead and an Egyptian flag wrapped around him like a cape. He stopped his bike beside us. He had a poor face, a tattoo dot on one cheek and worn-down teeth. Hassan, well drilled, engaged him in quotable conversation; the caped crusader used to sell secondhand clothes but he had no work now.

"We are fighting now for three days," he said amicably, passing commentary, as we continued to watch the crossroads. "We are not trying to destroy anything. Any fires started we are ourselves trying to put them out. We are saying peaceful peaceful. They take our truce and then they start firing at us again."

A chant went up, "Leave! Leave!"

"What happened in Port Said . . . ," began the unemployed superhero drawing his flag around him. "All of this . . ." He waved his hand expansively as if he wished to explain but then the sentence lapsed as another tear gas canister came sailing out of the sky.

Ahead through the smoke I could see the giant red Mina Daniel flag waving. The man with the cape and other middle-aged men standing around us continued to mull the events.

"It's not Egyptians, it's other people who planned these things."

"No," said another. "It's the SCAF who want to destabilize the country so that they can take it over again."

A volley of tear gas went up as a screen for two police vans firing shotgun pellets to push forward into the crowd and try to disperse it. The rock-throwing kids streamed back and crashed into the discussion. One of the middle-aged men told them: "Attacking those guys is not going to solve anything. Go back to the square and demonstrate, ask for your demands."

"We have sat on the square many times and it doesn't solve anything!" the kid said.

"Once twice three times. Go back and sit in on the square and things will sort themselves out!"

"Ehf, the square is full of vendors and people bringing their sweethearts to walk around and show off! You're not going to solve anything from the square!"

"But this . . ." The bearded older man swept his hand over the torn-up streets and milling discontent, the smashed shops and the hanging uncertainty in the air. "This—this is not going to solve it either."

"This—this is going to burn the country down!" another middle-aged man chimed in.

"No! This—this is going to change the country!" a young woman told him right back.

Just then a small street boy came running out of the cloud of smoke and, craning his head back to see who was chasing him, ran right into us. He was small, perhaps seven or eight years old, and very dirty, and he stood stopped and shivering for a moment against the railings. Hassan asked him, "Are you okay? Are you with anyone?" The goldfish shook his head. I put my arm around him and he leaned in close to the warmth like small things do in a storm.

"Ach, what are these kids up to?" said a middle-aged man standing behind us. "Why are they fighting the police? These officers are just doing their national duty."

The biker tousled the boy's hair and offered him a corner of his flag cape to wipe his tears.

"What are you doing here anyway? People are getting hurt! Aren't you with anyone?"

"We didn't throw anything at them!" said the boy defensively, "I promise, sir! We were not throwing stones or anything. They just started firing tear gas suddenly."

"Of course they are shooting! You are all pressing them! What are you doing here anyway, you should be at home!" The man did not say this unkindly. He meant to protect the child. "Do you want to die here?"

The little boy shook his head. "I just wanted to watch. I wanted to see the government."

Some of the middle-aged men among the crowd were Brotherhood. They began to hold up their arms to corral the kids. "Make a line, make a line!" They were trying to pull the protest back to Tahrir, away from the confrontation at the tax building crossroads. "To Tahrir, back to the square!" they called. "The police are our brothers too!" The kids snarled at them and pushed through their linked-arm cordon and clambered on top of one of the concrete-block walls they had toppled the day before. They shouted back at the Brotherhood men. "If you are afraid don't come here, stay at home!"

Amid the push and shove the graffiti artists continued to

paint their murals along the wall of the American University in Cairo at the mouth of Mohammed Mahmoud. Opposite, in the lee of the McDonald's, was a field hospital, a roped-off patch of overlapping blankets laid on the sidewalk. It was called the Clinic of the Martyr of Abd El Hadi, after the doctor who was killed at his post there during the First Battle of Mohammed Mahmoud. He had written his phone number on his arm in case he was killed.

A doctor in a white coat stood by the rope with a spray bottle in his hand spritzing the kids coming out of the fray with a mixture of flour and water. A nurse sat on a stoop ministering to a small street boy. He was as thin and fragile as a baby bird, hair shaved to a delicate scarred skull. He held out his tiny hands to the nurse and she was trying to wipe them clean with cotton wool soaked in sanitizer gel. The boy looked off into the fray where the motorcycle ambulances were gunning through the crowd, and the nurse touched his chin to bring him back to her. She was swabbing his hands too gently to make any difference to the ingrained grime, and so she found a rag and began to scrub a bit harder. The little goldfish boy winced and tried to pull his hands away. The nurse talked to him, chatting, trying to get him to smile. I stood against the McDonald's corner and watched this little scene. After a moment I saw the nurse stop talking and tilt her head up sharply, not to look at the sky but to stop her tears from overspilling the lower lids, because her hands were both occupied holding the boy's hands, and she could not wipe them away. Her mouth twisted and then set in a straight line, so as not to let him see her upset. She went on talking calmly and after a while she let the boy go and sent him to one of her colleagues to be given a small carton of juice. So I went over and said hello and I asked her, gently, sorry, what had made her cry?

"He's so small. He's too small to be alone on the streets," she said. "He has no parents, there is no one for him." The nurse had two children of her own. "He's too small," she repeated. "There are plenty of them and they are tiny. I cried because he pulled up the corner of his shirt and underneath there was a long scar around his abdomen and he pointed to it quite matter-of-fact and said that was from when they stole his kidney."

THE SKIN

CURZIO MALAPARTE; A CURIOUS PEN NAME. HE GAVE HIMSELF THIS moniker, the opposite of Bonaparte. Malaparte was the son of a German industrialist and an aristocratic Italian mother, fluent in several languages and well connected to high-born European circles. During the war he was *Corriere della Sera's* correspondent on the Eastern Front and he wrote *Kaputt*, described, not very convincingly, as a novel, from his time covering the other side of the war. Until very recently it was the only one of Malaparte's books that had been translated into English. It is half reportage and half fantastical; it doesn't matter about the facts, because it's so terrifying and true. Adrien told me to read it because most of Malaparte's books have been translated into French and he was a great fan. When we went to Naples we climbed up the staircase rock cliffs on Capri and saw the house that Malaparte built for himself on a jagged promontory above the blue Mediterranean. It is an extraordinary mix of brutalism and fun, shaped like a curved coffin with a roof flat and wide enough to ride a bicycle on.

When the Americans invaded Italy and occupied Naples, Malaparte, connected and well versed in the urbanities of diplomatic capitulation, offered his services as liaison. He wrote a book about his experiences called *The Skin*. Malaparte died in 1957; *The Skin* was made into a movie in 1981. Adrien and I watched it the night he came back from a week of war in Gaza.

Naples is starving and perfidious, its women given over to whoredom, its street urchins able to strip a tank for scrap in ten minutes flat. Vesuvius erupts and whole streets burn. Burt Lancaster, overdubbed in Italian, plays the American general with just the right amount of preening and blundering. One night, at an impossibly elegant dinner given by a local duke for the glamorous blond aviator wife of an American senator, Malaparte denounces the striped *tricolore* of the Italian flag (a gift from Napoléon, ironically enough) as fake and all flags that would incite men to war as false.

In the final scene of the movie the American army is marching on Rome. It is June 6, 1944, and its triumphal entry would be overshadowed by the news of D-Day. General Burt Lancaster rides among a column of tanks in an open-topped staff car. The sun is shining and the roads are lined with cheering liberated Italians. A father holds his small son in his arms; the small son waves a little American flag. "Welcome, Americans! Welcome, Americans!" the father cries as he dances into the parade and turns and stops suddenly and realizes he has got too close and is caught. The tank runs over him. His body disappears, inch by inch, descending from the frame, eaten. The tank halts. Malaparte jumps out of his jeep in horror. The little boy scrambles out unscathed, but when the tank backs up the father has been ironed into a smooth expanse of skin, a bloody piece of chewing gum stretched across the tarmac. "This," shouts Malaparte, furious, defeated, pointing at the ragged smear of gore, "*this* is the flag of Italy!"

THE STANDARD BEARER

Mostafa Sheshtawy

@msheshtawy

Mina Daniel flag is with us in #mansour, Mohammed
Mahmoud intersection. I really donno how, but it
energize people #MOI.

The police began another assault, driving their tin-can blue vans
at the front line to break it up. The tear gas came over and the
crowd began running and we ran too, Hassan and I holding
hands, tripping over running feet blind with our eyes streaming.
Out of the mouth of Mohammed Mahmoud Street into the ex-

panse of Tahrir, leaning against the doorjamb of Hardee's, crying into the gutter. Blurred red and coughing, I looked back down Mohammed Mahmoud toward the tax building crossroads. The tear gas billowed huge as white thunderheads, parted by the wind into curtains and softened at its edges by sunlight. Like an imperial eagle glimpsed through the cannon smoke at Borodino, proud in the center, I could see the great red Mina Daniel flag. Always at the van, where the gas was thickest, the Mina Daniel flag was touchstone, symbol, rallying point, sign of endurance, of fortitude. No matter the stench and the density of the tear gas, Mina Daniel, killed at Maspero, flew high and clear. The man who held the flag had a long black beard and yet his banner was stitched with the face of a Christian martyr. It was said the flagman was mysteriously impervious to the gas. The Big Pharaoh told me he knew him; he was known as the Standard Bearer and he was a kind of legend. This was Tarek.

Corduroy jacket over stripy sweater, woolly hat pulled back from his forehead, bushy black beard. A Salafi hipster math teacher look. Immediately friendly; Tarek talked fast and volubly, flashing glittery, almond eyes. "Let's go and have some tea nearby," he said, coming out of the battle. We walked a few streets away to a sidewalk café opposite the ruins of the Champollion Palace. Tarek's confidence shone brightly but it was tempered by a childlike excitement that was disarming. He was religious, but he wasn't a Salafi in any formal sense. He did not subscribe to any particular leader or collective view; he was not swayed by invective headline or pulpit sermon. He thought for himself. Tarek was straightforward and plainspoken, clarion.

"Revolutionaries are born revolutionaries," he told me. Handsome wide smile. Something about him glowed like a halo force field. He was born for this. His destiny swelled with the zealous certainty of youth.

On the morning of the twenty-fifth of January, Tarek took out the Egyptian flag he had stolen from the school flagpole years before and went down to the street. He had not expected to see so many people. The chanting electrified him. *Bread freedom social justice.* He found himself shouting his own proclamations. *Come on, Egyptians! Speak the truth! Say no! No to the oppressor!* The crowd around him roared his words back in a mighty echo. A year or more later we sat in a sidewalk café and he wiped his face, still rimmed with white flour-and-water paste against the tear gas, and remembered the beginning.

"The noise of the chanting was so loud the buildings shook."

For Tarek those first moments were a weird otherworldly floating feeling. It felt like a victory already just to be able to shout *no*. He knew he was not safe, but he was not afraid. He felt not happy but not upset either. He felt something deeper, akin to ecstasy. They marched toward Tahrir, all the time gathering numbers, and as they got closer the fighting with the police began. "Tom and Jerry; chasing and running." The protesters ran at the police and hurled into them, snatching away their helmets and their riot shields. If the police were cornered they would call out, frightened. "Don't hurt us! We are only following orders!"

Tarek was born the last of six children. Like Kamal the taxi thug, he grew up in the jumbly slum neighborhood of Shubra. As we sat drinking tea and smoking the tear gas out of our lungs Tarek told me stories of himself as a precocious boy who overturned the tables in the temple. When he was eight his father whipped him so hard for smoking that he blacked out. Afterward he went to his father and explained that he was not the one who had been smoking, it was his older brother, that he had not lied and his punishment had been wrong. It was the same at school. Tarek did not give himself up to the natural obedience a pupil owed a teacher. He was clever and naughty and butted violence back with his fists. He fought the kids who pushed the smaller ones in class, wrestling matches in break times. "I never lost." One time he and his friends kicked a football through the head-master's window. Tarek was the only one brave enough to go to retrieve it.

"Give me our ball back."

"No," the headmaster replied.

"Then tell me why the teachers can play football on the school field but we students are not allowed to!"

"Are you going to be a philosopher about this?" said the head-master. "There is no ball."

"Soon I will embarrass you and you will know that I am in the right about this!" Tarek told him. That night he stole the Egyptian flag from the school roof. The next day the headmaster assembled the school for the running up of the flag; "Ha!" said Tarek, re-membering. "They greeted the pole!"

His teacher nicknamed him the Annoying One; in the neigh-borhood he was known as the Strange One. He was political before he knew what politics was. He refused food before he knew what a hunger strike was. He gathered the signatures of students to complain about a teacher before he knew the word *petition*. People would say to him, "So you are the one who is going to change the universe!" And he would answer, "Yeah, I'm the one who's going to change the universe."

Once there were demolitions in the neighborhood. He saw an old man crying in the street. "All my money I put in that house. They are tearing it down and there is nowhere for us to live." Tarek picked up a stone and threw it. Then all the children in the neighborhood picked up stones and they pelted the government bulldozers and drove them back. The story became a local legend.

Tarek was one of those rare people who carry their own moral compass, intact and apart from the habitus of society. He told me, "I pitied the man who opened his drawer for a bribe because I saw that he was weak." When he went to the mosque as a child he saw the fear around him. Everyone knew that those who prayed five times a day were often arrested; everyone knew the torture stories of rape and electrocution. "When you hear these things you have goose bumps. The regime was very successful in suppressing humanity so that people accepted their lot to live like dogs." But Tarek never gave in to the fatalism of Islam. "People would talk about the rising prices and the corruption and then they would say, '*Inshallah*, God will fix it.' *We* should fix things! God created us to fix things ourselves."

On the twenty-fifth of January in the smoke and the cracking shotguns Tarek wrapped his flag around himself as a shield. But the bird shot still found him, seven or eight pellets. One was still lodged in his neck; he reached up to rub the nubbin to show me. When a protester fell beside him, he gave up his flag as a shroud. He fought his way onto Tahrir and did not go home for five days.

Tarek had met Mina Daniel on the twenty-ninth of January. "Every minute of his company," he told me, "is a memory."

In the middle of Tahrir, Tarek saw a Christian woman holding a banner that read, *We are all Copts!* He told her to take it down, telling her, "We are all Egyptians!" The woman, Maryam Daniel, was sitting with us that afternoon at the sidewalk café opposite the ruins of the Champollion Palace. She was wearing black and laughing as Tarek recounted their first meeting. She had replied that Copts *were* Egyptians and that saying "We are all Copts" was the same as saying "We are all Egyptians." Tarek told her he understood what she was trying to say but she should take it down because other people wouldn't read it in that way. Maryam stood her ground.

"The revolution is for everyone. There are Christians in the square and people should know we are here." Then she pointed to her brother, Mina, lying on the ground, wounded, with a bullet in his leg from the battles on the bridges the day before. "He's a

Christian. He was shot yesterday and he won't leave the square."

Tarek stopped arguing. He squatted down next to Mina. He saw the wound was bad and not just bird shot. He was worried about him and tried to persuade him to go to the hospital, at least for treatment; "I will come with you," he promised, "and then we'll come back to the square." This was the beginning of their friendship. They spent the rest of the eighteen days together on Tahrir, Tarek's long beard beside Mina's long hair, sleeping side by side, fighting side by side, talking, discussing everything. For Tarek, it was a revelation.

"For me to love someone like Mina is a miracle. It was love at first sight, like with a beautiful girl. Before, for me to love someone who was a Christian was just impossible. On Tahrir we shared our food; before it would have been impossible for me to eat with a Christian. Of course we are obliged, according the Koran, to treat Christians well and respect them in our neighborhoods. But Mina taught me humanity. To love someone who deserves to be loved whether he is Christian or Muslim. I saw that I had placed Muslims in a higher rank than everyone else and that I should change. It was a revolution inside of myself."

On the night of the storming of the State Security archives Tarek was knocked down by a policeman and handcuffed with several other protesters to a railing. Mina gathered a crowd and they chanted to release them. Finally the police got tired of trying to hold back the crowd and let the protesters go.

Mina was killed at Maspero. Tarek said, "I knew that either he would die or I would die. When they told me he was injured I immediately knew he was dead." Tarek went to the hospital where Mina's body was laid out and stayed beside it for six hours. Hassan and I were in the hospital that morning, and I remembered the courtyard full of wailing relatives. Tarek did not cry. Mina was fun, not sad. He did not feel that Mina had died. He smiled as he said this. Mina was with him still, a guardian angel, shielding him from the bullets and the choking gas. After he died Mina appeared to many of their friends in dreams. Each friend came to Tarek and told him Mina had left messages for him. "But when I dream about him, he doesn't tell me anything."

Maryam reached across the table and held Tarek's hand. She was his sister too now.

Tarek told me that when he was six or seven he used to raise chicks into chickens. He had a whole brood of chicks and he watched them carefully. He saw that one chick pecked another and then the pecked chick pecked a third chick and this third chick turned and pecked the first one. It seemed to him a circle, a symbol of God's design. He saw that it was justice that the first chick was pecked back, and when he understood this his eyes filled with tears. The next day was Friday and he went to the mosque and he heard the *sura* from the Koran that speaks of the seven categories of people that God will shade on the Day of Judgment, when there will be no shade. One is the man who cries when he remembers God and the small Tarek thought: *That's me!* In that moment he loved God and felt that God loved him. "I don't know why," he told me, "my father never went to the mosque; we did not read the Koran at home, but I felt committed by instinct."

Tarek saw justice in the first chick getting pecked. I, a Westerner, saw a psychological parable, a loop of abuse, abused turned abuser. I told him my theory that the abuses of dictators could warp whole societies by example. The first chick pecked the second and the second chick learned to peck the third and the third pecked back because that is what had happened to him. Action sanctioned in its reaction, transformed somehow into acceptable. Adrien and I would often argue about whether dictators were products of their societies or whether the inverse was true and societies were shaped by the trauma and repression of dictatorship. In Iraq I saw the kidnapping epidemic that swept through

Baghdad after Saddam fell—thousands, tens of thousands of children and women were kidnapped for ransom; literally every middle-class family had a horror story—and I tried to make sense of such widespread cruelty and criminality. Perhaps, I pondered, it was the product of an inculcated degradation of public morals. As the fish rots from the head, the example of a brutal corrupt regime had brutalized and corrupted its subjects. Adrien did not agree. He would say, "Yes, but Saddam was Iraqi. He came from that society. He learned brutality and corruption from other Iraqis . . ." Tarek also shook his head at my theory. Society was not a single thinking thing; neither was "the people." I decided that my new theory was that all theories were wrong.

I often saw Tarek in the Mohammed Mahmoud clashes. Beanie hat pulled down over his forehead, tired and blinking tears and grinning all at the same time. He was against SCAF, who were pushing their own agenda, proclaiming constitutions. He was against the Brotherhood, who stood on Mohammed Mahmoud and tried to persuade everyone to calm down and go home. He called them "the rotten toe" of the revolution. He called the black-uniformed riot police "the ravens." He veered between the glory of the confrontation, demanding, as it did, blood and broken

heads, and the principle of nonviolence. Sitting that afternoon in the middle of everything, in the sidewalk café with another cup of brackish tea in front of me, I could not reconcile his paradox. Undulating through days and weeks and months, the violence stopped and started up again to no order or purpose that I could see. Maryam sat with a bottle of Coke and absentmindedly ashed her cigarette into the flayed end of the cylinder of a spent tear gas canister marked *Made in the USA*.

"In the nights the ravens are attacking us," Tarek complained.

"But the protesters are throwing Molotovs and burning stuff," I countered.

"Burning things is wrong," said Tarek.

"But aren't you a part of that?"

"I would love to be peaceful," he said, "but there are things that have to be done." The new democratically elected parliament had only been sitting for a week. I suggested the protesters might give them a chance to do something.

"Democracy cannot be muddled through," Tarek said. "It is a single indivisible principle. All the people of Egypt say: we want to topple the regime. We went to the square for that right. I knew what was right because I saw what was wrong." Tarek would not be deterred by the niceties of incrementalism. His was the streamlined demand of sheer revolution.

Dusk began to creep up on long shadows. We left the café and walked back through the square. Tarek had been drawing up designs for Tahrir "when this is all over" and he described them to me: He would take away all the traffic and clear away all the green metal fencing. He would pave the whole space in granite inlaid with *25th January*, so big that you would be able to see them from space. There would be a monument for the martyrs with every name engraved upon it. There would be a dancing fountain in the center with lights and music, and over there—he pointed beyond the bobbing jostling crowd and the vendors selling popcorn and plastic cups of boiled samovar tea, to the building site in front of the Nile Ritz. "That would be for the tombs of the martyrs," he said. "I've told my family and my friends that if I am killed I want to be buried in Tahrir."

GRAFFITI

WALK THROUGH THE TUNNEL TOMBS IN THE VALLEY OF THE Kings, along the galleries painted in the rich royal colors of carnelian, ocher, turquoise; follow the processions of supplicants bearing tribute to sustain the Pharaoh in the afterlife, precious oils, platters of stuffed quail, heavy gold necklaces and quantities of clean pleated linen painted in lead white. Gilded stars glitter from the ceiling firmament, rendered in Egyptian blue, an ancient pigment made by superheating a mixture of malachite and salt and sand.

Walk through the alleys of any sand-drift slum neighborhood and you can see houses stenciled with stars and crescents to commemorate a pilgrimage to Mecca. Sometimes the details of the journey are recorded too: ships and trains and airplanes and crowds of stick figures faithfully circumnavigating the black-cube Kaaba. Walls as public message boards. Declarations of faith and hope and advertising: a stripy tiger jumping through a tire on the wall outside a mechanic's shop, *suras* swooping in calligraphy curves; blood handprints pressed in blessing against doorjambs.

A mar was a professor of fine art in Luxor. From time to time he made a little extra money painting orientalist dioramas for five-star resorts in Sharm el-Sheikh. On the Day of Rage he took a spray canister and aimed it at walls, making big furry caterpillar looping letters:

```
BEWARE OF MUBARAKS EVIL PLAN
--REVOLUTIONARIES ARE NOT THUGS --
                              EGYPT

                              IS

                              FREE

                              !
```

After Mubarak fell Amar went up to Cairo for the ongoing demonstrations on Tahrir. He saw a giant tank stenciled on an underpass wall on Zamalek. He saw a red and white chessboard painted with a toppled king in a downtown alley. These were the first moments of street art. As the revolution took back the streets, graphic designers and art students came out to deco-rate them. Something creative that had been held privately indoors, dormant winter wisteria, come spring had sprouted wildly, flowering all over the city's walls.

Over the next few months in Luxor, between the outbursts of riot and demo, Amar would design new stencils to commemorate the martyrs. There was a group of them from Luxor, friends, art students, artists, and they would travel to different towns and cities and meet other graffitists and share stencils and designs. I first saw Amar's work many months before I met him. Walking down Mohammed Mahmoud one night—after the first summer protests—I noticed a rash of new graffiti that excited me because it had crisp stenciling and was multicolored, which was something I had not seen before. Portraits of Mina Daniel garlanded with rainbow flowers; three monkeys in a row, see no evil, hear no evil, speak no evil; and cows everywhere, standing, recumbent, placid. Blue cows, green cows, red cows with green scarves around their necks. Around the corner there was a cow being milked with petrol pumps. "Yes, I did those!" Amar told me months later when the cows had long been painted over. "Egypt is the cow!"

Cairo graffiti evolved. I learned the tags of the more famous artists: Ganzeer, Sad Panda, Keizer. I would spot new images out of the taxi window and holler at Kamal to stop and then leap out to take pictures. Hassan got used to these interruptions. Every day I drove past Ganzeer's life-size tank under the underpass on Zamalek. In its original incarnation the tank pointed its turret at a *baladi* bread bicycle boy. Months later, when the army went through Tahrir with batons, other graffitists added protesters being crushed under the tank's wheels with red drips for blood. Shortly afterward the blood was mysteriously whitewashed. Over time and added daubings the bicycle boy lost his load of *baladi*, but the tank was beloved and remained more or less intact until after Morsi was elected.

I met Amar during the Second Battle of Mohammed Mahmoud. He was painting his favorite wall, the American University in Cairo wall, a long stretch of clean plaster opposite McDonald's, hoodie up, standing on a stepladder with a paint pot and brush in his hand. During the First Battle of Mohammed Mahmoud, protesters had climbed on top of the wall and smashed the windows of the adjacent library and sat up there swinging their legs with a view of the front line. When these protests subsided the AUC rebuilt the wall higher and workmen roller-painted over all the martyr faces and *Fuck SCAF* messages, making a new blank canvas. I called up hello and Amar climbed down from his stepladder and pulled down the scarf wrapped around his face to protect against the tear gas, and allowed himself a smile and told me, "When you see a wall that big it encourages us to make bigger paintings."

He was with friends and they worked as a team, together and separately. They were painting the whole wall green as backdrop and the first day of the battle I watched Amar paint the black outlines of portraits of the martyrs from the Port Said stadium riot. The next day when Hassan and I came we saw he had painted orange and yellow wings around them so that they became angels. When Muslim Brotherhood men stood on the curbs appealing to people to go home, Amar came down from his stepladder and shouted at them to leave the revolution to the true revolutionaries. On the third day Amar added gold frames around the portraits with a black sash across one corner. In between the green-faced martyrs, one of Amar's Luxor artist friends painted ancient Egypt in the style of the tomb paintings, elongated figures of Pharaonic myth, goddesses tumbling through the sky, bulls bowing before them, the free women who had gone before Ramses with their demands written on papyrus.

The fighting was sporadic; at any moment a volley of tear gas or cracking rubber bullets would send the crowd running back. But during the quieter midmorning lulls, when the tear gas was light, many people came to the intersection of Tahrir and Mohammed Mahmoud to see the portraits of the martyrs of Port Said for themselves. I watched them staring up at the giant faces of those who had died. Knotted discussions would ensue: maybe they were just thugs really, maybe it was all some foreign plot, maybe it was the police who were guarding the interests of the old regime by stirring up violence, maybe it was the army who wanted to destabilize the country so that they would have an excuse to stamp the revolution down with their boots. Amar would come down from his stepladder and talk to them about demands for justice and explain the hopes of Tahrir.

Word of the memorial spread and friends and relatives pressed photographs of their dead into Amar's hands so that he could add their portraits to the gallery. A small shrine of candles and flowers grew at the base of the wall. One morning I saw the mother of one of the martyrs there. She wore a black manteau and she was leaning against the shoulder of one of her sons for support. She stood in front of the wall for a long while just looking at it. The milling protesters stood at a distance out of respect. I watched her bend and reach out to touch the petals of a single pink carnation lying among a nest of candles; she brought her hand back and held it against her mouth for a few moments as she murmured her private prayers and then she reached out again to touch the flat black outline of her son's face.

When Amar and his friends got to the end of the AUC wall, they came to the wall of the French lycée next door. Here Amar painted a giant snake that looped over the tops of the blind oriental doorways. The snake had a triple head of army officers and its body was supported on uniformed legs. At the apex of an arched doorway Horus, the savior, was depicted stepping on the snake.

The story of the revolution was constantly being updated. If a wall was painted over it was only an invitation for the graffitists to come back and paint new stuff.

One day on Mohammed Mahmoud I noticed that someone had rolled new white paint in sections over the wall, even over the faces of martyrs. The next day I saw Amar and realized it was he who was painting over his own creation. A vast sentence that stretched all the way along the wall: *Forget all that has happened, now there are elections!*

Amar took a break and we wandered down Mohammed Mahmoud so that he could point out the work of artists he knew. As we walked past an enormous image of General Batran, who had tried to stop prisoners being released during the revolution as a way to intimidate protesters, we bumped into Tarek the Standard Bearer. Amar and Tarek embraced as brothers. They too had met on Mohammed Mahmoud in a cloud of tear gas. Amar had

needed charcoal and cardboard to make sketches and Tarek had gone with him to find some.

"No one can understand how he stands for four or five days in the tear gas," Amar said with wonder. "I fainted right here." He pointed to where we were standing. "Right here. Three times I fainted. Ah! There's a poet who has written a poem about you. You haven't seen it?" Tarek looked embarrassed and

shook his head. "Tarek the brave! The most decent man of Mohammed Mahmoud!"

"You give me more than I deserve," said Tarek modestly. That
week he was despondent. He felt the revolution had died in the
arms of the election. He looked up at the sky and then down at
the pitted tarmac of the street. "My Mina Daniel flag is at home in
tatters." Hassan told him not to be dejected. "Did you see on You-
Tube? There are pictures of a Mina Daniel flag in a demonstration
in Montreal!" Tarek smiled, a little wan, a little proud.

"In the next incidents I will fly a black flag."

"You really have to see what the poet wrote about you," continued Amar, and he began to recite: "'Tarek, standing five days,
Tarek, doesn't ever move back . . .'"

Tarek said, "Yes, now it's a state of depression. But this is a
phase that will pass. More blood will come, we know that."

"Yes," said Amar, softly, sadly.

BROKEN CAMERAS

ADRIEN LIVED ACROSS SINAI IN THE LAND THAT CAN'T BE NAMED out loud in Cairo cafés and I often visited him there. Sometimes I used to freak Hassan out by dropping shekel coins in the back of taxis on purpose. "Don't do that! If he sees you doing it the driver will take us straight to the police station and we'll be arrested as Zionist spies and the Americans will get you out after three weeks but I'll be stuck in prison *forever!*"

When the Egyptian revolution turned two years old two documentaries were showing at the Cinematheque in Jerusalem. *The Gatekeepers* and *Five Broken Cameras* were unintentional companion pieces.

The Gatekeepers was a series of interviews with the six previous heads of the Israeli domestic intelligence service, the Shin Bet. They discussed their methods, their operations, raids and assassinations. They made no apology; they were the front line. But they all, in different ways, acknowledged the ultimate futility of repression. They each said: *The Palestinians can be kept at bay, their terrorisms punished and frustrated, but if the political situation does not change, the threat will remain, swelling at times or receding, but extant. We punish them, they try to hit us back. This has become the status quo.* The Shin Bet leaders, retired and now able to speak their minds, did not believe the stasis was sustainable. The film is stark editorial. The opinions of the six former Shin Bet heads form a powerful indictment. "There are tactics but no strategy," one says bluntly.

Five Broken Cameras is the other side of the story. In the village of Bi'lin in the West Bank, Emad Burnat buys a camera at the same time as the birth of his fourth son. One of the first things he films is Israeli surveyors measuring village lands for the separation barrier. Next to the village is the expanding settlement of Ma'ale Adumim. Emad and his friends, Phil and Adeeb, decide to organize protests every Friday against the wall and the encroaching settlement. Five years, five cameras smashed by rocks, bullets and settlers. Every Friday rock and tear gas skirmishes with the Israeli soldiers. "No to the wall!" the Palestinians chant, and sing and clap and drum and wave flags. Mostly they are a small village band of thirty men and boys; sometimes they are joined by Israeli and European activists; later other villages begin to protest too and the movement grows. Gas canisters rain down in smoke streaks among the scattering crowds; gunfire cracks. The Palestinian villagers try every kind of tactic. They chain themselves to the fence, build an outpost in their olive grove, take their case to the Israeli Supreme Court. They plead with the visored humanity of the soldiers and hold fast as best they can to the principle of nonviolence. But their trees are burned and the legal decision to award the village part of the disputed land goes unimplemented for more than a year. Meanwhile, the settlement grows. Emad's three brothers are arrested one after the other, then he himself is taken. The settlers move into their new white apartment blocks. Every Friday, the village continues to protest.

"It's an endless cycle," one of Emad's friends admits at one point.

"People feel that nothing will stop the occupation from its course," says another.

The weekly confrontations become an almost ritualized dance. At the appointed time after midday prayer, the villagers set off for the olive grove and the soldiers line up across the track to block them. Press photographers crouch on the verges. An ambulance parks nearby in readiness. One day Phil is shot and killed. Another day Adeeb is taken and imprisoned for many months. The chain-link fence is replaced with tall gray concrete slabs of the wall.

"I have to believe," says Emad, piece to camera, almost broken by prison, injured, smashed up in a car crash, arrested twice, one of his friends detained, another dead, "that capturing these images will have some meaning."

M any times in the Tahrir melee with the rocks and the tear gas going over, Hassan and I would find ourselves running, coughing, retching, stumbling with the herd, and my stinging eyes streamed tears and I would wonder the same question implied but never asked in *Five Broken Cameras:* What meaning did this protest have at all? What purpose or efficacy? Can nonviolent protests really change

things or is it only violence that has the power to redirect history?

One day during the Second Battle of Mohammed Mahmoud, Hassan and I decided to walk around the front line and see what was happening on the other side. We made a big circle around downtown through ancient mazy alleys and looped back up Mohammed Mahmoud from the other direction. No barricades obstructed us; there was no battle here. The shopkeepers and café owners stood out on their stoops in the sunlight sniffing the dregs of drifting tear gas and muttering about the kids and thugs who were destroying the country.

We walked right up to the tax ministry crossroads from the opposite direction. A line of police cordoned the street; black-clad State Security gathered on the corners, flicking their batons against their armored knees; among them mingled plainclothes with leather jackets, walkie-talkies, mobile phones and guns jammed into their waistbands. The windows of the tax ministry had been smashed to the second story; its steps were striped with soot from Molotovs. The Interior Ministry was only a block away from where we stood, but the protesters were stuck fighting in the Tahrir neck of Mohammed Mahmoud. Why didn't they just walk around, as we had done, and attack from the rear? I stood there, careful not to take my notebook out of my bag in this Couch Party territory; lit a cigarette to look casual; and waved cheerfully at the police to say, "Hello!" so they might be preempted from bothering us.

"No camera!" snarled one of the locals, hawking a wad of phlegm onto the road. "Don't take pictures of this ugly Egypt."

"I have no camera," I assured him.

"Go and visit the pyramids. Not this shame."

As we walked back Hassan kicked at the rubble.

"They are not actually trying to attack the Interior Ministry," I said. "It's just a symbol—how many times have we stood outside the Interior Ministry with protesters chanting and shouting and climbing up the walls chipping off the big plaster national seals? But no one ever tried to get inside. Not really."

"So what are they doing?" Hassan asked.

"I don't know," I answered.

"What's the point?"

"I don't know."

For a while I had a theory that the fighting had its own logic. That it was a logic of confrontation that existed of itself.

ISLAM IS THE SOLUTION!

FROM KHAIRAT EL-SHATER'S FACEBOOK PAGE AS IT APPEARED BE-
fore the revolution. Khairat el-Shater was the deputy supreme guide of the Muslim Brotherhood.

Location	PRISON
Birthday	May 4, 1950
About	Free Khairat Elshater
Personal Information	Islamic leader & Reformist
	Passing the 19th feast in jail in
	Mubarak's era
	A significant businessman with a
	genius mentality

Loved by everybody
Personal Interests   Islam & Islam & Islam

The day after the day after Mubarak fell, Adrien and I went to meet a senior member of the Muslim Brotherhood. The Brotherhood's main office was in a nondescript dusty building at the sleepy end of the island of Roda, close to Dr. Hussein's maternity hospital. It was as unprepossessing a set of rooms as you could imagine, two or three offices around a desultory reception room.

"We are now on the long road," Essam el-Erian told us, sitting down at a borrowed desk that had no papers or computer on it, and then added: "We would like a short transition period." A few months later the Brotherhood moved their headquarters to a grand marble-columned villa on the Moqqatam Heights. A few months later mobs burned this building. Two and a half years after my first visit, I went back to the cubbyhole Brotherhood office on Roda and found the door smashed open and the place looted— but I am getting ahead of the story . . .

The Brotherhood did not go out to protest on the twenty-fifth of January, and when the revolution was successful, this initial reluctance was embarrassing. Journalists asked questions about it and el-Erian repeated the formulated answer to us: the Brotherhood had not wanted to invite the kind of crackdown that Islamist beards would provoke. "We led from behind," said el-Erian, without apparent irony.

The Brotherhood were not revolutionaries. They had never been revolutionaries.

Hassan al-Banna, a schoolteacher, founded the Muslim Brotherhood in the provincial city of Ismailia in 1928. On the wall behind el-Erian hung a sepia photograph of the founders of the Brotherhood with al-Banna sitting in the center wearing a lumpy white suit and a conical *tarboosh*. The Brotherhood was a social political religious movement, everything encompassed under the banner of Islam. Recruited among promising university students, organized in a strict hierarchy under a supreme guide with local cells or "families" and a strong tenet of obedience, funded by tithes and wealthy merchants in its upper ranks. At the beginning the Brotherhood opposed the British and colonialism and a Jewish state in Palestine. In 1952 the Brotherhood supported Nasser's Free Officers revolution-coup but was soon shut out of power, and then the organization was banned and thousands of its members put in jail. Sadat let them out and was assassinated by an Islamist plot from within the officer corps. Mubarak put them in prison again. Then the Brotherhood renounced violence and he let them out, then arrested a few, then let them out to contest elections— even though the movement remained banned—then locked them up again when they won too many seats. Let out by a swing door, disappeared in a trapdoor; it was an old intimate relationship, jailor and prisoner, almost codependent. Over time, it seemed, the Brotherhood and the state army had come to resemble each other, each secretive, hierarchical and dependent on the obedience of its members.

The first thing the Mubarak regime did when faced with the protests on Tahrir was to round up the usual suspects. On the twenty-seventh of January, el-Erian and thirty or so other senior Brotherhood figures, including Mohammed Morsi, were locked up. El-Erian spread his hands wide, almost nonchalant, as he brushed over this episode; he had spent a total of eight years in jail during the time of Mubarak. "This arrest"—he gave a small chortle—"was the shortest time." He and his colleagues had escaped from prison two days later.

El-Erian smiled a good deal at Adrien and I. Mubarak had just fallen after all. He dissembled and was disinclined to be direct, as was typical for the Brotherhood when they talked to foreign journalists. He employed an even-toned equanimity no matter the subject: his years of imprisonment under Mubarak, the youth of Tahrir, the army, Egyptian relations with Israel and America. Patter-patter, soft-pedal. The Brotherhood, he assured us, would take a backseat; they would not contest every constituency in a parliamentary election, and of course they had no intention of fielding a presidential candidate. El-Erian described the image the Brotherhood liked to cultivate: incremental and pragmatic. Slowly, carefully. "As Muslim Brotherhood our target is participation . . . we are not going to capture power and there is no reason the West . . . should be frightened."

Friendly always seems plausible when you're in the same room with it. But as we left the interview, Adrien jogged down the stairs shaking his head, not quite so taken in. "They say one thing in English and another thing in Arabic," he complained. And then he put on a funny squeaky voice and made a little song and dance out of the performance that el-Erian had put on for us: "We're so nice! We're so nice! We're so nice and quiet as mice!"

A year after Adrien and I met el-Erian, when the new parliament had been sitting for a few weeks, I went to the parliament building to meet another unctuous and blandly reassuring member of the Guidance Council. I was half an hour late because I couldn't find a way into the parliament building compound—the guards kept misdirecting me in circles around the concrete-block barriers, and a knot of Ultra fans were staging a sit-in by the main entrance. Saad al-Hosseini had been elected an MP and appointed chairman of

the Parliamentary Committee on Budget and Planning. He wore the same engineer glasses and short scratchy beard as el-Erian. I found him sitting behind an inlaid desk in a room lavishly decorated as haute Versailles with quantities of gilt plaster curlicues and medallions of pink roses set into a dove-gray damask wallpaper.

"This is a grand change in circumstances!" I said.

"Yes," Said al-Hosseini agreed with a half smile. He had been in prison many times. I looked down and saw that some of his fingernails were missing.

Al Hosseini was in charge of all the usual political platitudes. He said, almost dismissively, as if everything was already decided and set out in clear policy documents, "I think everything will be reformed now." Questions of executive authority, *sharia* law, the stated Muslim Brotherhood goal for the eighty years of its existence, were tidied into a rhetorical bonbon: "The Egyptian Islamic state we want is a democratic state, a constitutional state, a state of citizenship. A new state, a modern state."

The Brotherhood had reversed their position not to contest more than a third of parliamentary seats. When they won a majority in the parliament they declared they favored the parliamentary system over the presidential. Then after months of saying that they wouldn't, they entered a candidate for the presidential race. When they won the presidency they decided they preferred the presidential system.

I don't think the Brotherhood meant to go back on their promises. They were only reacting and adapting to the changing events the same as everyone else. They had to figure out how to maneuver between the liberals and SCAF and the vested interests that remained in the security forces and every bureaucrat with a desk in Mogamma. It was obvious that they wanted power. And that this was more important than any policy or *sharia*. The problem was that they didn't know what to do with power when they got it. They dominated all the major committees in the parliament but presented no reform program and virtually no legislation was ever passed. SCAF continued to appoint the cabinet, but when the protesters on Tahrir were screaming for the head of the interior minister and the resignation of the prime minister, the parliament, which at that time, popularly elected, was the only legitimate platform in the country, couldn't figure out how to challenge Tantawi's control. For a long time it looked as if neither the Brotherhood nor the military was doing anything other than reacting to events. The protesters on the street fought the police and shouted demands. Spokesmen made statements. Committees were formed. Few tactics, no strategy, each clinging to old paradigms for comfort. There was a lot of talk that the Brotherhood had come to an accommodation with SCAF.

In Café Riche on Fridays we began to talk about the deep state, the tendons and webs of patronage and supplication, several million state employees, enmeshed interests and fiefdoms. The parliamentary sessions continued to be televised every day but it had devolved to men talking into microphones, and no one could understand what they were saying because they were not saying anything. Sometimes the spectacle was funny, like when the Salafi MP was forced to resign because he lied about getting a nose job. The MPs spent their time arguing rubric and regulation and constitutional niceties even though the constitution had been suspended.

The Muslim Brotherhood had never had a plan. Hassan al-Banna was assassinated in 1949 and left a movement with a culture of resistance but no clear political theory. There is no structure of government laid out in the Koran, nor did al-Banna or any of his followers ever draw up a political diagram for what their Islamic state might look like. Throughout the spring I asked Brotherhood people and Salafis and commentators about the nature and logic of an Islamic state. My questions were about the framework: What is the ultimate legislative authority? Who decides what is *sharia* or not? What is the supreme authority in an Arab country without a dictator? Men's laws or God's law? *How does this work?*

Replies came mixed with quotes from the Koran, stories of the Prophet's mercy, tangents, non sequiturs and circumlocutions; a particular rhetorical favorite: "Let me explain to you in three points . . ." But there was never any answer.

"There is something missing in their ideology," Adrien mused. "They are engineers and doctors and merchants. They are more like a Rotary Club than a political party."

"They have no ideology," I replied. "'Islam is the solution' is only a slogan. I was thinking: the Muslim Brotherhood have been at the fulcrum moment of every Egyptian political transfer of power for the last eighty years and they have managed to screw it up or get screwed, every time."

MERRY-GO-ROUND

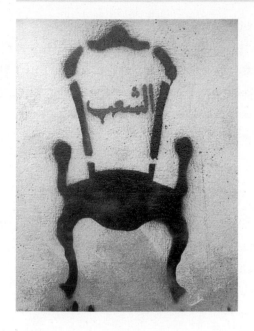

"A PARLIAMENT IS ONE THING," ADRIEN CONTINUED AS WE WAN-
dered, one slow afternoon, through the vaulted halls of
the Egyptian Museum, dazzled by the golden treasure of
the Pharaohs and then brought to weightier thoughts by the great
granite statues of the gods, "but a president is something else."
Fly-whisk whip, scepter, held in one chipped hand, the divine
ankh, key, in the other. "Suddenly you realize that one elected
man has more power in his hands than five hundred."

There was a new stencil graffiti of an empty throne on the
walls around Tahrir. Everyone had stopped watching the parlia-

ment; in Cairo the conversation was only about who would be the next president.

Hassan and I went to open-air meetings and listened to the candidates talk to assembled crowds. None of them was particularly charismatic, no towering demagogue, no great oration; campaigns were made out of string and posters and mobile phone connections.

Who are you going to vote for?

"I can't decide," said Dr. Hussein and Second Cousin Aly and Hisham Kassem and Nora and everyone else I asked.

One evening on Dr. Hussein's balcony: let it stand, composite, for every evening on Dr. Hussein's balcony that spring and summer.

"Who's going to be president?"

"Who can know?"

"Now that Baradei has confirmed he won't run . . ." Mohammed el-Baradei, Nobel Prize winner, former head of the UN's International Atomic Energy Agency, was the perennial hope and disappointment of the liberals; uncle of the revolution, too tired, or too canny, or perhaps just too disorganized to actually stand for—

"Baradei isn't running?"

"All he ever does is talk to CNN in his garden. He's always reacting. He hasn't led any debate since this whole thing started."

"I like Baradei—"

"I like Baradei too, but—"

"It's got to be Amre Moussa," said Dr. Hussein. Moussa was head of the Arab League, a foreign minister under Mubarak, and many believed he would be a good elder statesman, a safe pair of hands.

"Yeah, I know," I agreed. "But he's so *bland and billowy*. Which way is the wind blowing? Let me find a deck chair so that I can make sure it doesn't ruffle my hair—"

"But he would be acceptable to SCAF."

"He's too *feloul*, one of the remnants of the old regime," said Nora.

I had interviewed Moussa during the eighteen days on Tahrir. He was entirely diplomatic and noncommittal. "I was underwhelmed," I said, describing my impression, "plus think about it: ten years as head of the Arab League, and his achievements were . . ."

"What?"

"Exactly."

"I'm volunteering for Khaled Ali," put in Sally Sami, an Tahrir activist who was in the Egyptian Social Democratic Party with Dr. Hussein.

"I like him too," I said. I had first come across Khaled Ali in the Court of Cassation when he was arguing for an end to military trials. He was a human rights lawyer, secular, impeccable leftist credentials, "but he hasn't got a snowball's chance."

"I know," said Sally. "We've got no money in the campaign, and people have never heard of him—even in Cairo."

Dr. Hussein lit another cigarette and said, "Well, I only hope to God and hell and back it's not Abu Ismail."

Abu Ismail was an independent Salafi with a bushy gray beard and a wobbly girth. He had been a preacher on one of the religious cable channels before revolution and a fixture on Tahrir Fridays booming *sharia* from the stage. Hassan and I had gone to an Abu Ismail rally and heard him explain his economic vision. "Egypt is full of sand! And yet Egypt does not exploit its resources. The Germans make lenses from sand. Why don't we have researchers for this?"

"Did you see his supporters?" said Hussein's second cousin Aly. "They all have giant black beards and Abu Ismail T-shirts and Abu Ismail paper masks."

"But his mother is an American!"

"I know," I said, "this is my favorite plot twist so far this week."

It had been discovered that Abu Ismail's mother had immigrated to California and taken American citizenship. This was particularly amusing given his anti-IsraelAmerica rhetoric. More importantly, if this was proved, it would disqualify him from the race, because the rules stated that a candidate must have two Egyptian parents.

"But what about Fattouh?" Nora asked. Abdul Monim Fattouh was a candidate operating in the middle ground of moderate Islamism. He was former MB but had fallen out with the leadership. I had met him some weeks before in his office in the Doctors' Syndicate; he had a grandfatherly air but retained the Brotherhood habit of talking vague and happy sentiment.

"He hasn't got the organization."

"But at least he's independent," said Nora.

"He's MB."

"But the MB hate him; in their eyes he's not one of them. He won't get any of their votes."

"The trouble is the moderate vote is going to be split between Fattouh and Sabbahi." Sabbahi was a Nasserist.

"Shafik?" Aly Second Cousin threw another candidate's name into the hat.

Ahmed Shafik, former head of the air force, Mubarak's last-ditch prime minister who had resigned after Alaa Al Aswany shouted at him on live TV. Months before, when Shafik had first announced he was running, I had managed to arrange an interview. I was picked up by a handsome suave aide with an American accent and we drove in a gleaming chauffeured black limousine to a gated development off the Cairo ring road. Shafik received me in a summer house in the garden of the apartment house he shared with his daughters and their families. The room was full of souvenirs, stuffed animals and commemorative plaques and models of aircraft. Shafik had been politically pleasant, pretend relaxed, an open face, gold-rimmed glasses. I can't remember anything he said.

"No!" said Nora. "Shafik? No! We can't go back to a general-as-president."

"People will vote for him," said Aly Second Cousin.

"Who? The *feloul*?"

"The *feloul*, the Couch Party . . . ," replied Aly. Aly was a lawyer with corporate clients. "Don't underestimate their numbers . . . ," he warned.

"But even after all that SCAF has done!" cried Sally, impassioned. "Military trials, detentions of ten thousand civilians, Blue Bra Girl and virginity tests and—"

"People think what the state TV and the SCAF tells them to," said Aly. "That the army is the only thing that can protect the country."

There was a pause among us as we sadly digested the truth in what Aly had said.

"Anyway it's obvious the Brotherhood are going to win," said Sally soberly. "The Brotherhood has the best party organization."

"But they have lost a lot of support since the parliamentary elections," said Dr. Hussein.

"But Khairat el-Shater?"

There was a general liberal shudder. The Brotherhood had waited until two weeks before the deadline to announce Shater as a candidate. I spent a whole day sitting in a corridor in the Fairmont hotel in Heliopolis listening at the doorjamb while he gave interviews to CNN and Al Jazeera and Reuters and the *New York Times*. He was intelligent and combative. He looked like a gangster, furrowed heavy brow, pendulous lower lip. But as I eavesdropped, a vicarious interview, I realized he was the only candidate who could hold a room with any natural authority. At that moment, it looked very likely that Sally was right.

A week is a long time in politics and a week in Egyptian revolutionary politics was all change. The merry-go-round spun faster and the riders came off their horses. According to the strange machinations of the electoral committee, Abu Ismail was disqualified because of his American mother and so was Omar Suleiman, the bald intelligence chief who had made a surprise late entry, and so was Shater, absurdly enough, for being a convicted felon, even though his convictions were on charges

of voter fraud in an election that had been fraudulently manipu-
lated by the Mubarak regime. The Brotherhood put forward their
substitute candidate, Mohammed Morsi. He was chubby and no
one had ever heard of him and immediately he was dubbed "the
spare tire."

INTELLIGENCE

OMAR WAS A LIEUTENANT COLONEL IN MILITARY INTELLIGENCE. HE drove a low-slung sleek Audi with blacked-out windows and wore mirrored wraparound sunglasses. We met through friends—I don't want to be specific. Omar drank beer at the end of a hot day, whiskey later in the evening. "Among officers," he said, "it's almost a taboo if you don't drink." He was not large or small, a compact fit forty; his head was shaved, but he smiled readily and there was nothing menacing about him. In civilian company he held himself in polite check, but every so often, listening to the chattery gossip of revolution, he would be compelled to lean forward, hands over his knees, and interject to correct a rumor.

Omar and his wife, Dina, both came from military families. We had drinks at the Marriott one evening, and afterward, Omar offered to drive me home. Omar was momentarily worried because he had forgotten his permit for the hotel parking. But all was well: he flashed his military ID card and the guard straightened up, saluted and raised the barrier. Omar smiled at this deference, a little embarrassed, a little gratified. Dina laughed; she had grown up with the protections of a military ID card and she knew it afforded an insulated status even as she acknowledged this as a guilty privilege. She was the daughter of a general, and doors had always opened and queues been skipped by producing a military ID card.

"It's like now they are holding up my visa at the Swiss embassy!" she said, half indignant, half abashed at her own indignation. "I don't know why. We always get our family passports issued at Military Intelligence—I never have to go to Mogamma, thank God!—so the Swiss embassy know who we are. They know we are not ordinary people."

It seems to happen quite often that people who enjoy the freedom of privilege also enjoy teasing their stuck-in-the-status-quo relatives with liberal ideas. Dina had gone to Tahrir several times during the eighteen days. Omar pretended to admonish her for this, but in some measure he was proud of her too. He had spent the revolution in the Defense Ministry watching the live feed of the square from cameras and mobile phone footage. He did not go to the square—officers were forbidden—but Dina described the demonstrations, which were full of every kind of person, from the elite to street urchins, and that she, with her long tawny uncovered hair, had sat next to a man with a Salafi beard and he had called her sister and shared his rough *baladi* sandwiches. Initially Omar remained wary. Military Intelligence had reports of known Hamas individuals on Tahrir; they were dealing with the Brotherhood leadership in prison, then the Brotherhood leadership breaking out of prison, then negotiating with the Brotherhood leadership. There were high-level phone calls with the Americans and the Israelis, reports of foreign infiltrators, Islamists who were on terror watch lists spotted in the crowds—but later, as the mood of the country shifted in favor of the revolution and the crowds grew stronger and more celebratory every day, he was a little jealous. He would like to have lived, he once told me, in the 1940s, when Cairo was a cosmopolitan city. Dina's Tahrir seemed to have some of this spirit.

It was obvious to everyone, even obedient dutiful intelligence officers, that Mubarak's Egypt was sclerotic, but Omar did not give in to the optimism that followed Mubarak's fall. "You might call me cynical; I say I am realistic. Because then of course everything went bad again." What could you expect from Egyptians? Biting the hand because they didn't know what was good for them.

Omar was of the younger generation of officers. I used to tease him that he came from the same position of midrank frustration as Nasser and the Free Officers.

"Why don't you just take over with a few of your friends!" I joked. "You can put everything back in order again." Dina would chime in, encouraging. I could see that Omar believed in his own superiority and competence—after all, the army was the only institution in the country that got things done efficiently and could clear the swamp of corruption and bureaucracy. But he was a soldier: loyalty to his country, duty and obedience were ingrained.

Throughout the months of SCAF rule, Omar was frustrated with the slow-footed old-men generals, but he respected them as one respects a grandfather who is still chairman of the board. "We beg them not to go on TV!" he told me one evening when I complained about the general's finger-wagging as if the protesters on Tahrir were children to be admonished. SCAF came from a different mind-set, an elder echelon of officers that had been trained in the Soviet Union; Omar and his generation had been trained in America in a different era. But it was still Egypt; sons did not answer back to their fathers, nor junior officers question their superiors. Omar would come back from liaison exercises in France or the UK or Arizona and submit reports about a new satellite communications system he had seen or software that could process battlefield data, and the old-men generals would say no, no. They were frightened of innovation. They were cautious and stuck in their ways, but, Omar assured me, they were good men who cared deeply for their country and not the power-mongers the revolutionaries chanted against. Omar knew several of the SCAF generals personally, and he was friends with their sons, who would tell him, "Oh, my father is so tired, all he wants to do is to retire. After all his years of service to his country, now the crowds are shouting against him. He can't stand it anymore. But if he leaves, if they leave, who can they leave the country to?"

In the spring, as the presidential election campaigns were getting under way, Omar and Dina invited me to join them for a holiday weekend at a resort on the Red Sea. Dina flew ahead with the kids, and Omar and I would drive the five hours down together. Trying to get out of Cairo, we hit the traffic outside the Court of Cassation, where Abu Ismail's supporters were having a demonstration against his disqualification.

Haltingly we made our way to the Cairo ring road and then we took an exit I didn't know. The highway was strangely empty of cars, a smooth, wide, newly blacktopped road. Egypt and all its cacophony receded as Omar held the steering wheel steady with the gentle pressure of thumb and forefinger, opening up the engine and enjoying the power of it. The verges of the highway were decorated with mosaic scenes of Pharaonic fantasy. Hosni Mubarak's frescoed smiling face flashed past.

"Of course it's a good road," said Omar, thumping the wheel

with the heel of his hand. "The military built it!" He had one pistol in a holster on his hip, another in the glove compartment. The dun desert kilometers clicked past. We listened to music, we talked.

On one side the lumpy lion desert, on the other, a clean line of blue sea. World divided between yellow and blue, dry and wet. I tried to make a metaphor or some kind of theory out of this dichotomy, but the desert rolled over my thoughts with somnolent undulations, humps and knolls and stones, and I gave up and surrendered to the gentle hum of the car on the road.

Omar was careful; not cagey, but careful. He didn't tell me much, except to say there was much I didn't know. Which I knew. One of the things he told me was that the fighter jets that had buzzed so loudly over our heads that early revolution afternoon in Tahrir were actually trying to herd a group of escaped prisoners along a highway as an army unit deployed to recapture them. Another thing he told me was that there was a lot of Qatari money being poured into the Egyptian media and into the coffers of certain activists. He told me that they had found gas canisters stored on rooftops downtown to be thrown as bombs during the revolution, evidence of Islamist violence. I didn't know whether to believe him or not, but it was clear that he believed these things and the version of events that these things added up to. Once he told me that the Egyptian Revolution was nothing to do with people or being popular. It was an Israeli ploy to install Islamists to weaken Egypt.

Driving in the desert, he told me that twelve soldiers had been killed in the battle at Maspero on the night Mina Daniel had been killed. When he said this I looked at him hard.

"Twelve? Dead?" I remembered that early on, during the first hour of the violence, there had been TV reports of three soldiers killed, but nothing was clear or confirmed and later state TV apologized for false reporting and the dead soldiers were never mentioned again.

Omar nodded.

"How were they killed?"

"Most of them were beaten with shovels." Omar paused, hand on the wheel, gunning down the straight road that ran parallel to the shore. "With shovels. Can you imagine? This is the mob."

"Why was this information never released?"

"Because the army didn't want to affect the morale of its troops."

"So they hid this? Twelve dead soldiers hidden?"

"They are always very protective of the morale of the troops. What would happen next time soldiers are sent to a demonstration or a riot?"

The rubble of the sunny desert rolled my memory into the rubble of the dirty pavements, oil spotted, dust tramped, thick grime and murk. Hassan and I stood on the Sixth October Bridge looking down. It was dark. Shots and sirens, flares, Molotov fires, soldiers in riot gear, truncheons, sticks, rocks plinking against trapped cars, careening police trucks, ambulances, motorbikes revving skidding. Each moment was fractured into separate audio and visual. Close up: edge of curb, gutter, feet trip rubble, veering railing, spike slam shoulder. I was running and the scene jagged up and down with each footfall. Even when we stopped at the safe far end of the bridge and I climbed up onto a wall I could not see anything clearly. Light flashing shapes. Like people always described getting caught in a dense panic on Tahrir during a battle, the disorientation of falling and someone holding your arm too tight and it being hard to know if they were rescuing you or beating you.

I was not sure what to make of what Omar had said. It did not fit my assumptive narrative of the army as the bad guys and the protesters as the good guys. But at the same time Omar's explanation for why the army had kept their dead soldiers secret seemed plausible. Nondisclosure was in the army DNA. The army made its own lore; its official accounts were pitched as much for internal as public consumption. Stories evolve and are constructed over time, revising versions. Sometimes a story can take months or years to come to an end, either to bring about a conclusion, or more often, for some part of it to be revealed in a chance conversation or encounter. But a story, as you write, is never really finished.

Some months later, for example, it happened that I was in Shubra, where the Copt march to Maspero had begun, talking to the Fixer, Kamal's elder brother. We got talking about Maspero, and he told me he had gone to the hospital that night because Shubra people were injured and he had seen there the body of a dead soldier shot in the head.

Driving through the desert, I looked over to Omar to try to see something in his eyes but they were masked with the mirrors of his sunglasses. He did not add anything more. Further down the road the conversation resumed, this time focused on the presidential election.

Omar was supporting his namesake, Omar Suleiman, Mubarak's chief of Military Intelligence, who had, at the eleventh hour, announced his candidacy. "I agree with what Suleiman said: 'Egyptians just aren't ready for democracy yet.' Look at that mess outside the court! It's about security. We need a strongman."

Omar was not the enemy of the revolution but he was no friend to it either. He carried an officer's instinctive dislike of the rabble. "The people are a bomb," he once told me, scorn escaping from his mouth with cigarette smoke. "Whatever you give them they want something else." But he hated the Islamists more. He carried a visceral contempt for the Brotherhood. At some point in our journey, before we had reached our destination, I asked him what would happen if the Brotherhood ever came to power. Omar did not take his hand off the steering wheel or his eyes off the road. He said simply, "We will kill them."

ON THE BEACH

I N THE MIDDLE OF THE PRESIDENTIAL HOOPLA, NORA AND DAVID AND
several families and friends decided to take a weekend away
from it all and invited me along. There was a resort on the
coast at El Alamein that Nora knew, and we rented two adjacent
villas next to the main hotel. The beach was white sand and
the Mediterranean was clear turquoise and we put on our swimming suits and piled beer in the fridges and grilled sausages
on the barbecue. The kids ran around in a pack. We swam and
dived for sand dollars and made cocktails out of rum and grape-
fruit juice. In the afternoon Nora and I went for a walk along
the beach.

The sand was soft in between our toes; the sea breeze blew in our faces and cooled us so that we didn't realize we were getting sunburned. The main building of the hotel was balconied with sea views. On the beach in front were clusters of umbrellas and family groups; along the shore, boys threw themselves into the waves and came up gasping for air, happy yelping otters. Two women fully covered in *abayas* sat together in deck chairs. Volumes of black fabric blew into raven wings, and black cloth veils hung from their foreheads to cover their faces, except for a slitted opening that was so narrow even their eyebrows were covered. They leaned in to talk more intimately; one picked up a plastic cup of lemonade and drew it up beneath her veil to sip through a straw. Beside them children were playing, a little boy covered in sticky sand and his elder sister, perhaps thirteen years old but already fully covered in an *abaya*, who was building a sandcastle with black-gloved hands. Further up the beach I saw several more knots of black *abaya* women sitting on deck chairs or on plastic chairs dragged from the terrace to the sea edge. Their feet were in socks and sandals and they were careful not to get them wet. In front of us two men came out of the sea, furry chests, long black beards with shorn mustaches. One was wearing a pair of green swimming trunks. In the sea, men with beards were climbing up onto the swimming raft and diving off and splashing each other. I saw a woman among them, swimming in her *abaya*, with the expanses of black fabric flowing like seaweed around her. She clambered up onto the raft and pulled her dripping veil just below her nose so she could breathe.

"There are a lot of Salafis on the beach," I said to Nora. Nora was looking about too.

"There are *only* Salafis on the beach!" she said.

We walked among them in our bikinis, feeling a little strange about it. We walked and talked along the sea, to the far point where the wind had blown up drifts of trash and plastic bottles. There were remains of a bonfire burned down to soot, and behind a dune lay the desiccated carcass of a dead donkey.

When we walked back Nora asked one of the hotel waiters why there were so many Salafis there. He muttered an apology. Then the manager came over and asked us to stay on our section of the beach where the villas were, not to walk in front of the main building, because there had been complaints. Nora said, "But the beach is for everyone. There's no law against us and our bikinis." The manager looked a little embarrassed as he repeated, "Please," and pressed his hands together to implore us, kindly, to respect the wishes of their religious guests. He dropped his voice below the wind and explained. The Salafis all came from the same mosque in Cairo and they had paid in advance for every room in the hotel even though they only half filled them. They had been told that there were adjacent villas where other people would be staying but they had requested very specifically that there be no other guests at the hotel so that they would be able to holiday free from the sight of unclad women.

Nora waved her hands about and complained vociferously.

"I beg you, please, to be respectful . . . they have paid . . . ," said the manager apologetically.

The next morning Nora engineered a confrontation. She did not want to be shamed when she had nothing to be ashamed of. If they wanted to wear tents on the beach that was their right; if she wanted to wear a bikini that was her right too. Some of the Salafi men had rented Jet Skis, and they were launching them off the beach and revving them through the surf. Nora walked right up to a group of them, sarong wrapped around her waist, sunglasses as a headband on top of her long dark-blond hair.

"There are children swimming here and you guys are riding around really dangerously!"

The Salafis stepped back and turned their faces away.

"Look at me when I'm talking to you! It's not safe. You have to tell your friends to be careful."

The Salafis mumbled and dug their toes into the sand. One

of them kept his eyes carefully angled down as he told her she shouldn't speak like that.

"And this is the new Egypt!" Nora walked away and swept her hands up at the sky, half surrender, half furious.

An hour or two later two young *abaya* women walking along the beach stopped to talk to us. They were veiled, but their hands and feet were bare. They spoke excellent English and said they were medical students. We chatted with them for a few pleasant moments about their studies and the seaside and the clean air, not like Cairo smog. And I wondered at our funny bikini-*burqa* confrontation, two Egypts colliding. Not without grimaces, not without side glances and undertones, but we had, in some proximity, either side of a divide that was marked only by the end of one building and the villas next door, managed to share a beach for a weekend. Maybe this was something. Nora was not so optimistic.

That afternoon was the announcement of the verdict in Mubarak's trial and we all came in from the sun and gathered around the television to watch. *Après moi le deluge,* Mubarak had often threatened. If not me, then the Islamists will come. He lay on his gurney in a cage. Makeup-mahogany face, dyed black hair, arms folded across his chest, inscrutable sunglasses. The judge found him guilty of accessory to murder. But the conviction was equivocal; the legal rubric loopholed nuances. The court's judgment had not determined his responsibility for the killing of eight hundred protesters during the eighteen days, but only his responsibility for failing to stop the killing. Several senior police commanders on trial on the same charges were acquitted. I drove back from the beach through the scarred desert, still mined against Rommel's advance, and went straight to Tahrir to try to understand the mood. People had flocked to the square to protest the ambiguity of the conviction. I thought it was odd that the square was opposition instead of celebratory. A year ago they were protesting for Mubarak's indictment. Now they were protesting against the ambiguity of his conviction. Fists in the air, angry denunciations of the hand-in-glove, the judiciary, SCAF, the deep state. This was still Tahrir, this was still the people, incoherent mass, this was still the revolution that could smell expediency and continued to rail against the powers-that-still-were.

ELECTION

WHEN THE DAY CAME TO VOTE IN THE PRESIDENTIAL ELECTION, everyone I knew was still undecided. It was a five-way split between the top candidates, and the complexities of tactical voting were new or unknown. Nora changed her mind between leaving the house and arriving at the polling station. She had gone out having convinced herself of Moussa and ended up voting for Sabbahi. "Because the taxi driver talked me into it on the way. I said to him, 'Don't you think it's just a wasted vote?' and he said, 'No, everyone I know is voting for Sabbahi, after all you've got to vote with your heart.'"

The Big Pharaoh

@TheBigPharaoh

I am so undecided to the extent that I was at the
door and left the queue and went to its back. I
swear I did that. #EgyElections

The Big Pharaoh called me from the queue waiting to vote.

"Wendy, I'm literally tortured; I don't know who to vote for." I
could hear him half bemused, half desperate. "I reached the head
of the queue and then I backtracked." He had stopped and turned
around and gone back to the back of the queue to think some
more. "I want to vote for Sabbahi and yet I'm somehow sure there's
a conspiracy against Fattouh so if I give Sabbahi my vote I'm helping the MB against Fattouh and I don't want to do that. But I
don't want to vote for Fattouh because he's going to ban alcohol
manufacturing. I don't want to vote for Moussa, he's so old he's
practically dead." The Big Pharaoh ran out of breath and paused.
"Just tell me, Wendy, just tell me what to do!"

I said I didn't want to tell him how to vote because I was a
journalist and must remain impartial. The Big Pharaoh told me to
stop being silly.

"Okay," I said, "calm down," and I tried to talk him through
it. "The nice human rights lawyer Khaled Ali is the candidate who
best represents you—"

The Big Pharaoh had already discounted this option. "But he's
nothing and he'll never win."

"Okay," I said, "so if in the first round you don't just go pure
and vote for who you really want, then you need to be strategic and
vote for your next-best compromise candidate."

"So that's Sabbahi," said the Big Pharaoh, breathing a little
more regularly, going round the houses full circle. "But Sabbahi
will not even get to round two, so then the most obvious choice

is Moussa. But now what's my compromise vote? Is it Moussa or Sabbahi?"

There was a long pause.

"Okay," said the Big Pharaoh, approaching the ballot box for the second time, "I think I'll vote for Khaled Ali; at least I'll sleep tonight."

Half an hour later he texted me the picture of his ballot paper, with a tick next to Khaled Ali.

It's a disaster," said Hisham Kassem, throwing up his arms. No candidate had gained more than 50 percent in the first ballot. The moderate middle-ground candidates had split the vote ("I should have voted for Sabbahi," wailed the Big Pharaoh, "why didn't you tell me to vote for Sabbahi!") and now Mohammed Morsi, the Muslim Brotherhood's spare tire, and Ahmed Shafik, the former general with pastel sweaters, faced each

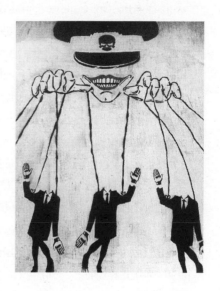

other in the second round. Hisham Kassem was, like all my friends, abject. "Shafik will try to restore the Mubarak regime. And my trust of the Brotherhood is minus zero . . . And what is happening now?" Hisham turned on the TV. The news footage showed a protest on Tahrir. The two of us watched for a minute or two without speaking.

"What does it mean?" I asked. Hisham Kassem, the expert, the great pundit, whom I liked to called the wisest man in the Middle East, had given up analysis months ago.

"What does it mean?" He repeated my question, still staring

at the pictures of the crowd. "What does it mean? Nothing!"
People, people, people; placards, flags, people. The same footage
over and over again. "A hundred thousand people with nothing
better to do."

"But this is Tahrir!" I said. "This is the Tahrir that we fought
for—" I caught myself and corrected this: "That Egyptians fought
for. This is the revolution, its locus, its conscience, its barometer. A
hundred thousand people must mean something," I said.

I believed in Tahrir. Talisman, wishful thinking. I still thought
that despite its violence, incoherence, Tahrir was the people, and
the people, with their mixed-up views and opinions, were the legitimacy, and their legitimacy was in their opposition and their
resistance. I did not want to think, as Hisham Kassem had begun
to realize, that the time of the crowds was over and the action had
moved to the corridors and negotiations.

Hisham Kassem let me air my muddles without commenting.
He apologized, laughing, for keeping the TV on.

"These days you can't help it. You go out and run an errand
for two hours and you come back—" He clapped, boom, anything
could have happened in that time. "Have you seen there is a new
graffiti on Mohammed Mahmoud?"

"Which one?"

"It's a verse from the Koran." I smiled and thought of Amar
on his stepladder painting the revolution. Hisham Kassem found
a picture of it on his mobile phone and translated for me:

*And they will say: Oh, Lord, indeed we obeyed our masters and our
dignitaries and they led us astray from the [right] way.*

The second round of the presidential vote was a rotten choice,
between devil and deep sea, between the past and Mubarak's
self-serving prophecy of the future. Even worse, it was a choice
between two men who were both second-rank, nether flun-

kies, equally mediocre. In the end Hisham Kassem decided he would vote for Shafik as the lesser of the two evils, because as a liberal he could never bring himself to vote for an Islamist. But when it came to the moment in the voting booth he could not bear to tick a Mubarak general so he scratched out both names and nullified his ballot. Dr. Hussein voted for Shafik because he thought he would be the easier president to contain from the street. Lina Attalah told me, "Could you imagine that your liberal Copt friend would vote for Morsi? I did! I voted for Morsi!"

The week between the vote and the delayed confirmation of the result swam in waiting liquid time. Never were the connections between cause, effect and consequence so plastic.

I can try to reconstruct events, but when I put them down in order they seem to take on a concreteness, a factualness, afforded by black-and-white type, that they shouldn't really be allowed. Because these "events" were really only gestures shaping a malleable conceptualization of power.

And then, by some obscured collusion of judiciary and SCAF, the parliament was dissolved . . . *And then* the country went to the polls in the second round of the presidential election . . . *And then* the Muslim Brotherhood said their exit polls calculated that Morsi had won . . . *And then* we waited because the electoral commission delayed confirmation of the result. *And then* tanks started moving to strategic points around the capital. SCAF announced a new emergency law so that officers had the power to arrest civilians. And at the same time a new addendum to the constitutional declaration. The Brotherhood sent their people to Tahrir for the first time.

Dr. Hussein called.

"God knows," I said.

"Things are happening. Happening very fast."

"Coup?" I said, tentatively, almost whispering.

"I can't go to sleep because when I wake up another something has happened that changes everything one hundred eighty degrees again."

And then SCAF held a press conference. *And then* Shafik held a press conference. *And then* Morsi held a press conference. Each began late. Each carried the urgency of an unresolved situation.

The general told the microphone, "We have called this conference to clarify everything." But nothing was clear at all. Hassan and I went back to Tahrir. What did the people think?

In the dim interior of a juice shop two men stripped lengths of sugarcane; a pile of discarded sticky orange halves gave out a fug of flies and rotten fruit. Milling Islamists, passersby, three high-ranking Interior Ministry police in black uniforms decorated with gold braid. Fag ends of conversation, snatched eavesdrops.

"Tantawi is saying the people don't even exist."

"This is the son of a bitch who wants to ruin Egypt."

"You know who supported Shafik? All the old NDP, all the old State Security people, because they want to get back to power."

"The scum! Pity the son of the scum. The scum! Pity the son of the scum!"

"In the name of Allah, they won't be able to do it."

A small march went by, maybe thirty people chanting, *Leave! Leave!* But who was in power to leave? The whole revolution was reduced to this word, shouted, *Leave!* Repeated so often it had lost meaning and become a mantra.

Hassan was disgusted. Hassan, who had shrugged *meh* through all the convulsions and convolutions. He said: "Don't they understand what would happen to this country without the army? There wouldn't be any kind of security at all. There would just be thugs everywhere on the street."

I looked at him askance to hear him defend the army like this—we walked away and went into the AUC bookshop to buy a copy of Wael Ghonim's book, *Revolution 2.0,* because I had to write a review of it. We sat in the air-conditioning for a bit to re-cover. Hassan was angry. I thought that he was angry with me, but he was angry at everything. He wanted to know why I had been upset when parliament was dissolved—"those idiots, they were doing nothing." And he wanted to know why I was happy that Morsi had—according to the exit polls, but still waiting, delayed, inexorable and agonizing, for the result to be confirmed by the election committee—apparently won. I tried to explain. I said that I believed in voting, in elections, in democracy. That the dissolution of parliament was a negation of this. That if Shafik had won we never would have known if he had really won or if the ballots had been stuffed and it was a coup.

Then it came pouring out of him.

"Yesterday it happened like that with the taxi driver. He asked me who I voted for and I said Shafik and then he called me a son of a bitch. Suddenly the meter went to zeros and I said, 'What's wrong with your meter?' He said: 'No no, it's all fine, it does it like that sometimes.' So I go from my house to Nasr City, no distance, and all I had was a twenty. So I gave him the twenty and he wants five more. Five more? I said, 'You should give me five as change.' He just said Shafik people are all sons of bitches. He was yelling at me. He said, 'Keep your twenty,' I said, 'Fine,' and got out of the car. And then he wanted more money again and he kept shouting at me, 'Shafik people are sons of bitches.'

Before the revolution it was bad and I wanted to leave and get the hell out of this country. But it was okay. Now if it's Morsi it's just going to be another dictatorship with beards. You only understand the freedoms you had under the dictator when you feel they are going to be taken away from you. I hate this country. That's why I didn't go out on the twenty-fifth. Egyptians are all rude and rip you off and shout at you. It's a really bad country. It's a really bad country." He repeated it, shaking his head. "They won't let me pass my exams, they won't let me have a job. It's a really bad country. I've never been to another country, but I know this one is really bad." He pointed to his index finger on his right hand. "I had to scrub the skin off to get rid of the election ink. It disgusted me."

I wanted to make him feel better, so we went to McDonald's in Mohammed Mahmoud.

The McDonald's cashier struck up a conversation with a kid ahead of us in line who ordered a cheeseburger combo meal. "I hope you didn't vote for Shafik."

The kid said, "I did actually."

"Agh," said the McDonald's man, making a grimace.

"Did you want me to vote for Morsi?" asked the kid.

"What's wrong with Morsi?"

"The Brotherhood, it's just another NDP, man."

We ate our hamburgers and went back into the waiting room of Tahrir. It was later in the afternoon now and it was filling up with Brotherhood people coming in minivans from all over the country. This was the first time the Brotherhood had ordered their people to the streets. They brought tents and blankets for a sit-in, demanding Morsi be confirmed president, demanding SCAF remove its constitutional addendum that would hamstring presidential authority. Hassan was still muttering under his breath. The scree of scratchy beards did not improve his mood. We talked to some people and listened to the Muslim Brotherhood official line and then when it got dark we went to Café Riche to have coffee with Dr. Hussein. Desultory conversations of absurdist ironies. And then a rumor came over Twitter that Mubarak had slipped into a coma in his hospital prison and was clinically dead.

Dr. Hussein looked up from his beer and remarked, "Mubarak's been clinically dead for years."

MORSI IS THE PRESIDENT

THE STREETS WERE EMPTY; MANY SCHOOLS AND OFFICES HAD closed early. On Tahrir the crowd stood sun-baked in silence. Waiting. It was hot, and I was worried I would get heatstroke. The crowd was almost all men and almost all Muslim Brotherhood. They were friendly and nervous, half smiles, tensed. One gave me his sweaty baseball cap to wear, another held an umbrella over my head. Others were spraying water from bottles to cool everyone down.

I looked at my feet. Grubby blue sneakers, apparently attached to me. Beneath them anodyne galaxies of grit and sand set in asphalt. Next to them a pair of box-toed leather lace-up shoes and a pair of rubber flip-flops and callused heels. I looked up, first at the impervious sky god above, then at the faces around me. There was a strange intimacy to this moment, all of us hemmed in close, waiting to see if history would tip revolution or return. The Brotherhood calculations put Morsi nine hundred thousand votes ahead, but this was roughly only 2 percent; the electoral commission could easily "correct" the exit tallies. Shafik. Or Morsi. Back. Or forward. We stood, leaning on one leg, and then shifted weight to the other. The man who held the umbrella had three careful stitches in his frayed collar; his face was sweating under his beard, and he wiped a handkerchief across his forehead. Hassan passed me the water bottle. I poured a little on the back of my neck. Elsewhere I could see men around me biting their nails. One man in front of us crouched on the ground, his hands interlaced behind his head, bracing the tension.

I was standing on the raised stoop near the Hardee's corner. It was tiring and boring to wait in the heat, and I turned to look behind me. At the edge of the square by the wall of the Mogamma I saw a garbageman. He was small and stunted, almost too short to be a man. An old man with a burned black face and a child-size body. He wore a shirt too big for him that was shiny with grease and dirt and billowed over a pair of filthy trousers. He was manhandling two large sacks, almost as tall as he was, and poking in the seeping smelling garbage piles for cans and bottles. He came to the corner but didn't raise his head or look about him; he was not interested in the crowd or the spectacle but only in the redeemable glass bottles he might find. I watched him wrestle one of the sacks to prop it against the wall so that it wouldn't topple over. There was no fastening and the cans would have spilled out otherwise. He rooted around in the garbage pile, unnoticed.

Finally, the head of the electoral commission addressed the country. His speech was broadcast through loudspeakers in metallic disembodied tones. Hassan strained to hear and whisper the translation. Several rows of the more devout continued to kneel for their midafternoon prayer. The head of the electoral commission recapitulated at length the procedure of Egypt's electoral transition and the difficult circumstances and accusations his judicial committee had dealt with. From time to time someone called out, "Hurry up!" or "Get on with it!" only to be shushed by the crowd. The head of the electoral commission turned his attention to the appeals, lodged by both camps, over voting irregularities. He detailed several investigations into discrepancies—for example, between the number of ballot papers counted in a particular polling station and the number of voter signatures registered. His pace, case by case, polling station by polling station, at times describing how complaints about the process in a single room of one polling station had led to the disqualification of this number of votes or that number of votes, was agonizing. Finally he admitted the mistakes did not substantially alter the initial tally. He recited the final figures. Morsi had won.

A great overwhelming cheer erupted.

"*Allahu akbar!*" shouted the man with the umbrella, waving it at the heavens. All around men wept openly and embraced each other. Several fell to their knees in spontaneous prayer. Everyone had their mobile phones clamped to their ears, nodding furiously and grinning and repeating *God is great God is great*. A little boy roared, "Morsi is a lion!" Above, fireworks sparkled in the blue sky like false raindrops. I felt drops in my eyes and I began to cry. I don't know why. Because the army had, despite everything, ceded to the ballot box. Because this meant there *was* a revolution. I wiped away my tears with the back of my hand but as my eyes blinked open, I caught a man looking at me. He smiled broadly and pointed and clapped his hands together—*Ha! Even the foreigner is weeping with joy!* Hassan looked at me with disbelief; I am sure he would have walked away at that moment but the crowd was too dense.

LIE DOWN FOR A BIT

MORSI WENT TO TAHRIR TO SWEAR HIMSELF PRESIDENT OF THE people. Hassan and I stood in front of McDonald's and watched his motorcade approach the square from Mohammed Mahmoud, graffiti portraits of the martyrs on either side. The police moved everyone back. Black SUVs with blacked-out windows drove past.

Then we went to Café Riche to watch his speech on TV. Egypt's first democratically elected president. He hailed the revolution and the legitimacy of the people. Then he stepped forward in front of his bodyguards and opened his jacket wide to show that he was not wearing a bulletproof vest. Dr. Hussein stubbed his cigarette out and said nothing. I experienced no high, not even the down after the high. I was passive with exhaustion. I left Cairo the next day.

In Adrien's apartment in Jerusalem I lay down on the sofa and did nothing for a whole month. It was hot outside, everything quiet and closed for the summer. Adrien was in Syria. I was alone and unthinking. I tried to write but my brain had shut down. At the end of July Morsi fired Tantawi; two hundred senior officers retired with full military honors and pensions. It seemed the Brotherhood had trumped the army. How or quite why this had happened was not clear; the army remained implacable, apparently quiescent. Then Omar Suleiman was reported to have died in hospital in America. Reading Egyptian news was like swimming further and further out to sea. Whenever anyone asked me to tell them about Egypt and the Arab Spring I found I could muster no analysis and certainly no theory. All the memes and themes had broken down into a thousand voices, shifting sands and a postcard of the pyramids.

1900: TWO TRIBES

ADRIEN HAD A VERY LARGE AND EXCELLENT COLLECTION OF DVDS. I watched a lot of Terrence Malick and began to believe that trees were the fundamental element of life. Trees stood, apart from any metaphor, as grand wisdom. They never acted or commented, but they watched all the follies of man and history and they were eternally beautiful and godly and moral, unspoiled by original sin.

One of the DVDs I watched was an old Bernardo Bertolucci film; *1900* tells the story of two boys born on an estate in the Po Valley on the same day at the turn of the century. One is the heir to the *padrone*, the other is a bastard child of a peasant. The bastard grows up to be Gérard Depardieu, a big and brave communist

organizer. The heir grows up to be Robert De Niro, soft and plea-
sure seeking, kidding around, weak. They are the representatives
of the polar political forces that shaped the twentieth century and
grow up best friends on opposite sides of the argument. Feudalism
to modernization, pastoral to war, an epic of the poor against the
landowners. The film is more than four hours long; the first half is
personal and intimate, human scale, but as time marches through
the twenties the story is overtaken by Fascist violence. Donald
Sutherland is the evil Blackshirt overseer of the estate. He pinions a
cat to a doorpost. "If this cat is communist," he cries to his hench-
men, "this is what I do!" and he rams the cat with his head so hard
that his grinning face with its malevolent tombstone teeth is covered
in blood. Adrien was very upset about the cat scene and complained
that the character was a cipher, too obviously evil: he abuses and
then murders a boy, he murders an old lady for her villa, he shoots
the peasants in the mud. In the final scenes the sun comes out for
liberation day in the spring of 1945. Dog roses bloom; the great red
flag is dug up from its hiding place. The peasants take their revenge
on Donald Sutherland, who is pitchforked, dragged into a pigsty
and shot. Gérard Depardieu convenes a people's court to judge his
birthday brother, the vacillating, ineffectual, good-man-who-stood-
by-and-did-nothing Robert De Niro. The peasants want to execute
him but Depardieu says that the *padrone* is already dead; the man
may be alive, but the title is gone and that is enough. The red flag is
carried out to the fields in celebration; the two old playmates are left
alone in the courtyard. "The *padrone* is not dead," states De Niro as
a matter of fact. Depardieu lunges at him and they tussle, kicking at
each other's legs, wrestling like boys. They are still wrestling in the
final scene, thirty years later, old men, in their seventies.

*C*ommunism and *fascism* are words consigned to the last century.
How do ideas turn into violence? I went out onto the balcony.

Adrien's apartment was in a neighborhood on the old green-line divide between East and West Jerusalem. I could see the golden Dome of the Rock and the crosses of the Christian quarter and the black-hatted figures of the ultra-orthodox hurrying through the Damascus Gate to pray at the Wailing Wall. I was not thinking straight; I was looping ideas that would not knot. A cat walked carefully across an adjacent roof, picking up his paws delicately from the hot tile; the afternoon was still. Isn't it funny that to think that hostility must first be imagined before it can be realized? That enmity is all in our heads? It is only a concept. It isn't tangible, but yet it manages to be real . . .

DOWN WITH
THE BROTHERHOOD

SIX MONTHS AFTER BECOMING PRESIDENT, MORSI ANNOUNCED, AS SCAF had before him, his own constitutional declaration. The declaration would put presidential decrees beyond the legal reproach of the Constitutional Court. Repeat. Circular. Just as fascism and communism, apparent polar opposites, bend toward each other and meet at the same totalitarian point. The revolution took to the streets again. Adrien and I flew back to Cairo.

Hassan picked us up from the airport and we drove straight to the scene of the recent protests, the presidential palace at Heliopolis. It was afternoon and quiet. We wandered around the walls and I took pictures of the new graffiti, Morsi with devil horns and a red nose, Morsi's head on an octopus body. The police wore their blue winter uniforms. The central security wore black uniforms. The military police had red berets, the Presidential Guard had sky-blue berets, the Republican Guard had helmets painted forest green. A protester in a *V for Vendetta* mask stood in a sentry box. Behind the gate a soldier with a camouflage forage cap leaned on the stoppered gun turret of his APC.

"What's the difference between the Presidential Guard and the Republican Guard?" I asked.

"Nothing," answered Hassan, "except mistranslation." Two weeks before, *Time* magazine had put Morsi on the cover with the headline "Is This the Most Important Man in the Middle East?" after he had negotiated a ceasefire between Hamas and the Israelis. Hassan had translated the interview. Morsi had sat on a gilt chair with a high curved back and golden armrests. "It really was a throne!" recounted Hassan. "The presidential palace is huge. You walk in and the floors are marble, but really clean, super shiny. Men in suits and big generals with briefcases walk past. There's a reception room all in Louis Farouk furniture and gold painted with pictures on the walls of European things like a woman feeding ducks or a man fishing, shit like that. There were even pictures of naked women! Then there was a large hall, then

a room with columns. The toilets had door handles made of brass lion heads. Did you know that Mubarak used to address the nation from a podium in front of a blue curtain? Morsi changed it for a red one."

Adrien tuned in to his singsong satire voice that sounded like munchkins singing in *The Wizard of Oz:*

"Now we are changing the decor. Now *I* sit on the throne. Now *you* sit in the tanks, now *you* do the chanting and *we'll* be the thugs."

"I still hate them though," said Hassan cheerfully. "Even more after they tried to arrest me for singing."

Hassan had sung front man one night at a heavy metal concert and a Muslim Brotherhood lawyer had filed charges of apostasy. Hassan woke up to find himself on the cover of every newspaper with his big floppy Afro, pulling the microphone close, underneath the headline "DEVIL WORSHIPPERS." The Ministry of Interior sent two police investigators to ask questions. People recognized Hassan and pointed at him on the metro. Hassan didn't think the prosecutor would take the case further. "In any case my picture was bigger than Morsi's on the front page," he said, shrugging, meh-heh, "which I consider a victory."

I was not frightened of the Muslim Brotherhood. But I was not an Egyptian and I didn't live among them. My feelings about them were pity and exasperation. I felt sorry for them because they had built and maintained, often at great personal cost, a network that supported and sustained, financially and in terms of spirituality and community, many thousands of families. I acknowledged their long and difficult effort of resistance against dictatorship. I remember Dr. Mohammed Beltegi living in the fetid travel agency on Tahrir throughout the eighteen days. I remember him staying all night on the square during the Battle of the Camels because his sons were defending the barricades,

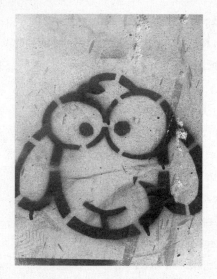

and he didn't want to leave them. But I didn't like the Brotherhood. It was based on obedience and hierarchy; dissent was expelled and discussion eschewed. They never understood pluralism or tolerance. They never acknowledged the validity of a different opinion. They did not really believe that other people had the right to have other ideas. Worse, they didn't have any ideas of their own. When Morsi became president, the Brotherhood had only the idea of power. "We are the majority, and democracy means that the majority rules," I heard one of the Brotherhood say on TV once.

When I had first met him the Big Pharaoh had been excited to reach one thousand followers on Twitter. Now he had twenty-one thousand and he had stopped bothering to check the number. But still he had never told his Couch Party family about his activism. For two years he had resigned himself to his double life. He did not tell his parents or his brother when he went to protests because he knew their fear for him would paralyze him. When political discussions came up at home, he would say, "Oh yes, but I read on Twitter that . . . ," or "On Facebook there was an article that said something else." He lied every day. He said he had to go to a business dinner in the evening or that he was meeting friends in a restaurant in Zamalek. He was very good at lying, and his brother and his parents were never suspicious. He would tell them he was staying late at the office and when he got home his mother would say, "Oh, you always come home so late, you work too hard!" Once he came home from a protest with a bruise on his forehead and he told them he had fallen down at work. When he got hit with bird shot in his leg he never mentioned it.

More marches were called. The Big Pharaoh's brother called him as he was leaving work.

"Are you going to go to the demonstration?" His brother said he was thinking of going. His brother had never gone to a demonstration in his life before. But this was a march against the Muslim Brotherhood.

"No," said the Big Pharaoh, lying, "I don't think so. I'm pretty tired."

Of course when he went to the demonstration he immediately bumped into his brother and his father in the crowd.

"Well I thought I would just come and check it out," he told them, trying to look casual about it.

"Stay right beside me," his father, a former paratroop officer, cautioned him. "In case something happens. It could get dangerous." The Big Pharaoh pulled his head down into his collar in case any of his revolutionary friends in the crowd recognized him. He tried to walk a little ahead of his father and his brother to lose them.

"Stay close!" his father called out.

The march advanced toward the presidential palace. The Big Pharaoh and his brother and father walked along the Heliopolis light railway track, stepping from one wooden tie to another. Along the way people peeled off from the crowd to spray-paint *Fuck Morsi* on the walls of the presidential palace. They stenciled Morsi's face and added rabbit ears and devil horns. Several puffy sheep appeared: the Brotherhood were all sheep to follow a supreme guide blindly! The Big Pharaoh's father was very taken with the placards and slogans and jokes and kept deciphering the chants that the Big Pharaoh knew well.

His father found his own milieu in the crowd, an older guard, well dressed in blue blazers with gold buttons and high patrician foreheads, all of them out on the street for the first time. The avuncular Couch Party members began an amiable debate.

"This is a mess because the Brotherhood are fascists and they are going to apply religious law! Maybe Mubarak was corrupt but at least he didn't use religion to curb our freedoms."

"The Brotherhood are not so bad," the Big Pharaoh tried to counter. When he was blind, his eyes streaming from the gas in Mohammed Mahmoud, it was a lady in *niqab* who had bathed his face with the flour-and-water mixture. He could understand why his parents were frightened when the TV showed pictures of crowds of beards shouting *Allahu akbar!* But he had been on the front lines with them. The night before he had been watching TV with his father.

"Look at that bastard Brotherhood!" his father had said, pointing to a certain Dr. Khalid Hanafi pontificating on a talk show.

"Dad, this Dr. Hanafi is a good man," the Big Pharaoh had said. "He was the head doctor at the clinic inside the church behind Tahrir all through the clashes on Mohammed Mahmoud. You can say what you like about all the rest of them, but this one I respect." His father cocked a side glance at him. The Big Pharaoh put his hands out in defense. "I read about him on Twitter!"

The Big Pharaoh's father had watched the melee of the last two years and put his faith in the steadying hand of the army. Ranks of the Presidential Guard stood outside the gates to the presidential palace. The protesters called out to them. One woman heckled, "Leave your positions and join us!" A soldier called back, "Take this guy out and put whoever you want inside!"

The crowd swelled and stood and shouted. The Big Pharaoh's father fell silent for a few moments and became anxious as the crowd funneled denser, calling out to his sons, "Stay close! Don't get lost here!" Ahead, unseen beyond the mass of heads and flags, lines of riot police waited, swinging their arms inside their new plastic armor. The Big Pharaoh saw his chance to escape.

"I'm tired, I think I'll go home," he told his father, and he pretended to leave down a side street. Almost immediately he ran into a friend of his.

"What am I going to do?" He told his friend all about bumping into his father and his brother at the demonstration. "This is a disaster!"

"Don't worry," said his friend. "The same thing happened to me! This is what you do: you go home tonight and talk in bright amazed tones about how wonderful and extraordinary the demonstration was and how you had never seen anything like it."

So this is exactly what the Big Pharaoh did. When he got home later that evening, he told his father: "Wow! What a demonstration! There were so many people! Did you see how big the crowd was? Wow! It was so exciting to be in the middle of all those people! Did you see the tear gas, Dad? Could you imagine that the police would throw tear gas at us?"

I met the Big Pharaoh for dinner in Heliopolis a few nights later. The Belgian Baron's oriental-Italianate porticos and colonnades and balconies looked cracked and down-at-heel under the unforgiving streetlights and the streets were emptyish while the demonstrations were still going on at the presidential palace every evening. We met at Le Chantilly, a Swiss restaurant with green and white checkered tablecloths, waiters in black waistcoats and *rosti* and cordon bleu veal on the menu. The waiters were anxious and wanted to close early because of the nearby disturbances. They ushered us, tutting, to a table, tapping their watches to indicate that we should eat quickly and go home early to be safe. We ordered fondue. The Big Pharaoh was a bit despondent. "There weren't huge numbers on Tuesday," he lamented, "it was nothing, it was carnival." The waiters twitched and refilled our wineglasses promptly.

"Right after the revolution we were dreaming about electing the regional governors," said the Big Pharaoh, putting his elbows on the table, leaning forward, forceful. "But according to the Brotherhood constitution, the president still appoints the governors. Right after the revolution we were dreaming of purging the police; Morsi is talking about purging the judiciary but he's leaving the police untouched. Right after the revolution we were dreaming that the police would be independent like in the U.S. or the UK, but the new constitution states that the police are answerable to the president. We dreamed that the judiciary would be independent but here is Morsi appointing his own prosecutor general. They have filed espionage charges against Baradei, Sabbahi and Moussa! We just changed Mubarak for a guy with a beard."

"Hey," I said, trying to cheer him up, "it's not over yet." I tried to pull back to a wider view. "I know that now it looks messy, violent, awkward, confused, full of shouting. But the street still holds a certain legitimacy. The street is still holding out for the original demands of Tahrir. Dignity. A better government, responsive, responsible, accountable, fair. These were the hopes, badly articulated, distracted by events, but they remain, I think, bedrock. Think about it. Every time the authority—Mubarak, Tantawi and now Morsi—tries to impose their will from above, the street pushes back."

The Big Pharaoh shook his head at me. We finished our fondue. The waiters were turning off lights, agitating for us to leave. It wasn't yet eight o'clock.

"Let's go and smoke *shisha*," said the Big Pharaoh, and we walked around the corner to his second-favorite *shisha* café.

"I myself have my doubts," he continued, thoughtful. "Was it worth it?" The café was almost empty. The man brought two glasses of tea. The boy brought the water pipe and the hot coals.

On the TV behind us the news of the day was turned down low: footage from the funeral procession of a journalist who had been shot in the clashes.

"My friend," continued the Big Pharaoh, "my very close friend Malek lost his eye in Mohammed Mahmoud. I remember when I heard. A friend called me and told me he was in hospital. I was on the street. I ran into a doorway and I sobbed. You asked me what I remember most clearly over the last two years? This moment. I was sobbing loudly, then someone came past and I tried to be quiet. I was walking through the streets just crying and everyone thought I was crying from tear gas. I thought, Malek, this great cheerful young man, will have to live with one eye. And that's when I started to doubt things. And this is the question that I want to ask him, but I just don't have the guts: Malek, was it worth it?" The Big Pharaoh stopped himself for moment; it was unlike him to be angry. "He lost his eye for this? Was it really worth it?"

I found Jehane in the same place I had seen her exactly a year before. She was again finishing an edit before a Sundance deadline. Again there were ongoing protests.

"So, it's getting better," said Jehane, about the edit, not the political situation. "But the ending has still got to be figured out."

Karim had a beard now, but the same grin. Laughing at all the tangled constitutional wranglings. Laughing at all of us trying to make any sense of the whole shebang. At me writing a book and them making a movie.

"If I could make my ideal film about this situation," said Karim, "it would be *The Canterbury Tales*. Every story is connected but each is separate. Every incident is part of the revolution but you can't link them with this-means-that-happened or this-happened-because-of-that."

He ran his hand over his face. Many times over the past year editing, reediting, they had found themselves focusing on someone, and then that person would disappear from the story for several months, only to pop up again in a new plot twist.

"Like all the problems we had with trying to figure out where to put Shafik. At one point we had a big section with Shafik and now he's not in the movie at all." Karim mimed tearing his hair out. "And everyone thought he's going to be the next president and the army are going to anoint him in a coup and then he lost—by one percent, one percent!—and now he's disappeared again."

Jehane brought me a cup of tea and we went into the viewing room. "So I haven't seen this new version yet," she said. "It's not perfect. We want to add a new ending. The old ending was Morsi's election, now it's 'Leave, Morsi!' The full circle."

"I had the same problem," I told her. "This is the third act."

"But is this a three-act play or a five-act play?"

We sat down to watch. The film echoed the version I had seen a year before, but now, with a little distance, the episodic protests dissolved into each other naturally and made a continuous swell. Jehane had not tried to explain anything. Shorn of exposition, the revolution was the square. People talking in the quiet waiting early hours, an arguing knot under a blazing overhead sun, a pointing finger jabbing for emphasis, someone making a sandwich, tent pegs and garbage underfoot, an old man spooning *koshari* from a plastic tub, two glowing cigarette tips meeting to light each other. Prosaic moments. Cut. The camera jolts, angled toward the ground, veering tarmac, running among the running protesters. Day into nighttime and then sunrise again, running protesters, running lines of police, rocks going over, bandaged hands, blood trails across the rubble, revving engines of the blue police vans with their tiny square grilled windows, switch reel, cut edit, another day, running again, flared sparking fires, many scenes cloudy with tear gas . . .

Karim said: "How can two years of my life be reduced to ninety minutes?

As the months of the demonstrations repeated each other on-screen and the debates revolved, army and Brotherhood and constitution, I saw my own memories from another angle, and the gaps between my memories filled. I saw, for example, the officers on the square on the eighth of April. That day I had walked past them without stopping. Or I think I tried to talk to one of them and he had backed away. Maybe at the time I had not thought the presence of the officers was significant—and maybe, looking back, it wasn't; Jehane's film rewound my memory with hindsight. *The officers look very frightened,* I thought, watching, looking back, *in their olive-green fatigues, standing in the crowd without their guns.* There was footage of the army storming the square at two o'clock in the morning. At the time I was asleep. Shouts of "Protect the army officers" go up as the soldiers advance. In the next shot Tahrir is completely empty. I never saw the square completely empty. In the following scene soldiers are relaying sod on the central traffic circle. This I had seen firsthand; it was midafternoon, I was walking back from an interview in downtown and the soldiers planted flowers within a circle of military police who stood shoulder to shoulder guarding the new grass.

Spring to summer. Ah, I remember that billowing white parachute-silk set pulleyed over the central traffic circle for shade during the July sit-in. Handsome Khalid Abdalla, actor, activist and one of the recurring characters in the documentary, is talking to the camera. Watching him I realized I had actually met him on the square that July; he was screening revolution footage and every evening a crowd would gather and watch the police vans run over protesters on the Sixth October Bridge again or the camels bouncing through Tahrir. And I remember thinking, watching my memories then, that summer night, how strange it was that I felt moved with so much nostalgia for events I had lived and consumed and already half forgotten.

I reached over for Karim's lighter.

"It's wonderful," I told them. "You get a sense of the to-and-fro, the ongoing struggle, the strange cycles of it all. Again and again you see the military trying to clear the square. Again and again the police and the protesters throw rocks and tear gas at each other."

"This is what Khalid the actor says," Karim agreed. "He's been giving a lot of lectures and he talks about the revolution coming in waves but says the pattern of the waves is not logical. An act leads to a reaction but the reaction can come months later and be connected to something else. But the boiled-up anger pushes the revolution forward toward its goals."

The protests against Morsi at the presidential palace now formed the final sequence, denouement, riposte or just another chapter. It was only last week. Ahmed, one of the revolutionaries whom Jehane had followed through two years, is in the back of a car driving away from the protest. He describes how the Muslim Brotherhood came beating people just like the pro-Mubaraks came beating people. Ahmed is shaking, hunched small in the darkened backseat, delivered from the violence behind him. He looks over his shoulder at something unseen and receding behind him. There is a pause as he returns to the narrative.

"And then I threw a rock."

"That's it!" I said, jumping up and clapping my hands. "'And then I threw a rock.' Cut!" It is everything, it is the sum of the revolution. 'And then I threw a rock! Fade to black. Roll credits!"

CITADEL

THE PROTESTS SUBSIDED. MORSI'S CONSTITUTIONAL DECLARATION was superseded by a referendum on a new constitution. The country voted yes, apparently in the tradition of voting yes in referenda; something-anything was better than the unknown future of no. There were also complicating details and farce: the liberals on the constitutional committee had walked out of the proceedings and there was a court case pending charging that the constitutional committee was unconstitutional because it had been convened under the authority of a parliament that had been dissolved . . .

What did it matter anyway what was in the constitution? I am half American and half British. I revere the vision of the Founding Fathers' contract, but in England we have never had a written constitution and my British half has more faith in an informal contract based on precedent and an indefinable commonality. "The American Constitution is the exception," I might have said to the Egyptian Social Democrats, Dr. Hussein and Aly, sitting on Dr. Hussein's balcony. "No other constitution has lasted—look at the French! It doesn't matter what is written on a piece of paper; what matters more, what determines a political culture, the *governance* of a country, is more to do with expectations, mores, norms, than with legal rubric. What is acceptable, what is reasonable . . ."

"But you can't sanction the unacceptable and the unreasonable without laws . . ."

I can't remember who I was arguing with, or if I made up this debate, walking along, kicking at scree on the sidewalk, talking to myself.

"The rule of law, yes, this is the most important thing," I might have continued, "but the enforcement of law does not depend on a constitution. The 1971 Egyptian constitution that Mubarak operated under has a perfectly good set of checks and balances, but they were either not applied or abrogated by thirty years of a state of emergency."

"So we need to write regulations to prevent dictatorship," Aly's second cousin, the lawyer, might have replied.

"But dictatorship will always circumvent regulations. What are regulations to a dictator?"

"In Egypt," Omar the intelligence officer might have said, reflexively resting his thumb against his pistol, "there is only the army that can do anything."

"Ah," interrupted Adrien, stepping forward one afternoon that December, as we were walking around the old Citadel, "now we are back to our debate about who creates polity: the leader or the people. Is there even such a thing as politics?"

The Citadel was quiet. We wandered around Saladin's ramparts. Here was military centuries past, built on a hill above the inundations of the Nile. Beneath us, balconies and rooms strung on washing lines, spread across the city. We wondered at the history of Egypt that stretched unbroken through every age and empire and I told Adrien a story I had heard: that when an Egyptian general went to visit another Egyptian general he brought a gift of a solid-gold pyramid.

"Even if it's not true, it might as well be," I said. "Patronage."

"It's very Ottoman," commented Adrien. "Each rank pays its tribute to the rank above." We gazed over the dun cubism of the city spread before us, poked here and there with Abbasid minarets. There were no other tourists in the Citadel and we were alone.

"Perhaps the culture of the Ottomans remains underneath the khaki and gold they copied from the British. As if each age lays down a layer of culture like sediment."

"The modern idea of Egypt comes from Napoléon," mused Adrien. "The French were only here for three years but they had a big impact. They brought with them scholars and ethnographers and cartographers and they found the Rosetta stone and cataloged all the Pharaonic ruins that were half-covered in sand and squatters. They started Egyptology."

"And chopped off the Sphinx's nose," I put in.

"No," said Adrien, who always knew these things better. "That's a myth. It wasn't done by French soldiers. It was a religious zealot in the fourteenth century who was furious that the local people were bringing offerings to the Sphinx like a shrine. That's another strand that seems to recur, religious extremism. The idea of religion as a superiority that has to destroy everything other." Adrien stopped to bend down and touch the nose of an elegant marmalade tabby. "Are you looking for good tourist garbage, cat?"

"Meow," answered the cat.

"Before the French," Adrien continued, "Egypt was ruled by the Mamelukes for four hundred years. Foreign slaves made into boy soldiers and raised to commander caste. Then the Ottomans sent Muhammad Ali to take charge. He was an Albanian born in Macedonia. He invited all the Mameluke feudal leaders and warlords to a great dinner here in the Citadel and then he killed them all."

"Saddam style."

"And he turned out to be a good military ruler too, he was inspired by the French, he modernized the army, he created a national army out of conscription, he modernized the state, he began taxation. Then he sent his son to Arabia to defeat the Wahhabis—"

"It is a long tradition," I said, thinking aloud, "the conflation of Egyptian military with Egyptian state is much older than Nasser—"

"And they were successful; they were a big strong army of the time: Muhammad Ali invaded Arabia, he sent soldiers to Greece, they conquered Palestine . . ."

When we had walked Saladin's ramparts we went to visit the National Military Museum in another part of the Citadel complex. It was housed in the emir's former harem, a grand building with no windows. Inside was dimly lit and dusty gilded gloom, the ceilings and walls painted with the orange groves and fountains and rose arbors and river vistas, trompe l'oeil scenes, perhaps in compensation for the lack of freedom to walk abroad in real gardens. On the ground floor, directly opposite the entrance, was a vast mosaic, an epic scene of beloved supreme leader Mubarak walking in front of a group of generals surrounded by a crowd of smiling Egyptians holding out flowers in gratitude.

In a couple of rooms the wall paintings of pastoral courtyards and topiary had been painted over with murals of missiles and satellite radar dishes or tanks and fixed-wing aircraft. We toured the hall of the paratroops, the hall of the air defense corps, the diorama of the 1952 revolution . . . cabinets filled with bullets and guns, bronze busts of generals and walls of portraits of martyrs. Many of the exhibits had been roped off and lay dormant in darkened unlit rooms.

NAPOLÉON

THE ASSEMBLÉE NATIONALE DEVOLVED INTO UPROAR, GIRONDISTS against Montagnards hurling treachery at each other, insults flying like paper darts that unfolded into arrest warrants; the guillotine waited on the Place de la Révolution. There is no dialogue. This film was made before talkies. The screen flickers black and white, the camera chops from one side to another, faster and faster, like a speeded-up tennis match. It doesn't matter what they are saying. Every deputy is shouting, each an argument unto himself. The words are replaced by an orchestra playing clashing discord. The edit cuts back and forth with such speed that the blur of intercut suddenly explodes into six images all at once, all yelling, all pointing, furiously gesticulating. I do not know which one to look at: the fat curate in the periwig or the scrawny lawyer with a hank of greasy hair who is rattling a sheaf of papers or the stentorian powder-white profile of Robespierre.

Abel Gance made *Napoléon* in 1927. He originally planned to film Napoléon's life as a six-part epic, but he spent all the money on the first episode, five and a half hours, which covers only childhood and his early career through the Italian campaign. In 1792, the French Republic is proclaimed, the king is imprisoned and the Assemblée Nationale fractures with the challenges of governance, law and order, regicide and civil war. At the same time, Napoléon flees the anti-French faction in his native Corsica.

From the roiling Assemblée Nationale, cut to Napoléon's nighttime escape as he is galloping to the coast. The rain lashes at his face, and water from his bicorne's runnels drips off his long nose. He comes to a cove where there is an old rotted rowboat tethered to a pontoon. He turns his horse loose in the maquis and sets out to sea, to France, rowing. The storm swells, the waves roll. Abel Gance invented many new techniques for *Napoléon*: the split screen, panorama vision, the triptych. To film the debate in the Assemblée Nationale he hoisted his cameras on pulleys and swung them over the faces of the crowd so that when he cuts back from Napoléon bailing water out of his little boat with his hat, the audience is pitched forward, rocking like the storm-tossed boat across the faces of the arguing deputies. The wind howls, the debate rages, the camera veers close-up and pulls back again, the waves climb and crash. Napoléon, drenched, hoists the *tricolore* as a sail. Finally the sea is soothed; shafts of sunlight pierce the clouds; the revolution has expended its fury.

My father took me to see *Napoléon* at the Barbican in London when I was thirteen. The film was being shown around the world after being lost for many decades. *Napoléon* was a victim of history, apogee of the silent era; just as it was finished, the talkies arrived, and microphones anchored all action into drawing-room stasis.

The film historian Kevin Brownlow had managed to reassemble it from bits of footage lost in archives and flea markets; the composer Carl Davis wrote a new score.

When it was finally shown to an audience in 1979, Abel Gance was ninety years old, still alive, just for two years yet, to see his masterpiece finally triumph. Screenings were theatrical events with a full orchestra. *Napoléon* cannot be bought on DVD, and screenings, considering its length and the need for an orchestra, are rare. The film made such a strong impression on me that I can still recall Gance's montage of revolution and flight almost frame by frame. The tumultuous rhythms of Abel Gance's fluid-motion camera work carry a raw power and a fury that I have never experienced in the cinema again. I remember my father and I taking our seats at eleven thirty in the morning; there were intervals for lunch and tea and dinner, and we emerged, reeling, saturated, shattered, at eleven thirty in the evening.

Sometimes I would think of *Napoléon* in the tear gas blur on Tahrir. And I would try to apply my history lessons. *Whiff of grapeshot.* And I wondered too if some lieutenant or colonel or general, a character yet unknown to us, would step out of the wings and take the stage. Then I would remember that I had given up theories, and the theory of history repeating itself in particular.

REASONS TO BE CHEERFUL

MORSI HAD BEEN PRESIDENT FOR A YEAR. ADRIEN CONVINCED his editors to let him write a travel-history story about the French in Egypt. I wanted to go back to Cairo to see my friends, and because I had heard a big national demonstration had been called against Morsi for the thirtieth of June.

The first thing I noticed driving in from the airport were petrol queues two hundred cars long.

"Everyone hates the Brotherhood now," said Hassan triumphantly. He was doing well working for foreign journalists and had bought a car. Still the same loose black T-shirt, the same shaggy fro, but he had lost his meh and was now all enthusiastic about the gathering anti-Morsi momentum. A group called Tamarod, which means "rebel," had collected seventeen million signatures on a petition against Morsi. "I went to see them," Hassan told me. "They are nice middle-class boys. Not the English-speaking elitey Twitterati revolutionaries . . ."

"Yes, but seventeen million—seriously?" I was skeptical. "A national grassroots organization from nothing to seventeen million in two months? Just logistically, practically, there would be enough paper to fill warehouses!"

Hassan shrugged, but he liked the Tamarod kids; they were sincere.

"Tamarod are calling for everyone to go out on June thirtieth, to demand Morsi's resignation."

"And then what happens?" I asked.

Hassan shrugged again.

Adrien counted out loud 213 cars in one petrol queue.

I said, "So is the traffic better now because no one can get gas?"

Hassan laughed. "No, it's worse! Because the gas lines are blocking all the roads."

"Why is there a shortage?" asked Adrien.

"If you ask the minister of petroleum he says there is no shortage and the shortages are only psychological," said Hassan, repeating the government pro forma.

"Huh?"

"If you talk to the economists," he continued in a new voice, a honed professional briefing voice, "they say it is because the environment ministry stopped allowing the river to be used for transporting oil and the trains aren't carrying oil because there have been too many accidents recently and so the only way for the oil to travel is by road, but there had been a shortage of diesel. But then if you ask the petrol station guys they say they have enough petrol," said Hassan, regaining his mischievousness, "but they admit they are rationing each car to twenty liters to create a perception of shortage to undermine Morsi . . ."

"So no one knows why there are gas lines," I concluded, not very surprised.

And no one knew what would happen on the thirtieth of June. Flights out of Cairo were fully booked, families massed in the departure lounges with mountains of luggage. Shopkeepers pulled down their metal shutters and made sure they were double locked. People said there would be violence because the Brotherhood would send rival marches and thugs; people said no one would go out onto the street because people said there would be violence.

There was a lot of white-noise disquiet: stories of mugging and carjackings, balaclava gangs that appeared in the midst of demonstrations; *V for Vendetta* masks were selling like hot falafel . . . Morsi had appointed an Islamist as culture minister and the liberals were camped outside the ministry villa to stop him taking office . . . a tax on alcohol had been mooted, but this was to do with the IMF loan that was a long negotiation that had been going on for more than a year and kept breaking down . . . just the previous weekend four Shia were beaten to death by a mob in Giza and Morsi had said nothing . . . sexual harassment on Tahrir was epidemic, mob attack, rape—"I wouldn't advise you to walk around downtown alone," Hassan told me soberly.

"Oh," said Hassan, adding incidents as many headed hydra as ever, "and did you hear Morsi is being indicted for escaping from prison during the revolution?"

I called all my friends. Axiomatic that no one answered their phone. The city seemed the same as always, sand colored and full of people and traffic. Adrien and I went to the pyramids for his history-travel story. There were no sightseers and we shoed away the camel boys and the souvenir vendors who hovered like flies. We felt harassed and defensive, subject to the same guilt and irritation, pity and exploitation, that

has been the lot of foreign visitors in Egypt since Napoléon invented tourism.

One night we bumped into Ramy Shaof and his wife, Ragia
Omran, the red-haired human rights lawyer, at a restaurant in
Zamalek. I was drinking mojitos, the better to clear my head.
Ragia, cogent as always, discussed Tamarod and the looming
thirtieth of June. Ramy was uncharacteristically quiet. Ramy,
the original revolutionary, Ramy who talked a mile a minute
of elaborate analysis and whom I had always seen in constant
motion, setting up another political party or organizing a solidarity convoy of aid to Gaza or debating on Tahrir on a Friday
afternoon—and I would ask him where Ragia was and he would
answer, "My wife?" and laugh, looking about him pantomiming
a search for something that had been, just a moment ago, right
beside him. "I have no idea! She's busy busy, all the time, too
many people arrested who need defending." And then he would
sigh, the revolution unfinished—Ramy whom I had first met
after the Battle of the Camels, staring up at the giant edifice of
Mogamma and pointing to the window of the State Security office where his file was kept, *this Ramy* had recused himself from
activism. He had quit Baradei's party and stepped back from
politics.

"There's something dirty on both sides of this June thirtieth
thing," he told me. "I'm having a kind of break, time to get back
to life a little."

In the time of Mubarak, Ramy Shaof's name had been on a
State Security list for twenty-two years. He was forced to renew
his passport annually; every year he went to a special section of
Mogamma to submit an application; every time he went through
the airport, leaving or arriving, he was taken to the security office for interrogation. Several times he had been placed under a
travel ban. His life had been circumscribed by State Security. At

the end of December 2010, as Tunisians were revolutioning, he
went to a meeting of activists in the town of Minya to discuss
how to organize protests for Police Day on the twenty-fifth of
January. They had organized protests for the previous couple of
years; maybe this time, they hoped, more people would turn out.
Two days after this meeting, Ramy received a call from his State
Security case officer.

"How was Minya?" his State Security case officer asked.

"Very nice, thank you," answered Ramy.

"Well I think you should come to the office and tell us
about it."

Ramy went to the State Security office, where he had been
questioned many times before. He always fought to keep his
mood buoyant. He treated it like a game: he smiled at them, he
presented himself as an open book—"Yes, I am, yes, I was. And
so?"—and hoped to belay their aggression with a kind of guile-
less friendliness.

His State Security case officer questioned him for some time.
Ramy told him some things but not many things. The State Secu-
rity officer growled his irritation and finally dismissed him, saying,
"Get out of here! Go away and play!"

After the revolution Ramy brought a lawsuit against State Security to expunge his name from the travel-ban list and to rein-
state his passport privileges. Ramy won the case and returned to
the State Security office to get his new passport. He came in front
of his old case officer, the same man sitting behind the same desk
in the same office in Mogamma. The officer was still irritable and
belligerent. Ramy presented his documents and notification of the
court ruling, smiling pleasantly, and was careful not to betray a
twinkle of gratification. The State Security officer displayed his
superiority, in the manner he had always done, by banging his fists
on the table and shouting.

"Why are you angry?" Ramy asked him sweetly. "You told me to go away and play—so, we did what you told me, we played."

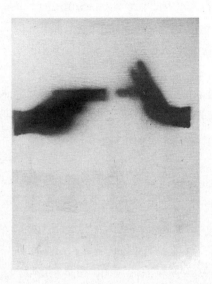

In the evenings, according to habit, I typed up my notes. I put them in a file I labeled *Reasons to be Cheerful.* Ramy's victory over State Security was one. A conversation with Aly Second Cousin was another. Aly told me that his law firm, which dealt mainly with high-end corporate clients, was super busy. Mergers, acquisitions, small-medium businesses opening, activity. "Heineken had a record year last year!" Perhaps this was a sign that amid the messiness there was a space that had never existed before, a little elbow room, chinks between the blocks; a place where people could do things that they had not been able to do before—"Yes," continued Aly, lowering his voice, "but I almost don't want to say it out loud. There is a sense of something opening and growing where once Egypt was just stagnant. Watch Bassem Youssef . . ." Bassem Youssef was an Egyptian Jon Stewart who lampooned everyone, Brotherhood sheep and judicial hypocrisies and stentorian generals and bombastic imams. I remembered Adrien telling me: *Dictators fall when people can laugh at their ridiculousness.* "You can feel it in odd ways," said Aly, "for example there are Egyptian atheist groups on Facebook—no one would have ever admitted to such a thing before! And another thing, I have several gay friends who have come out recently."

"Really?"

"Just to their friends, some not yet to their parents—but!"

I had always held fast to my optimism and my faith in the revolution. The week before the thirtieth of June I was still inventing reasons to be cheerful. I thought that the revolution was still there, a mess, a political flowerbomb, but somehow blossoming slowly in people's hearts and minds. The revolution on Tahrir had toppled the authority of the dictator and in so doing it had challenged the assumption of authority—from the police to the army to the headmasters and fathers and husbands too. I believed that the street (as violent and incoherent as it inherently was) could continue to push back against the powers-that-be and create a space in which aspiration and innovation and reform and justice could grow. Egypt's future would depend on the will and mind-set of its people more than it would ever be dictated by the proscriptions of a constitution. If the revolution lived, it could change Egypt's relationship to government and to the state simply by changing the expectation of that relationship. If the revolution lived, if it honored differing opinion and individual rights, it could change society too. This was the example and the promise of the utopia of the eighteen days on Tahrir.

Lina hovered between tired and somehow not-weary-yet. We met for our customary lunch; she paid and I was sure it was not her turn and I felt bad about this. The English version of *Egypt Today* had been closed down, the management said it was too costly, but she was starting up a news website called Mada with her old staff. It was due to go live on June thirtieth. I found her ambivalent about Tamarod's calls for people to go out on the street. Something had shifted in her feelings about the relationship between the protests and the revolution. Six months before when Morsi tried to declare his own constitution and the revolutionaries took to the streets again she had told me: "The rowdy elusive street fights have played a role in changing the higher political dynamics. Although those fighting on the streets didn't care about politics, even though it was more between street vendors and police and young revolutionaries. They delegitimized SCAF and now they are delegitimizing the rule of the Brotherhood."

But now Lina felt Tahrir had lost its meaning for her. The square had eroded into a place that only represented nostalgia. Whenever she walked across it, picking her way over the sandpit sidewalks and broken curbs, she found herself unmoved by the fragments of tents and scratched-up graffiti, the detritus of left-over protests. She was only irritated at the eyesore.

A few days before our lunch, she had, by chance, driven through a demonstration supporting the Tamarod campaign. The small crowd was chanting: *The people and the army are one hand!* As she slowed down, one of the protesters had slapped a sticker on her car that read, *Go Down on the Streets on the 30th June! Don't Be a Coward!* When she got home she immediately scraped it off, angry at being labeled, appropriated. And as she caught herself desperately scratching at the glue, she remembered that five years ago she had voluntarily driven around

Cairo with a bumper sticker that read: *Stop Bitching and Start a Revolution!* She tried, in an article she wrote, to articulate the irony:

"Last night I recognized the hysteric moment of removing the bumper sticker insistently as an unspoken declaration of 'I am not one of the people today.' I recognized the Kafkaesque instance where a metamorphosis of self or revolution was unfolding. It is either that we have become the counterrevolution or that the revolution has become the counterrevolution."

The Big Pharaoh was in Amsterdam, but he was planning to return for June thirtieth. The white noise was gathering intensity and three days before the date, Morsi addressed the nation. At the same time, the Big Pharaoh was eating a big juicy rib eye in a steak restaurant beside a canal and following the broadcast on Twitter. Morsi railed at the unseen forces against him. He kept denouncing the *feloul*, the remnants of the old regime. The *feloul* was undermining Egypt, deep state and *feloul* with foreign agendas, maneuvers and conspiracies, hidden hands . . .

Morsi was right about all of this. We knew it at the time even as we derided his monotony and his paranoia. After all, he was a Brotherhood spare tire, unsympathetic, insincere. His appeals for a committee of national reconciliation fell on deaf ears as they had always done. The Twitterati rolled their emoticon eyes. After a while the Big Pharaoh finished eating and paid the bill. He left the restaurant and walked back to his hotel. He took in the pleasant early summer evening, the coolness next to the canals, the elegant houses that rose on either side. He took his time, and, after half an hour, he reached his hotel. He went up to his room, brushed his teeth, had a bath, put on his pajamas, got into bed, opened his iPad, clicked onto Twitter and discovered Morsi was still speeching.

The Big Pharaoh thought: *This is worse than Mubarak.*

I woke up the day after Morsi's speech and went out onto the balcony. Adrien and I were staying at the Marriott in Zamalek and the view gave out over the green lawn tennis courts of the Gezira club. I leaned against the railing and turned my head upside down so that the sky was the ground and the street was the sky and the tennis players and the pedestrians were walking upside down on clouds. Adrien looked at me and asked: "What are you doing?"

"I am trying to look at the world from a different perspective," I answered.

WAVES AND SEA

CROWD WAS SEA. STAND WAIST-HIGH AT THE POINT WHERE WAVES break and watch the swells as they come in irregular intervals and varying strengths. Successive rise, curl, crash, fizz. The undertow pulls through your legs, sucking backward, and the wind blows landward currents that drag the salt water against your body. The swells grow larger and you have three choices: to dive clean through the wave, to stand and let it knock you over and swirl you around in its washing machine, or to paddle to catch the wave and ride it, surfing into shore.

Me making metaphors to pass the time, sitting in a café, waiting for history to march past.

On the thirtieth of June Adrien and Hassan and I went out to the presidential palace in Heliopolis to gauge the numbers. Tamarod had called people to occupy every square in Egypt. The crowds gathered, as enormous as an ocean.

There were middle-aged men and kids and little kids too, begging with missing fingers, goldfish darting among the reeds of legs. *Feloul* with smart sunglasses and Ralph Lauren Polo shirts, unveiled women with glossy tossing hair who admitted to supporting Mubarak, Couch Party types, older women who twisted their rings into their palms to hide them when they were pressed too much in the crowd, people who had never been to a protest before, men with mustaches and small prayer calluses and Christian women in T-shirts with bare arms and families holding hands with their children like a daisy chain, Twitterati activists from the twenty-fifth who worried about the pro-army contingent and plenty of people who had voted for the Brotherhood but who now said they hated them for bringing Egypt down, policemen waving Egyptian flags and people chanting, "The people and the police are one hand!" Hassan showed me a picture on his phone of police being hoisted on the shoulders of protesters in Alexandria. Cars roared past us, honking and streaming flags from their windows. "It's massive," said Hassan, scrolling through Twitter. "It's all over Egypt! I never felt Egyptian, but today I feel hope. Look! Everyone is smiling!"

We left Heliopolis and drove back into the center of the city toward Tahrir. There was little traffic except at the intersections, where the marches were thick. At these we inched our way through. The atmosphere continued to be one of high holiday celebration. Along the Corniche we passed an army barracks and I saw four soldiers inside the guard booth dancing and waving at the marchers as they went past. "Look!" Adrien pointed. Behind us a kid was standing on the roof of a moving bus, surfing the slipstream with his palms. Father, mother, two kids all crammed onto mopeds; two boys washing a horse in the Nile. It was the golden hour of sunset; kites flew against the pink sky. A group of children at a crossroads were having their own little protest and jumping up and down delightedly. An elderly couple sat in front of their house holding flags in solidarity. Every café was full to overflowing on the sidewalks and when the Corniche became clogged with buses and marches we turned into the mazy alleys of Bulaq. It felt like the whole country was on the street and Hassan was right. *Happy.* We passed a trinket stall selling balloons.

"Why is SpongeBob everywhere?" I asked. "This is a strange phenomenon!" Hassan posited that there was an Arabic Sponge-Bob song that had become wildly popular. Adrien laughed, "In Aleppo SpongeBob is painted all over the schools—it is a little incongruous now because the schools are rebel headquarters and the cartoon walls are stacked with homemade mortars. Sponge-Bob also has several friends," he added, "there is a starfish and a lobster and a jellyfish."

Tahrir was full and the crowds were packed even along the bridges over the Nile and along the Corniche. The crowd was too dense to fight our way through; we stood in our old spot, out-side McDonald's at the neck of Mohammed Mahmoud. March-ers were still arriving and there was no room for them. It was the same in Alexandria and Asyût and Suez and Port Said. Egyptians gathered outside Egyptian embassies in Montreal and London and in five cities in Italy and in front of the UN building in New York and in front of the White House in Washington. Millions and millions of people, too many to count. They said there were fourteen million Egyptians on the streets that day. They said it was the greatest demonstration in human history.

Hassan was exultant.

"Do you see? Do you see!" he said. He raised his arms to the sky to the people to the great mass all around us. Hassan was standing, by coincidence, next to a huge mural of a martyr who looked like him with the same slim smooth face and the same big floppy Afro. Two days before, we had been walking about and I had taken a picture of Hassan next to this graffiti doppelgänger. Hassan was annoyed at my taking his photo; he looked sad-eyed. Now he was smiling and jumping up and down. Hassan's dead twin looked on with an unchangeable expression.

"Ah, good old McDonald's!" Old faithful, windows boarded up, guard posted on the door, but always open no matter the mood or crush or tear gas outside. We went in.

"The last time we came here together was a year ago when Morsi was elected and we sat at this same table," said Hassan. "And you cried!" Hassan pointed at me. "I'll never forget that you cried! And I sat here and yelled at you and said, 'They don't represent me and I don't feel a part of this country,' and you said, 'No, everything is fine and Egypt has elected a new leader,' and you cried!"

I remembered the week waiting for Morsi's election to be confirmed. Parliament dissolved. Tanks surrounding the capital. I ate my trustworthy cheeseburger that always tasted the same in every different country. Something skipped over itself in my head like an echo. Chanting reached us through the boarded-up windows from the street, a scratched record jumping over chorus lines.

Everything that followed was as clearly written and predictable as a train timetable in August 1914. Or, if you preferred, you could have consulted more recent Egyptian history, opening the textbook at the chapter entitled "Nasser and the Free Officers," and read the plot. I had once thought history doesn't repeat itself. Another theory down the toilet.

The next day General Sisi, a character as yet unknown to us, who had replaced Tantawi as head of SCAF and minister of defense, announced a forty-eight-hour deadline: "If the demands of the people are not met within this period it will be incumbent upon us to announce a road map for the future and oversee measures to implement it."

He wore sunglasses beneath the gold-laureled brim of his officer's cap.

It was a coup.

Several million people shouted back: "No! It is a revolution!"

The next night Morsi addressed the nation for the last time. Dr. Hussein and I watched the broadcast at Café Riche. Morsi spoke as Mubarak had. Doomed, and doomed by the same forces. These forces were not unseen this time; in fact, they were visible and obvious. "*The army and the people are one hand!*" chanted the marchers going by on the street. I had imagined history as an impartial observer or as a blank page on which people (those who survived to tell) wrote themselves. But that night in Cairo history felt like an omnipotent force, a god, arranging the inevitable. What was happening was a reiteration, a compare-and-contrast essay question in a school exam.

The crowds protesting Morsi were many times larger than the crowds that had toppled Mubarak. The numbers were overwhelming, and to us liberals, beguiling. In the original land of the Muslim Brotherhood, here was a popular repudiation of political Islam. Dr. Hussein and I talked in tones that alternated between excitement, schadenfreude and misgiving. That night I think I said stupid hopeful things like: "This could be the reboot the revolution needs. Rewind the tape back to the beginning and start afresh. A transitional committee and consensus to organize the political process properly . . ."

I watched Magdi lock the door to the café against the careening mob outside. Filfil brought us coffee without comment.

When the forty-eight-hour deadline was up General Sisi announced, without taking off his sunglasses, that Morsi had been taken to a secure location for his own safety.

Tahrir went crazy. Cheering yelling singing chanting fists pounding the air in victory. So many, many people. So much noise. So loud! Honking horns, vuvuzelas, whistles, tambourines, sticks chinking railings. Dr. Hussein and I walked the streets around Tahrir because the square was jammed and I was afraid of being attacked. Ultras with fiery red flares and deep bass drums drumming; girls with bare arms (!) dancing, reaching up and waving. Muggy buzzy cacophony. Swerving motorbikes pimped up with lights like electric jellyfish, a whoosh of a firework rocketing up and showering sparks. Bang bang crack of poppers and diesel smoke from a growling bus stuck in the fray. People held up stuffed toy sheep on poles and wore *V for Vendetta* masks on the backs of their heads. The dusk drew slowly, coloring the sky purple, and green lasers (the latest protest accessory) swooped the square as if it was a disco. The national anthem played through loudspeakers. Across the broad concrete face of Mogamma, a giant laser wrote enormous letters: *THIS IS NOT A COUP!* And then the letters morphed into an eagle,

and the eagle became the flag of Egypt. And then the helicopters came over and a great roar went up from the crowd and they
waved madly and pointed their green lasers upward so that the
circling Apache was turned into a silhouette of wriggling green
worms. I saw a group of police in their white summer uniforms.
I had never seen police not in riot gear on Tahrir before. People
stopped to shake their hands and their posture was relaxed, hand
on hip, and they were smiling. All the time fireworks went up in
a constant fusillade of sparkling chrysanthemums. And louder
came the F-16 jets, screaming, flying low and in formation, trail-
ing smoke in the colors of the Egyptian flag, banking, coming
back again roaring, roaring.

I did not feel any connection to their World Cup jubilation.
The volume was turned up so loud that Dr. Hussein and I could
not hear each other speak. I felt, for the first time on Tahrir, like
a separate and almost disinterested observer. I did not understand
what I was looking at. Was this democracy or *demo*-cracy, "the
people," a many-headed hydra or mass hysteria? We walked away,
both quietly uncomprehending. I could still see the scrim of anti-
SCAF graffiti from the year before visible underneath portraits of
new martyrs.

Days waited for the nights. When the sun went down and the
heat left the day the marches would start and the microphones
would scream and the violence would flicker in pockets, on the
verges, in side streets. Hundreds of Brotherhood were detained.
The supreme guide was placed under "house arrest." Islamic TV
channels went black. Dr. Hussein and I made a bad joke about
calling it the Gillette revolution because so many people were
shaving off their beards.

Egypt was now two revolutions: the anti-Morsi and the pro-
Morsi. The ante-Morsis held Tahrir. The pro-Morsis settled at a

crossroads in Nasr City. The first held pictures of Morsi with a big red cross over his face; the second held pictures of Morsi without his face crossed out. Both groups held up placards denouncing the American ambassador. *Send that crone home!* The anti-Morsis accused America of pandering to the Brotherhood, the pro-Morsis accused the Americans of supporting the army over democracy. Egypt had divided, but it was nice that everyone could still agree that America was the bad guy.

Every evening the helicopters flew over Tahrir and the jets wrote hearts with their contrails and screamed triumphalism across the sky. Overnight the vendors selling roast potatoes and fireworks were all selling pictures of General Sisi in his generalissimo hat and his black sunglasses. No one knew who he was but he was already the reproduction of a dictator. Several months later, thinking back to this scene, as Adrien and I finished watching the film Z, I said, "Maybe Sisi is only an image, a cardboard cutout. There is nothing individual about him; Sisi wearing *mufti* could walk past us on the street and we would never notice."

"It is all projection," said Adrien, waving his cigar at a poster on his wall of Saddam smoking a cigar. "People see what they want to see."

"People get the government they deserve," I said, repeating the old shibboleth I had never liked because it implied the people were passive, like children.

"I don't know," Adrien replied, thinking through the cigar smoke, "maybe people get the government they want."

"We had no choice," said Dr. Hussein.

"We had no choice," said the Big Pharaoh.

A Tamarod kid on the street outside the empty palace in Heliopolis told me, smiling, "It is a very nice intervention by the army and I think everyone likes it."

"But this is the same army that fought protesters, the same SCAF of military trials and constitutional declarations."

The Tamarod kid cocked his head to one side. "It's different this time," he said. I recognized the hallucinations of hope. Hope burrs hold fast after all, buried in our hearts.

The Big Pharaoh now had forty thousand Twitter followers. Baradei was mooted as interim president. Lina launched her new website. Jehane was reediting another ending to her documentary. Dr. Hussein was sending out Social Democratic Party announcements and organizing meetings with foreign diplomats. Alaa Al Aswany tweeted: *Democracy must accommodate the Muslim Brotherhood and the Salafis and all the political currents but anyone who bears arms or incites violence, whatever their affiliation, their natural place is in prison.* Omar the intelligence officer pasted messages on his Facebook page asking the protesters on Tahrir not to send up fireworks :))))) to allow the helicopters to fly low so that they could drop more flags.

Every night the TV channels showed a split screen with nine frames of the crowds and clashes, Alexandria, Suez, Tahrir, Nasr City. Fighting in traffic jams, boys thrown off a roof in Alexandria, churches burned in Upper Egypt, guns seeded through the marches . . .

I went from one crowd to the other. The army had cordoned the Brotherhood sit-in at the crossroads in Nasr City with armored personnel carriers. The Brotherhood barricaded themselves behind razor wire and walls built out of hexagonal paving stones.

The crossroads the Brotherhood occupied as their Tahrir was an ordinary junction. On one corner was a mosque, on the opposite corner there was a military administration building. Brotherhood men camped along the military walls in lean-to shelters made of sticks and blankets and blue tarpaulins. It was a strange proximity. The Brotherhood (and a few among them who were not Brotherhood) were middle-aged, middle-class men wearing rayon trousers that held a crease. Some had hard hats and reflective vests, which made them look like construction workers. Some carried flimsy zinc shields that looked like they had been run up in a back-street metalworkers' shop overnight. A few held walking sticks with tape wrapped around the handles. They were very friendly to me because all the Brotherhood website and media channels had been shut down and they were desperate to get word out to the wider world. They gave me dates to eat and one man kindly held an umbrella over my head against the sun. Some were angry and defiant, others were quieter, shocked. Some were clean shaven, some had hard dark prayer calluses. All of them had a furrowed brow, the rancor of betrayal.

"We will defend democracy until the end!"

"The problem is the *feloul* and the secularists."

"The secularists?" I queried. I had not heard this label before.

"Some of the bad Christians."

"We are the power, not the army!"

"This is the democracy you told us to make?"

Faces heavy and troubled. Their eyes flickered from my notebook to the line of armored personnel carriers.

"We want Islamic rule. This is the last chance for us to realize our dream of Islamic law."

"After the protests our place will be in jail," one man said. "Tell our families and supporters to come down here to gather with us. Don't leave us alone."

A radiologist from Alexandria told me, "If the Brotherhood does not call for force I will go with *jihad*. I will join Gamaa Islamiya or the *jihad* in Sinai. They have pushed us to this. We took eighty years to tell everyone in Egypt that this is the only way, and now they cancel the ballot box—"

But another man replied, "We will not fight. We don't have anything to fight with."

"We have faith in God and whatever he wills will be."

"There will not be elections now, there will be only a spectacle put on by the army."

"After the protests our place will be in jail."

Voices pleaded, incredulous, imploring, impassioned, against the injustice.

"Our democratically elected president is kidnapped and no one knows where he is or what will happen to him."

I saw that a line of Brotherhood hard hats stood in a semicircle by the gate to the military administration building, guarding it. When I asked, they pointed to a patch of blood on the tarmac. In the night some of the protesters, angry and chanting, had tried to push against the gates, and shots had been fired from inside. Now they were making a cordon so that this kind of incident would not happen again. They were curiously at pains not to provoke the army.

I looked at the military gate being protected by the Brotherhood against the Brotherhood. Above the gate there was an advertising billboard for National Chicken, a brand owned by the army, with a picture of a juicy, golden roasted chicken. Next to the chicken was a bronze statue of a soldier with his hand resting protectively on the Sphinx of Egypt, and gathered at his feet, cast as half the size of the soldier, were the people of Egypt.

A final scene:
Near midnight, Dr. Hussein came back from an emergency meeting of the Egyptian Social Democratic Party. They had met in Café Riche, but there had been so many of them they could not fit around a table. Magdi had let them go down into the cellar

bar. An Egyptian Social Democrat leader, Ziad Bahaa Eldin, had been put forward as a compromise candidate for prime minister. The meeting was to discuss whether to accept this poisoned chalice or not.

Several of us had gathered on Dr. Hussein's balcony that evening, waiting for him. Several more had not been able to make it because the bridges were blocked with tanks. Our conversation had been rueful and jagged. When he came in we all asked him at once: "So? What is happening? Who is the prime minister?"

Dr. Hussein opened his arms wide to embrace the welter.

"What is happening? Lots of things are happening! Lots of things are happening!" He sat down and everything came out in a rush:

"The generals want to get the Brotherhood off the streets, but their commanders are telling them no, to wait. The Salafi Nour Party has rejected Baradei for prime minister but now they are saying okay maybe Baradei for vice president. I was against Ziad becoming prime minster, because we will end up taking all the blame, especially when something against human rights happens, when the army shoots people. Now the Nour Party guy is tweeting that he is pro-Ziad. Tamarod is pro-Ziad. Ziad himself is actually in Canada—"

Someone asked him if there was any negotiation between the Brotherhood and the army.

"No," said Dr Hussein, "there's absolutely no contact between them at all!"

"Yes, but you would put your trust in the army," I said to him, "after everything, after SCAF and military trials and all their pushing their own constitutional declaration proclamations through—and now they just remove a democratically elected president?" I shook my head. I had always been on the side of the revolution; now I realized I didn't know which side

I was on. "The army and its road maps! Again! Do you know there aren't any road maps in Egypt—no, really, there are no maps of roads."

"It's true," Dr. Hussein admitted.

"So if you want to go from Cairo to Alex or Luxor or Asyût or wherever you want to go, the only way is to stop and ask people directions—it's the people—"

"But the people brought down Morsi!" someone answered.

"Yes." I conceded. "But there will be consequences to what you have done, to what you have condoned. Don't you see? There will be those who will want to go back to the violence. It will start up again, assassinations, car bombs . . ."

Dr. Hussein nodded his agreement, but he did so looking into the depths of his whiskey.

"I know," he said, as I had heard him say before, "but there was no choice."

We talked until late. At two or three I went to bed.

I reached for my notebook and wrote the scene above, and then added:

And you get to the end of these days and cannot remember anything because everything passes through your brain like a hurtling train.

I went to sleep very tired. And when I woke up it was all over Twitter that the army had killed fifty-one Brotherhood at the sit-in.

AFTERWORD

THERE ARE ALWAYS SIGNS, THERE ARE ALWAYS THINGS YOU COULD have seen, there are many things you miss. Afterward it is too late, understanding comes only after it was possible to do anything about it. The army killed fifty-one Brotherhood protesters on my last day in Egypt. At the end of Ramadan they got fed up with the Brotherhood sit-in at the Rabba crossroads and went in with bulldozers and guns. Among those killed was the seventeen-year-old daughter of Mohammed Beltegi, the senior Brotherhood member who had spent all night on Tahrir during the Battle of the Camels. He was arrested a few weeks later, dragged from where he had been hiding in a house in Giza, sleepless in a gray *galabia*, a wry smile on his face, shut up with the rest of the Brotherhood leadership. Hundreds were killed imprisoned died in custody sent for trial executed. When Morsi appeared in a glass cage in court and tried to shout his denunciation of the proceedings, the judge turned the microphones off so that he could not be heard.

Bassem Youssef went off the air. Human Rights Watch was closed down. Liberal activists were arrested and intimidated. When Dr. Hussein and I coincided in New York one afternoon the following summer we walked around the new 9/11 museum, amazed. Monument to loss. Sisi had been elected president. I asked him if he felt that the new repression in Egypt made him careful about how he expressed himself in public. He reluctantly said yes. In the headlines the people of the world demonstrated against their governments in Bangkok São Paulo Moscow Istanbul Kiev Greece Spain Indonesia. The images were all the same: lines of armored police, clouds of tear gas, orange flames in the black night, angry bloodied faces.

Hassan and I stayed in touch; all our Facebook messages were about how he was trying to get out of Egypt.

NOTE ABOUT THE GRAFFITI

When Mubarak fell, graffiti sprang up all over Cairo. Some of the best ones were done by art students and graphic designers and street artists. Many were spray-painted stencils downloaded from the internet. The images told the story of the revolution and memorialized its protagonists and its martyrs. I wanted to use them in this book to illustrate a visual narrative that was being sprayed and played with on Egyptian walls.

Most graffiti was anonymous, but where possible, I have tried to identify the artists (or their monikers) whose images appear in the book. I apologize for any mistakes or omissions.

Ganzeer, which means bicycle chain, was responsible for the most widely used Mubarak stencil. I met him in 2011. He had started a project to memorialize the martyrs of the revolution with portraits in red and yellow and black. It was Ganzeer who painted the great tank under a Zamalek underpass. After Morsi's fall, he moved to New York.

Keizer was a student of Banksy's political satire. Keiser designed many of the most iconic images and slogans of the Egyptian revolution: the video camera gun, the fist replacing the military eagle with the slogan Resist Imperialism, the fuel-o-meter registering from war to fear to peace, I Love Chaos, We Are Watching Back, Colonel Sanders with devil horns, girl with flowing hair,

Vodamoan, Tutankhamen Che, the child on the swing, stick man helping another stick man over a wall, line of stickmen holding hands, man with his mouth taped shut, Mubarak with his face blacked out and covered in polka dots, female protestor in hijab with her arm raised, TV personality whispering conspiracies into ears, marching ants, Brotherhood Bullshit.

El Teneen, which means the dragon, designed the famous chessboard with the king being toppled, as well as the tank being smashed by a fist (look closely and you will see a crescent and cross on the wrist), Tantawi with a Salafi beard and the Molotov cocktail stencil.

Amar Abo Bakr, who I write about in the chapter on graffiti, was responsible for the stencil of Mina Daniel, the see-no-evil speak-no-evil hear-no-evil monkeys, the mothers in mourning holding photographs of their martyred sons, the Maspero building morphing into a cobra, Mubarak looking very mean, the protestors with angel wings and the girl with the upside-down military eagle on the back of her shirt.

Adham Bakry stenciled the no entry sign over the image of a couch and TV.

4SprayCans came up with the Statue of Liberty wearing niqab.

Sad Panda did the portrait of the man with the downturned mouth—it was pasted on paper on the wall and one eye had been torn away when I took the picture—the child in the striped shirt with a slingshot and Salafi-Che.

Hossam Shukrallah did the diptych of the man shooting his television.

Zeft announced the revolution will not be tweeted and stenciled the Kalashnikov shooting doves that appears on the cover of the book.

Mohamed El Moshir painted the boy holding his knee.

Alaa Awad painted the ancient Egyptian figure climbing a ladder.

Mohamed Khaled painted liberté fraternité egalité.

Nazeer was responsible for the signposts to Tahrir.

Alaa Awad painted the head of a general on the body of a snake.

Folan did the megaphone and the microphone.

Ahmed El Masry, Ahmed Abdallah, Saiko Manio and KIM did the joker grinning military holding the puppet strings of presidential candidates.

Omar Fathi drew the morphing of Mubarak into Morsi, the portrait of Morsi shadowed by a question mark and the Mubarak-Tantawi followed by Morsi and a question mark.

Moshir designed the martyr's funeral scene that appears on the cover.

ACKNOWLEDGMENTS

Those friends of mine who appear as themselves in the book have given me permission to use their names; public figures who are quoted knew they were talking to a journalist. Some names (and a few minor identifying details) have been changed to protect identities.

I would like to go through my notes and memories and write a long thank-you list, over several pages, to all the Egyptians I met who befriended me, talked to me, fed me, explained things, yelled, questioned back, argued, discussed, and voiced opinions. But I fear that many would be wary of having their names associated with a foreign journalist. It is a very miserable thing to have witnessed such a joyous cacophony of national excitement during the turbulent years after Mubarak's fall and then to see all this possibility quashed with the installation of his successor, President Sisi. I guess I hope that at least this new phase will bring stability, which is the next best thing (and not a small thing, frankly, considering the neighborhood) to proper, pluralistic, ballot-box democracy.

Instead, let me thank all the Egyptians who inspired me and so many others. From the mother of the martyr killed during the eighteen days, who I found sleeping in a tent on Tahrir in full hijab to protest in his memory, to the kind Salafis in Agamy who patiently explained their vision for a new Egypt under sharia law, to the brave reckless kids on the Square who shared their water and their Internet connections. I know that all of them want to see a better, fairer, and more prosperous Egypt. I hold out hope that the experience of those crazy times will have lodged in the hearts of those of us lucky enough to have witnessed them, and that someday debate will be dusted off again and used to build a country that everyone can share.

ABOUT THE AUTHOR

WENDELL STEAVENSON wrote for *The New Yorker* from Cairo for more than a year during the Egyptian revolution. She has spent most of the past decade and a half reporting from the Middle East and the Caucasus for the *Guardian*, *Prospect Magazine*, Slate, *Granta* and other publications. She has written two previous books, both critically acclaimed: *Stories I Stole*, about post-Soviet Georgia, and *The Weight of a Mustard Seed*, about life and morality in Saddam's Iraq and the aftermath of the American invasion. She was a 2014 Nieman Fellow at Harvard. She currently lives in Paris.